Change and Stability in Thesis and Dissertation Writing

Also available from Bloomsbury

What Is Good Academic Writing?: Insights into Discipline-Specific Student Writing, edited by Melinda Whong and Jeanne Godfrey
Expressing Critical Thinking through Disciplinary Texts: Insights from Five Genre Studies, Ian Bruce
Academic Writing and Genre: A Systematic Analysis, Ian Bruce
Academic Writing: At the Interface of Corpus and Discourse, edited by Maggie Charles, Susan Hunston and Diane Pecorari
What Makes Writing Academic: Rethinking Theory for Practice, Julia Molinari

Change and Stability in Thesis and Dissertation Writing

The Evolution of an Academic Genre

Brian Paltridge and Sue Starfield

BLOOMSBURY ACADEMIC
LONDON • NEW YORK • OXFORD • NEW DELHI • SYDNEY

BLOOMSBURY ACADEMIC
Bloomsbury Publishing Plc
50 Bedford Square, London, WC1B 3DP, UK
1385 Broadway, New York, NY 10018, USA
29 Earlsfort Terrace, Dublin 2, Ireland

BLOOMSBURY, BLOOMSBURY ACADEMIC and the Diana logo are
trademarks of Bloomsbury Publishing Plc

First published in Great Britain 2024
This paperback edition published in 2025

Copyright © Brian Paltridge and Sue Starfield, 2024

Brian Paltridge and Sue Starfield have asserted their right under the Copyright,
Designs and Patents Act, 1988, to be identified as Authors of this work.

For legal purposes the Acknowledgements on p. ix constitute an
extension of this copyright page.

Cover design: Charlotte James
Cover image © Dmitrii Maslov/ iStock

All rights reserved. No part of this publication may be reproduced or transmitted
in any form or by any means, electronic or mechanical, including photocopying,
recording, or any information storage or retrieval system, without prior
permission in writing from the publishers.

Bloomsbury Publishing Plc does not have any control over, or responsibility for,
any third-party websites referred to or in this book. All internet addresses given
in this book were correct at the time of going to press. The author and publisher
regret any inconvenience caused if addresses have changed or sites have ceased
to exist, but can accept no responsibility for any such changes.

A catalogue record for this book is available from the British Library.

A catalog record for this book is available from the Library of Congress.

ISBN: HB: 978-1-3501-4657-0
PB: 978-1-3503-8103-2
ePDF: 978-1-3501-4658-7
eBook: 978-1-3501-4659-4

Typeset by Integra Software Services Pvt. Ltd.

To find out more about our authors and books visit www.bloomsbury.com
and sign up for our newsletters.

Contents

List of figures		vi
Acknowledgements		ix
1	Introduction	1
2	The doctoral thesis/dissertation as an evolving genre	5
3	Investigating change and stability in doctoral theses and dissertations	29
4	The evolution of thesis and dissertation types	43
5	The 'new humanities' PhD	65
6	Professional doctorates	103
7	Practice-based doctorates in the visual arts	133
8	Practice-based doctorates in music	167
9	Doctorates by publication	193
10	Genre evolution in thesis and dissertation writing	227
Appendix A		248
References		250
Index		281

Figures

2.1	An extract from Wittgenstein's *Tractatus Logico-Philosophicus* (Wittgenstein 1922: 25)	11
2.2	An extract from Stewart's (2016) PhD 'Indigenous architecture through indigenous knowledge'	12
2.3	A 'simple' traditional thesis (Fox 2019)	18
2.4	A 'complex' traditional thesis (Green 1997)	19
2.5	A topic-based thesis (Jung 2015)	20
2.6	A thesis by publication (Cotterall 2011)	22
2.7	Examples of practice-based doctorates (Fenton 2007; van Niele 2005)	23
4.1	Summary of thesis types (based on Paltridge 2002)	44
4.2	Typical sections of thesis types (Paltridge 2002: 135)	45
4.3	Table of Contents for Palmer's (1894) PhD from Yale University	49
4.4	Table of Contents from an Astronomy traditional complex dissertation (Powell 2019)	51
4.5	Table of Contents from a topic-based History dissertation (Decker 2017)	52
4.6	Table of Contents of Ayres' (1923) topic-based thesis	54
4.7	Table of Contents from an English topic-based dissertation (Clucas 2014)	55
4.8	Contents of Parks' (1900) topic-based thesis	56
4.9	Contents of Gao's (2019) topic-based thesis	57
4.10	Contents of Webb's (2019) topic-based thesis	58
4.11	Contents of Cerfeda's (2019) topic-based thesis	59
5.1	Table of Contents topic-based new humanities thesis (Robinson 2002)	69
5.2	Title page new humanities thesis (Wessell 1999)	72
5.3	Table of Contents topic-based new humanities thesis (Wessell 1999)	73
5.4	Table of Contents history thesis (Scharen 2000)	74
5.5	Table of Contents (Bok 2017)	85
5.6	First page of Table of Contents (Carlin 2016: 4)	88
5.7	Table of Contents history thesis (Zubrzycki 2018; first 5 chapters)	91

5.8	Table of Contents from a history thesis (Egan 2019)	92
6.1	An example of a Columbia Teachers College simple-traditional EdD dissertation (Liu 2021)	107
6.2	An example of an Arizona State University simple-traditional EdD dissertation (Brady 2020)	109
6.3	Poole's (2012) simple traditional EdD thesis submitted at the University of Bath	114
6.4	Chapter titles in Nixon's (2007) University of Alberta EdD thesis	116
6.5	Chapter headings in Perkin's (2012) University of British Columbia EdD thesis	117
6.6	Chapter titles in Buis' (2015) EdD thesis from the Queensland University of Technology	121
6.7	Section headings in Leonarder's (2016) EdD portfolio from Western Sydney University	122
6.8	Typical structure of the Western Sydney University EdD by portfolio	123
7.1	Table of Contents of a Rensselaer PhD dissertation (Pirler 2019)	137
7.2	Table of Contents of Fortais' (2018) Slade School practice-led doctoral report	141
7.3	The acknowledgements page in Fortais' (2018: 5) doctoral report	142
7.4	Table of Contents Gaietto's (2018) Slade School doctoral report	145
7.5	Page 26 of Gaietto's (2018) PhD report showing landscape formatting	147
7.6	An image from 'The Whisper' in Segal's Slade School PhD (2020: 112)	151
7.7	An image from 'The Fabric of Memory' in Segal's PhD (2020: 116)	152
7.8	Table of Contents from Flanders' (2014) dissertation	153
7.9	Page 50 from Flanders' (2014) dissertation showing Illustration 24 of Mourning Dove	155
7.10	Table of Contents of Robertson's (2018) SCA PhD	160
7.11	Emma Robertson, Exhibition Overview (2017: 167)	161
8.1	Table of Contents of Lander's (2017) DMA UC San Diego dissertation	172
8.2	Table of Contents of Yahav's (2018) performance submission	176
8.3	Table of Contents of Liu's (2019) composition submission	177
8.4	Table of Contents of Ascenzo's (2020) simple traditional DMA performance submission	180
8.5	Table of Contents of Wright's (2020) DMA composition submission	182

8.6	Table of Contents of Lim's (2018) Sydney Conservatorium performance thesis	184
8.7	Front cover of Heaton's DMA recital program	186
8.8	Table of Contents from Heaton's (2020) DMA submission	187
8.9	Table of Contents Kay's (2019) composition thesis	190
9.1	Texas A&M guidelines for organizing a doctorate by publication	196
9.2	An example of a manuscript type dissertation (Okuda 2017)	198
9.3	An example of the two-part model of PhD by publication (McGrath 2015)	199
9.4	An example of the sandwich model of PhD by publication (Stevenson 2005)	200
9.5	An example of a US sandwich-style dissertation (Thacker 2020)	205
9.6	An example of a US two-part style dissertation (Jamil 2013)	206
9.7	Table of Contents for Ali-Khan's (2011) dissertation	208
9.8	Table of Contents of Hirst's (2019) Middlesex University two-part PhD by published work	211
9.9	An example of a Canadian sandwich-style manuscript dissertation (Jackson, P. A., 2013)	215
9.10	An example of an Australian two-part PhD by published work (Di Mauro 2015)	219
9.11	An example of an Australian sandwich-style PhD by publication (Cowden 2012)	221

Acknowledgements

In the course of writing this book, we have read many PhD theses and dissertations. We would like to thank all the former doctoral students whose work we refer to in our book for making their theses publicly available, thus facilitating our study. In particular, we would like to acknowledge to the students whose interviews enrich the discussion of change and continuity in the thesis genre that form the core of our book. Several doctoral supervisors also participated in interviews and we would like to thank them for their thoughtful contributions. We also need to thank the wonderful librarians across the globe who facilitated our online searches and acknowledge all those who have worked tirelessly to develop the online repositories which store the theses and dissertations we examined.

We would also like to thank the reviewers of the proposal for our book that we took to Bloomsbury and to our editors at Bloomsbury for their support throughout.

To our families and friends who supported and encouraged us as we worked on our book, our grateful thanks are also due.

Finally, we would like to thank each other for being such incredible writing partners over many rewarding years. We couldn't have done it all by ourselves!

Every effort has been made to trace copyright holders and to obtain their permission for the use of copyright material. However, if any have been inadvertently overlooked, the publishers will be pleased, if notified of any omissions, to make the necessary arrangement at the first opportunity.

The third-party copyrighted material displayed in the pages of this book is done so on the basis of 'fair dealing for the purposes of criticism and review' or 'fair use for the purposes of teaching, criticism, scholarship or research' only in accordance with international copyright laws, and is not intended to infringe upon the ownership rights of the original owners.

1

Introduction

Doctoral theses and dissertations,[1] for many years, have been a relatively stable genre. This has begun to change, however, especially as doctoral degrees are being offered in an increasing range of academic disciplines where alternate scholarly forms are now being accepted for the award of the degree, and when doctoral students need to be prepared for a diversity of careers on completion of their degrees beyond the academy. There has, however, been little research which examines these changes in doctoral degrees and how these impact on the nature of the doctoral thesis/dissertation, the focus of our book. To do this, the book reviews theories of genre change, focusing on the concepts of evolution, innovation and emergence and considers their relevance to an examination of change and stability in the production and reception of doctoral theses and dissertations more broadly, then in the humanities and social sciences. In particular it examines new humanities dissertations, the Doctor of Education, the PhD in the visual arts, the Doctor of Musical Arts and the PhD by publication. The doctoral thesis/dissertation, then, is an evolving genre, the focus of Chapter 2 of our book. We examine the doctoral thesis/dissertation as a distinct research genre and typical dissertation types (see below) and trace their development over time. We also consider the extent to which new technologies and their multimodal affordances are reshaping theses and dissertations.

Chapter 3 reviews research methods and approaches that have been employed to research doctoral theses dissertations in the past. It then provides a detailed account of our choice of investigative approach to studying genre change in doctoral theses and dissertations. We discuss our adoption of ethnographically oriented research strategies and the affordances they offer to genre-based research within the academic context and the doctoral thesis/dissertation. In particular, we discuss textography (Swales 2018), an approach which combines elements of text analysis with ethnographic techniques such as interviews, observations, document analysis and other data sources. A textography is, thus, something more than a traditional piece of discourse analysis, while at the same time less than a full-blown ethnography (Swales 2018). It aims to get an inside view of the worlds in which texts are written, what guides the writing and the values that underlie the texts that have been written. A particular goal of a textography is to examine the 'contextualization' and the 'situatedness' of written texts (Swales 2018). It aims to do this through an exploration of the texts' 'contextually embedded discursive practices' (Swales 2018: 112). A textography, thus, aims to provide an understanding of the context in which a text is produced in order to gain an understanding of why texts are written as they are as well as extend students' understandings of the purposes for which they are writing (Evans 2022).

Previous research has identified four main thesis and dissertation types that students typically write: 'simple traditional' dissertations which have an 'IMRD' (introduction–methods–results–discussion) pattern of organization; 'complex traditional' dissertations which report on more than the one study; 'topic-based' dissertations which commence with an introductory chapter which is then followed by a series of chapters based on sub-topics of the topic under investigation; and 'theses by publication' which are based on a compilation of published, or publishable, research articles. Most of this research, however, was carried out some years ago and in some cases was based on theses and dissertations submitted for examination at the university where the researcher was working. In addition, earlier research into thesis and dissertation types does not reflect changes in types of study which are now part of doctoral research and academic disciplines which have moved into the area of doctoral studies. Chapter 4, then, reports on research carried out using a larger and more international data set than was the case with previous research on this topic to explore changes in thesis and dissertation types over time.

In a study of sociology and history PhD theses, Starfield and Ravelli (2006) identified a cluster of 'new humanities' texts that could be seen to challenge the conventional thesis in these disciplines. At the time, they questioned whether the changes they observed at the macrostructural level and in terms of the presentation of the researcher's identity constituted a passing 'fad' or were indications of more longer-term change. Chapter 5 revisits this study and extends it with a more recent set of doctoral theses to chart more recent developments. Interviews with student authors aim to enrich the textual analysis as they seek to understand motivations for choices made in relation to perceived generic expectations.

Practice-based and professional theses and dissertations represent perhaps the most significant diversion from the conventional doctoral thesis/dissertation. These types of doctorate are the focus of Chapters 6, 7 and 8 of the book. Chapter 6 examines the Doctor of Education degree, while Chapters 7 and 8 examine doctoral degrees in the Visual Arts and Music. The use of ethnographic interviews illuminates the ways in which students and supervisors navigate the challenges inherent in these theses.

Chapter 9 examines the doctorate by publication, typically a compilation of journal articles either previously published or destined for publication. This form of doctorate is relatively new in the humanities and social sciences. This iteration of the genre shares features of both the prestigious research article and more conventional features of the doctoral thesis. This chapter draws on textual analysis of recently submitted theses by publication and interviews with students and supervisors to investigate the challenges they face and the choices they make as authors and supervisors in what is relatively uncharted territory.

Chapter 10 discusses change and stability as well as the future of the doctorate in the humanities and social sciences. It considers the 'dissertation of the future' which paves the way for a new generation of doctoral students and changing kinds of doctoral submissions. The chapter also pulls together the themes identified in earlier chapters on the book and considers implications for the evolution of doctoral theses and dissertations as a genre.

Note

1   The terms thesis and dissertation are used differently in different parts of the world. In the UK and Australia, for example, PhD students write a thesis, whereas in the United States they write a dissertation. In Canada, however, both thesis and dissertation seem to be used for doctoral students' submissions. We have tried to refer to thesis when referring to doctorates awarded in the UK and Australia and dissertation when the doctorate has been awarded in the United States. Whenever we use the terms thesis and dissertation however, we are, in all cases, referring to doctoral submissions.

2

The doctoral thesis/dissertation as an evolving genre

Institutional genres such as doctoral theses and dissertations change slowly and change is often highly contested. In this chapter, we chart the emergence of the doctoral thesis/dissertation. We discuss the concept of genre 'evolution' and its relationship to changes in this genre. The concepts of prototype, inheritance and intertextuality are also discussed as they relate to genre change and evolution. The notions of typology and taxonomy are discussed in relation to doctoral theses as is the context of thesis and dissertation writing. We also consider the extent to which new technologies and their multimodal affordances are reshaping theses and dissertations. This chapter, thus, sets the scene for the chapters which follow.

History of the PhD

The first PhD in the world was awarded at the University of Berlin (now Humboldt University) in 1810. In the same year, PhDs were awarded at what came to be called the Pierre and Marie Curie University and is now part of the Sorbonne University in Paris. The Netherlands introduced the PhD in 1810 and the University of Zurich awarded its first PhD in 1833 (Bogle 2018). The first PhDs awarded in English medium universities were at Yale University in the United States, the University of Oxford in the UK, the University of Toronto in Canada and the University of Melbourne in Australia.

Yale University awarded its first PhDs in 1861. These were in the areas of Physics, Classics, and Philosophy and Psychology (Rosenberg 1961; Yale University 1961). The title of the PhD in Physics, awarded to Arthur W. Wright, was 'Having given the velocity and direction of motion of a meteor on entering the atmosphere of the earth, to determine its orbit about the sun, taking into account the attractions of both these bodies'. A copy of this dissertation, however, no longer exists. The title of the Classics PhD was 'Brevis Vita, Ars Longa' (Life is short, art is long). It is also, however, not available in the Yale library. The PhD in Philosophy and Psychology was awarded to Eugene Schuyler. It has not, however, been possible to locate the title of his dissertation (Rosenberg 1961). After Yale, the University of Pennsylvania, Harvard University, the University of Michigan and Ohio State University followed and by 1900 the PhD had become the essential requirement for university teachers in the United States (Buchanan and Hérubel 1995; Park 2005; Simpson 1983). An important requirement of the PhD in the United States, from its early days, has been that the dissertation has to be published, first in print form, then through micro-filming and now in digital form (Noble 1992).

The University of Oxford awarded its first DPhil[1] in 1914 to Lakshman Sarup for a thesis in the area of Sanskrit philology. His thesis, however, is not held in the Oxford libraries nor is there a record of his thesis title (Simpson 1983). The first woman at the University of Oxford to be awarded the DPhil was Evelyn Simpson in 1922 for a thesis on the prose works of John Donne. In 1919 the University of Cambridge introduced the PhD after which other universities in the UK offered the degree with practically identical regulations to those of Oxford (Simpson 1983). A key requirement of the DPhil at Oxford when it was first introduced was that the 'work constitutes an original contribution to knowledge and is of a sufficient standard of merit' (Tidlen 1918: 183). This was later rephrased as 'a significant and substantial contribution in the particular field within which the thesis falls' (Simpson 2009: 172), a criterion which continues for the award of doctorates through to the present day. This can be seen, for example, in the UK Quality Assurance Agency for Higher Education's statement that a doctorate should demonstrate the candidate's 'original contribution to knowledge in their subject, field or profession' (QAA 2015: 3).

The PhD was introduced at the University of Toronto in 1897, prior to which students had gone to the United States to undertake doctoral studies (Noble 1992). The University of Toronto's first PhD was awarded to John Cunningham McLennan in 1900 for a thesis titled 'Electrical conductivity in gases transversed by cathode rays PhD in physics'. In the same year William Arthur Parkes was awarded a PhD for his thesis 'The Huronian of the basin of the Moose river' and Frederick Hughes Scott for a thesis titled 'The structure, micro-chemistry and development of nerve cells, with special reference to their nuclein compounds' (Noble 1994). McGill University offered the PhD nine years after the University of Toronto, in 1906. The University of Toronto regulations stated that the PhD should be 'the results of original investigation' and McGill that the PhD represent 'a distinct contribution to knowledge' (Noble 1992: 41), in line with the requirements for the award of the PhD at the University of Oxford and other universities in the world.

PhDs were first awarded in Australia at the University of Melbourne in 1948. Prior to this, students went to the UK, United States and Canada to undertake doctoral studies (Noble 1992). The first PhDs at the University of Melbourne were in the areas of Chemistry, Biochemistry, Literature and Physics for theses titled 'The chemistry of the ethylene sulphides and some related topics' (Chemistry); 'Biochemical aspects of the virus hemagglutination phenomenon and the related immunological and serological problems' (Biochemistry); A French-Australian writer: Paul Wenz (Literature); 'Virus haemagglutination: A review of the literature' (Biochemistry); and 'The preparation and properties of tantalum and some of its alloys' (Physics) (Noble 1994). The University of Sydney awarded its first PhDs in 1951 and the degree is now available at all universities in Australia.

The number of PhDs awarded across the world has increased dramatically since the early days with 52,250 doctorates being awarded in the United States in 2021 (National Science Foundation 2022), 21,000 in the UK in the years 2020/21 (Higher Education Student Statistics 2022), more than 7,000 per year in Canada (Torunczyk Schein 2019), and over 9,000 in Australia (McCarthy and Wienk 2019). Beyond this, there are now a number of other doctorates such as practice-based doctorates, professional doctorates and doctorates by publication (also referred to as manuscript-style theses and theses by compilation) which are becoming increasingly common (see Chapter 9 for further discussion of doctorates by publication).

Newer forms of the PhD are awarded at long-established as well as newer universities. Yale University, for example, has had a Doctor of Musical Arts degree since 1968 which has professional performance as its prime focus (Noss 1968). The University of Oxford offers a DPhil in Fine Art at its Ruskin School of Art with a focus on art making. The University of Toronto has a Doctor of Musical Arts available in the areas of composition and performance, and the University of Melbourne offers the PhD in areas such as visual art, dance and design through the Victorian College of the Arts and composition, jazz and music performance through the Melbourne Conservatorium of Music. The University of the Arts, London, a newer university, offers a PhD with a focus in areas such as design, illustration, media and communication, fashion, theatre, creative computing and fine art. In the United States, the PhD in Rhetorics, Communication and Information Design at Clemson University allows students to submit alternative types of work for their degree, aiming to produce graduates who can work in 'departments of English, rhetorics, composition/writing, communication studies, writing centers, new media – and other innovative academic departments and centers whose names and definitions have yet been determined' (Clemson Rhetorics, Communication and Information Design 2019 online). Many Canadian universities accept non-traditional content and forms for the PhD, such as Hussey's (1999) thesis 'Of swans, the wind and H.D' submitted at McGill University which was based on a set of letters between the student and the American poet Hilda Doolittle. In Australia, the University of Technology Sydney, also a newer university, offers a PhD which can include professional or creative work such as visual artefacts, an exhibition, performance or a portfolio of professional or creative work (University of Technology Sydney 2019) as do many other Australian universities.

It should also be added that doctoral theses and dissertations are now being written in English in non-English-speaking countries as well. In some of these countries it is a requirement that parts of a dissertation have already been published in order for a student to graduate. Stevenson's (2005) PhD by publication 'Reading and writing in a foreign language: A comparison of conceptual and linguistic processes in Dutch and English' at the University of Amsterdam which she wrote to meet her university's requirements (published as Stevenson et al. 2003, 2006) as well as to enhance her employment prospects on completion of her PhD is an example of this. Lisa McGrath's (2015) PhD 'Writing for publication in four disciplines: Insights into text and context' from Stockholm University is also based on a set of research articles (Kuteeva and McGrath 2015; McGrath 2014, 2016a, 2016b). Lian Malai Madsen's (2008) PhD 'Fighters and outsiders, linguistic practices, social identities, and social relationships among urban youth in a martial arts club' completed at the University of Copenhagen which was subsequently published as a book (Madsen 2015) is a further example of a PhD being written in English in a non-English-speaking country. Humboldt University of Berlin also produces PhDs written in English such as Yumin Zhang's (2017) PhD 'Masculinities in transcultural spaces – Negotiations of masculinities in Ang Lee's films'. PhD students in Hong Kong also write theses in English. An example of this is Ting Fai Yu's (2017) PhD 'Class differences among gay men in Hong Kong: Local history, queer modernity' submitted at the Chinese University of Hong Kong (published as Yu 2018, 2020). In China, English and Foreign Language Department PhD students often write their thesis in English, for example, Min Zhao's (2014) thesis 'Distribution of appraisal resources in English newspaper texts' submitted in the

School of Foreign Languages at Shanghai Jiao Tong University and Ye's (2009) 'Homing in and reconstructing native American identity' submitted at Fudan University in China.

Beyond this, the traditional doctorate is changing. Generally, in the past the doctorate was a single piece of work which resulted in an 80,000–100,000 word thesis which is not now always the case. There are newer forms of doctorates being introduced, as mentioned above, and in the UK, for example, taught components have been introduced into the PhD in what is termed the 'new route' PhD. In some cases, students are able to do their doctoral studies by distance using the affordances of electronic communications. As a result, students may be located a long way from their home institution. In addition, a more diverse range of students are now undertaking doctorates and students have a wider range of reasons for doing a PhD than has been the case in the past (Thomson and Walker 2010). And the doctoral thesis itself has changed from its early days to the range of doctoral types and possibilities that we are seeing today, the subject of the next section of this chapter.

Genre emergence, change and evolution

Emergence, change and evolution are features of research genres as they are with all genres. Genres emerge in response to new social practices and communicative situations (Luckmann 2009; Miller 2017) and existing genres can be 're-purposed, re-designed, and re-deployed' (Allori et al. 2014: 10) in the development of new genres. The emergence and development of the research article have been examined by a number of researchers (see e.g. Atkinson 1999; Bazerman 1988; Berkenkotter and Huckin 1995; Luzón and Pérez-Llantada 2019; Pérez-Llantada 2013) (see Chapter 3). Atkinson (1999) discusses the development of the conventional genre form of research articles in the *Philosophical Transactions of the Royal Society of London* from 1675 to 1975. He found that reports on research in *Philosophical Transactions* in the seventeenth and eighteenth centuries were in the form of 'polite letters' and from this they evolved so that by the nineteenth century the reports were clearly marked by section titles and headings, and with increasingly developed descriptions of the methods employed in the studies being reported on. By the twentieth century the research articles were closer to what today is considered the basic form for a research article, the IMRD format, that is, an 'introduction', 'review of the literature', 'materials and methods', 'results', 'discussion' organizational structure.

Not all of the earlier articles, however, were based on empirical research, whereas by the twentieth century they nearly always reported on experimental studies and, increasingly, more than a single study. More recently, Pérez-Llantada (2013) has discussed the 'article of the future' in which she both tracks changes in the research article due to technological innovations and proposes ways in which the research article might further change. Parallel developments can be seen in the development of doctoral theses, as will be seen in this book. Genres, then, are only 'stabilised for now' (Schryer 1994: 108) and there are a number of forces at play that can bring about changes in academic genres.

Miller (2017) discusses genre emergence and evolution in a way that has implications for the study of thesis and dissertation writing. The doctoral thesis, for example, emerged to meet the need of a higher-level research qualification to provide evidence of research capacity beyond that of the master's degree. In doing so, it re-purposed and re-deployed features of other ways of disseminating and endorsing the quality of research and, in particular, the research article and the process of peer review. The doctorate has since become a qualification that is 'recognised internationally, as the standard qualification for entry into the research and academic professions' (Park 2007: 4). As such, it plays an important part in the formation of scholars as well as ascribes holders of the degree with a formal and institutionalized academic identity.

In terms of genre evolution, Miller (2016) discusses diachronic change which involves the inheritance of genre features from earlier exemplars of the genre. An example of diachronic change is the more transparent ways in which research methods are presented in current Science theses and dissertations compared with early PhDs in this area where they were present but not so clearly outlined. Miller also discusses synchronic variation in genres where alternate forms of a genre are accepted as being part a genre category by viewing them from the point view of prototype (Rosch 1983) and family resemblances (Rosch and Mervis 1975; Wittgenstein 1953), as discussed above (see prototype, inheritance and intertextuality below).

Molinari (2022), in her book *What Makes Writing Academic*, describes a number of PhDs which illustrate how the notions of prototype and family resemblances help us understand how, despite the alternative nature of the submissions, they are still members of the genre category of doctoral dissertations. Sousanis's (2014) PhD titled 'Unflattening', for example, which was awarded by Columbia University was a graphic novel in comic book form about the relationship between words and pictures in literature. Carson's (2017) PhD 'Owning my masters: The rhetorics of rhymes & revolutions' from Clemson University combined rap, audio-visual media and recorded interviews. The dissertation he submitted for the degree was seventeen pages long and contained only thirteen references (see Chapter 10 for further discussion of these two PhDs).

Harron's (2016) PhD in mathematics from Princeton University was titled 'The equidistribution of lattice shapes of rings of integers of cubic, quartic, and quintic number fields: An artist's rendering'. She wrote three versions of her dissertation: one for lay readers, one for mathematics school teachers and one for her examiners. Harron describes her work as 'A fascinating tale of mayhem, mystery, and mathematics' (iii) and that it is 'in many ways, not very serious, sometimes sarcastic, brutally honest, and very me' (1). Notwithstanding, her submission met the knowledge requirements of Princeton University for the award of the PhD (Molinari 2022). Beyond this, however, Harron's thesis 're-configures the *standards of excellence* of a doctorate to include social justice in the field of mathematics because she introduced a new standard of excellence: being accessible to an audience that transcends her examining committee' (Molinari 2022: 128, italics in the original).

These less usual dissertations are not, however, that recent with Molinari (2022) pointing to the PhD awarded to Ludwig Wittgenstein by the University of Cambridge in 1929 based on his (1922) book *Tractatus Logico-Philosophicus*. Figure 2.1 shows extracts from Wittgenstein's text. His book is a philosophical work which deals with the relationship between language and reality. Rather than being written as a traditional thesis, it is a collection of numbered sentences and paragraphs, from 1 through to 7, with very many subsections within each

1	The world is everything that is the case.
1.1	The world is the totality of facts, not of things.
1.11	The world is determined by the facts, and by these being all the facts.
1.12	For the totality of facts determines both what is the case, and also all that is not the case.
1.13	The facts in logical space are the world.
1.2	The world divides into facts.
1.21	Any one can either be the case or not be the case, and everything else remains the same.

Figure 2.1 An extract from Wittgenstein's *Tractatus Logico-Philosophicus* (Wittgenstein 1922: 25).

section. Some of the subsections, further, are equations and images rather than text. His text is just under 20,000 words long. Despite being written in an unusual style for a PhD, the philosopher G. E. Moore, who was one of his examiners, left no doubt that Wittgenstein's thesis was acceptable for the award of the degree. He said, 'It is my personal opinion that Mr. Wittgenstein's thesis is a work of genius; but, be that as it may, it is certainly well up to the standard required for the Cambridge degree of Doctor of Philosophy' (Goldstein 1999: 512).

The language of doctoral theses is also something that is changing. For example, Patrick Stewart, a First Nations student in Canada, was awarded a PhD by the University of British Columbia in 2016 for a dissertation titled 'Indigenous architecture through indigenous knowledge'. Parts of the text in his 52,438-word dissertation contained no punctuation, no full stops, no commas and no semi-colons. In addition he ignored conventions such as the use of upper case at the start of a sentence and writing in standard paragraphs. His reason for this, he explained, was that he wanted to make a point about aboriginal culture, colonialism and 'the blind acceptance of English language conventions in academia' (Hutchinson 2015, online). Figure 2.2 is an example of Stewart's (2016: xi) writing. The layout in this extract is unusual in the way the text is spaced across the page with gaps in unexpected places. Sentences do not commence with an upper-case letter and there are no full stops at the end of sentences to indicate where they end. Not all of the dissertation is written in this way but there are enough examples of this to challenge the conventions of traditional academic writing in the way that he intended.

Thus, as Molinari (2019: 4) argues, what makes writing acceptable for academic purposes (and indeed whether a text is acceptable for a PhD) 'is not a static property of texts but one that is emergent and open to change'.

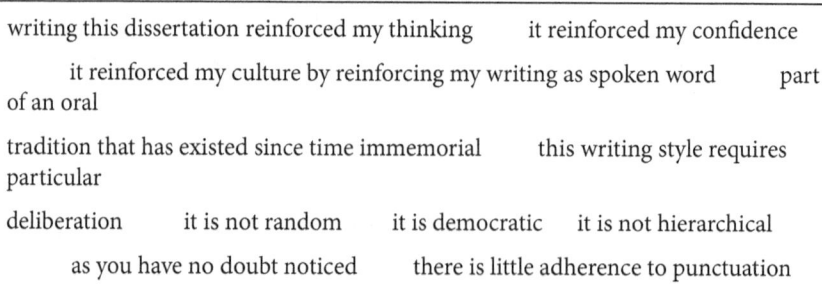

Figure 2.2 An extract from Stewart's (2016) PhD 'Indigenous architecture through indigenous knowledge'.

Prototype, inheritance and intertextuality

Prototype

Important concepts for discussions of genre change are those of prototype (Rosch 1983, Rosch and Mervis 1975; Swales 1990), inheritance (Hudson 2015) and intertextuality (Prentice and Barker 2017). A prototype is a typical example of a particular object, in the case of the subject of this book, a doctoral thesis. The work of the psychologist, Eleanor Rosch, suggests that when people categorize objects, they do so on the basis of a prototypical representation of the particular object. An exemplar may, or may not, however, be prototypical (Swales 1990). Thus, the extent to which an exemplar relates to a prototype depends upon the extent to which qualities or properties are inherited from other texts. Intertextuality describes the process by which a text may 'echo and re-echo' aspects of other texts (Crombie 1989) and so be seen as a successful (or otherwise) example of a particular genre.

Rosch's work led to a theory of 'natural categorization' (Rosch 1977) wherein people are shown to categorize in relation to prototypes which have a common core at the centre and fade off at the edges. This, plus the notion of family resemblances (Wittgenstein 1953), allows language users to see instances as being more or less typical of a particular genre category. A text, thus, may contain features and characteristics which occur in many, but not necessarily every, instance of the text but still be a member of the particular genre category; that is, there will be a 'family resemblance' (Rosch and Mervis 1975; Wittgenstein 1953) relation between the text and other instances of the genre. When we apply the notions of prototype and family resemblances to doctoral theses, there are a number of characteristics that doctoral theses are expected to display which are reflective of criteria which are given to PhD examiners. These include, among other matters, originality, contribution to knowledge, and a high standard of literary quality and presentation. Importantly, however, these criteria do not state that the thesis should be in a particular *form*. Thus, there are a range of acceptable forms for a doctoral thesis based on how they have been typically written in the past as well as a number of newer ways in which doctoral theses are now being presented (see typology and taxonomy in thesis and dissertation writing below). Indeed, as Guerin (2020: 138) points, doctoral student writers

> need to conform to the 'generic form' [of doctoral theses] only *sufficiently* for readers to recognise where their work fits in with the conventions and expectations of the genre – they do not need to slavishly repeat them. The real

achievement for doctoral writers is to find a balance between what they want to say and the conventions of their discipline. This is always a matter of judgement and can't be dictated by adherence to strict rules.

Inheritance

De Beaugrande and Dressler (1981: 91) describe inheritance as 'the translation of knowledge among items of the same or similar type of sub-type'. Thus, an instance of a text inherits all the characteristics of its class unless expressly cancelled. For example, we assume that a doctoral thesis is based on some kind of research even if this not explicitly stated because a doctoral thesis is a member of the category 'research genres'. Hudson (2015) describes this as 'default inheritance' because we assume this property by default 'in the absence of any more specific information to the contrary' (8). He also discusses shared properties which are inherited from other instances of a text which contribute to the formation of a prototype. There are, of course, exceptions and, at times, 'quirky' cases. These still remain instances of the particular genre category because the research community (or in the case of a PhD, the examiners of the thesis) have agreed that this is the case, as with the Wittgenstein and Stewart PhDs described above. As Booij (2017) explains, the idea of default inheritance 'has the advantage of enabling us to specify the regular properties [of a text]' while at the same time allowing for exceptions without the need to create other categories to account for alternate types of texts. Miller's (2016) use of the notion of inheritance draws from the work of Mayr (1982) in the area of evolutionary biology. Miller discusses the move from essentialism where variation is seen as sign of imperfection as opposed to taking unique examples as the starting point for analysis, 'valuing diversity and variation rather than stable abstractions' (Miller 2016: 6). This is in contrast with the essentialist view which assumes a single orderly system, linear hierarchies and an order of perfection. Genres, rather, are fluid and no longer seen as static, universal categories which do not change over time; a view, Miller points out, has implications for genre studies and, in the case of this book, the doctoral thesis.

Intertextuality

All texts, whether they are spoken or written, make their meanings against the background of other texts and things that have been written or said on other occasions (Lemke 1992). Texts may more or less implicitly or explicitly cite other texts; they may refer to other texts, or they may allude to other past, or future, texts. We thus 'make sense of every word, every utterance, or act against the background of (some) other words, utterances, acts of a similar kind' (Lemke 1995: 23). All texts are, thus, in an intertextual relationship with other texts. The notion of intertextuality draws from the work of Bakhtin who presents the view that the 'linguistic significance of a given utterance is understood against the background of language, while its actual meaning is understood against the background of other concrete utterances on the same theme; a background made up of contradictory opinions, points of view, and value judgements' (Bakhtin [1935] 1981: 281). The actual term intertextuality, however, is usually attributed to Julia Kristeva (1980) who brought the work of Bakhtin to the West. Kristeva argues that a text is kind of a 'productivity' in which various semiotic codes, genres and meaning relations are both combined and transformed.

The notions of intertextuality and inheritance, then, are crucial to understanding the relationship between instances of genres in the production and interpretation of texts. The notion of prototype (together with the notions of intertextuality and inheritance) is, thus, an essential element for discussions of genre change. Assigning a text to a prototype genre, as mentioned above, does not necessarily involve an exact match in terms of characteristics or properties. Rather, it involves the notion of 'sufficient similarity'. In the absence of a sufficient number of properties which match the stereotypical properties of the prototype, we then assign texts on a pragmatic basis, that is, on the basis of whether conditions such as, in the case of a doctoral thesis, the text was written by a student working in the field, has been submitted for the award of a research degree and has been accepted by representative members of the community as a successful instance of the doctoral thesis. Rosch's work suggests that when people categorize objects, they do not expect them to be on an equal footing. Thus, while many doctoral theses might be somewhat conventional, other doctoral theses might be considered instances of the genre without, necessarily, that expectation.

Typology and taxonomy in thesis and dissertation writing

The notions of typology and taxonomy also have important implications for discussions of thesis and dissertation writing. The basic difference between these two terms is that typology is a conceptual category while taxonomy is an empirical one (Bailey 2011). Thus, in terms of thesis and dissertation writing we might see the doctoral thesis as a typological category and instances or kinds of doctoral theses as taxonomical categories. A typological view of theses and dissertations, thus, might include the features we expect a thesis or dissertation to contain and a taxonomical view examines ways in which this kind of academic writing is realized based on particular features or characteristics.

One way of taking a typological view of theses and dissertations is by considering criteria that are applied in the examination of them; that is, what are the 'ideal' features or characteristics of a doctoral thesis or dissertation (remembering that 'ideal' may vary according to discipline and area of study). When doctoral theses are examined, universities typically draw on a list of criteria they expect the thesis to meet. These normally include the following or some kind of variation of it. That is, the thesis should show:

- an awareness and understanding of relevant previous research on the topic;
- a critical appraisal of previous research on the topic;
- a clearly defined and comprehensive investigation of the topic;
- the appropriate application of research methods and techniques;
- a thorough presentation and interpretation of results;
- appropriately developed conclusions and implications that are linked to the research framework and findings;
- a high standard of literary quality and presentation;
- a contribution to knowledge on the particular topic.

A study carried out by Holbrook et al. (2004) looked at 803 examiners' reports on 301 theses from three different universities. From their analysis they identified a set of qualities as being characteristic of 'high quality' doctoral theses. These qualities include:

- significance of the research topic;
- potential of the thesis for publication;
- use of the research literature in the design of the study and writing of the thesis;
- logic and clarity of the reporting and discussion of findings;
- the extent to which the findings can be applied in the field.

Holbrook and her colleagues also identified characteristics of 'low quality' doctoral theses. Features of low-quality theses included:

- inadequate coverage of the literature on which the study is based;
- inaccuracies and omissions in referencing;
- editorial inadequacies.

Other weaknesses in a low-quality thesis might include:

- a lack of critical evaluation of previous research;
- arguments in the thesis which are intrinsically weak;
- limited understanding of appropriate statistical analyses and their interpretation;
- insufficient detail on how the data analysis was undertaken;
- unfounded conclusions that have little or no basis in evidence.

(Evans et al. 2014)

From the point of view of prototype theory, the features of high-quality doctoral theses are those which a 'best' example of a doctoral thesis should contain, in addition to having met the examination criteria listed above. If a thesis includes features of a low-quality thesis, the student is often asked to revise their thesis so that it moves closer to being a 'best' (or better) example of a doctoral thesis, showing how, notwithstanding the discipline in which the thesis is written, there is a broad understanding in the academy of the features that a doctoral thesis should contain from a typological point of view. All of these qualities of a 'good doctoral thesis', further, are inherited from previous examples of 'good' doctoral theses and the thesis being examined is in an intertextual relationship with previously successful doctoral theses.

Looking at doctoral theses from a taxonomic point of view, previous research has pointed to a number of thesis types within which many doctoral theses sit. Dudley-Evans (1999), for example, describes a 'simple traditional' thesis which has an IMRD (introduction–methods–results–discussion) structure. Thompson (1999) further refines this category by dividing traditional theses into those which have 'simple' and those which have 'complex' patterns of organization. A thesis with a 'complex' traditional pattern is one which reports on several empirical studies with the chapters which report on research having their own IMRD patterns of organization. The table of contents of a typical 'simple' traditional thesis (Fox 2019) is shown in Figure 2.3. This thesis is a case study of the craft brewing sector in Portland, Oregon. It is important to note, however, that not all the chapters in a simple traditional pattern will have IMRD chapter headings and that they will always be separate, clearly demarcated chapters. For example, in Fox's thesis Chapter 1 is both an introduction and outline of the methods used in the study. Chapter 2 is a review of the literature, Chapters 3 and 4 are results and discussion chapters, and Chapter 5 sums up the study, considers its implications and makes suggestions for future research.

A thesis with a 'complex' organizational structure typically commences with 'introduction' and 'review of the literature' sections, as with the simple traditional thesis. It might then have a 'general methods' section which is followed by a

Study area: Geography

Title: Craft and the Contemporary Geographies of Manufacturing: Local Embeddedness, New Workspaces, and the Glamourization of Work in the Craft Brewing Sector.

Chapter 1: Introduction The Contemporary Geographies of Craft Manufacturing

1.1 Three Waves of Craft Revival
1.2 Geographies of Craft Manufacturing in the 'Third Wave'
1.3 Research Design
1.4 Methods
1.5 Dissertation Outline

Chapter 2: Becoming 'Beervana' Institutions and Materiality in the Evolution of Portland, Oregon as a Craft Brewing Hub

2.1 Introduction
2.2 The role of institutions and the material in an evolutionary economic geography of craft production
2.3 The road to 'Beervana:' the history of brewing in Portland
2.4 'Beervana' takes shape: the rise of craft brewing in Portland
2.5 Conclusion

Chapter 3: 'Glorified Janitors' Creativity, Cachet, and Everyday Experiences of Work in Portland, Oregon's Craft Brewing Sector

3.1 Introduction
3.2 Craft production as creative manufacturing work: creativity, precariousness, and glamour
3.3 Background and methods
3.4 Glamourous work? Cachet and the everyday experiences of being a craft brewer
3.5 Overappreciated and underpaid: the implications of craft brewing's 'cool' status
3.6 Conclusion

Chapter 4: Placing Production in Cultural-Economic Policy Craft Brewing and Urban Policy in Portland's Central Eastside Industrial District

4.1 Introduction
4.2 Placing production in cultural-economic policy
4.3 Urban policy and Portland's Central Eastside: the changing face of an industrial sanctuary
4.3.1 CEID becomes an industrial sanctuary: 1970s–1999
4.3.2 Remaking the CEID: 1999–present
4.4 Craft brewing and urban policy in the CEID
4.5 Conclusion: the future of craft breweries in the CEID?

Chapter 5: Conclusion

5.1 Key Findings
5.2 Contributions and Implications
5.3 Future Research
5.4 Concluding Thoughts

References

Figure 2.3 A 'simple' traditional thesis (Fox 2019).

series of sections which report on each of the individual studies, the methods they employed, the results of the individual study and a discussion of the results in relation to previous research. The thesis concludes with a general overall conclusions section. A sample 'complex' traditional thesis is shown in Figure 2.4. This thesis reports on community perceptions of the notion of town character in

---

Study area: Planning, landscape architecture and surveying

Title: Community perceptions of town character: A case study

Chapter 1: Introduction
The concept of town character
Research strategy
Thesis structure

Chapter 2: Byron Bay: from sacred sites to tourist attraction
Regional setting, natural history and cultural history
Concern with maintaining town character

Chapter 3: Place character: a theoretical framework
Spirit and concept of place
Models of place
Dimensions of place character

Chapter 4: Methodological considerations
Community involvement in assessing town character
Landscape assessment paradigms and methods
Research design

Chapter 5: A threat to town character
Club Med development proposal
Research questions
Method
Results
Conclusions
Limitations of the study and future research

Chapter 6: Community description of town character
Survey aims and research questions
Method
Results
Discussion

Chapter 7: Identifying town character features
Research questions
Method
Results
Discussion

Chapter 8: Relating landscape features to town character
Research questions
Inventory of town character features
Randomly selected landscape scenes
Part one: respondents and rating scales
Analysis and results
Part two: respondents and rating scales
Analysis and results
Discussion and further research
Conclusion

Chapter 9: General discussion
Addressing the research questions
Concluding remarks

Figure 2.4 A 'complex' traditional thesis (Green 1997).

a small coastal town in Australia. Even though the thesis is titled 'a case study', it actually reports on a number of case studies (five in all), each related to its overall topic. The thesis starts with a general introductory chapter which presents key notions relevant to the study, a general description of the research strategy employed and an overview of the thesis. This is followed by two chapters which provide further background to the study. The five case studies are then presented. The thesis concludes with a general discussion chapter which draws the findings of the study together, makes suggestions for future application of the findings as well as discusses limitations to these findings.

Dudley-Evans (1999) refers to a further kind of thesis, one of which he terms a 'topic-based' thesis. This kind of thesis typically commences with an introductory chapter which is then followed by a series of chapters which have titles based on sub-topics of the topic under investigation. The thesis then ends with a 'conclusions' chapter. The example of a topic-based thesis shown in Figure 2.5 was written in the area of Education (Jung 2015). It examines consequences of test-focused education in Korea through the indigenous Korean concept of Hakbeolism, social status that is achieved on the basis of a shared academic background. This thesis has no observable literature review chapter, although Chapter 2 draws extensively on previous research to discuss the themes her thesis is based on. There is, further, no methodology chapter although she does discuss in her thesis the methodological approach, autobiographical inquiry, she is working with for her study.

A further kind of thesis is based on a compilation of research articles, or what is often termed a 'thesis by publication' or manuscript-style thesis or dissertation. The number of articles that are required to go in this kind of thesis can vary from institution to institution as well as between disciplines. Whether

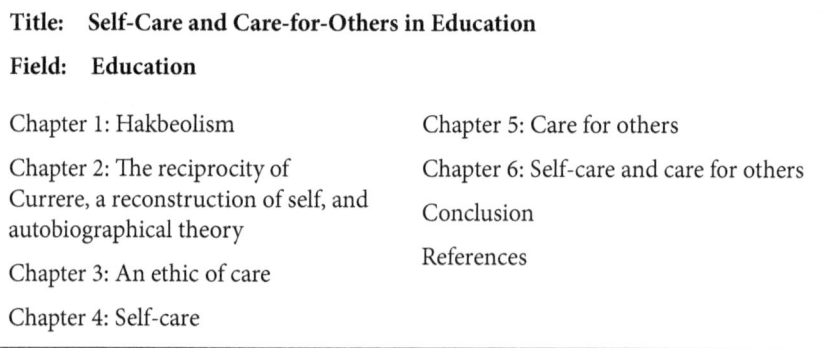

Figure 2.5 A topic-based thesis (Jung 2015).

the papers actually have to have been published or accepted for publication when the thesis is submitted for examination can also differ. The papers which are included in the thesis can be research articles, book chapters and papers from refereed conference proceedings. In some cases, the papers may be joint-authored with the student's supervisor, although there is often a regulation which says how many of the papers must have the student as the lead author. A student may choose to do a thesis by publication to build up, or to continue, a publication track record while they are doing their research which will help them get a job when they finish their degree, or it may be that the university (or supervisor) encourages the student to do this kind of thesis to help increase the publication output of the institution (Guerin 2016). A complication with a thesis by publication, however, is that the student is dependent on the outcome of the peer-review process for the completion of their thesis as well as the extra time all this will take. The student, further, may not have had experience with the peer review of their work and may find it a difficult and challenging process to deal with (Guerin 2018; Kamler and Thomson 2014) (see Chapter 9 for further discussion of the thesis by publication).

Theses by publication, then, are quite different from other sorts of theses. The research article chapters are more concise than typical thesis chapters with less of the 'display of knowledge' that is often found in a thesis or dissertation. Further, in terms of audience, they are written more as 'experts writing for experts' than novices 'writing for admission to the academy'. In this sense, they are quite different from the 'Traditional: complex'-type thesis described above. The thesis by publication summarized in Figure 2.6 was based on five discrete but related research articles, two of which had already been published at the time of submission, with the other three having been accepted for publication and 'in press' at the time the student submitted the thesis for examination. Chapters 4 and 7 of the thesis were book chapters while Chapters 5, 6 and 8 were journal articles. While Chapter 6 has the most recognizable 'shape' of a research article, the other chapters, at times, use topic-based headings in place of more conventional headings such as 'What writing experiences do the students encounter?', 'Emotion episodes in participants' narratives' (for Results) and 'How do the students' writing experiences measure up?' (for the Discussion).

Beyond this, there are also theses written in practice-based disciplines such as art, architecture, music and design which are different again from the theses described above. A key feature of doctoral submissions in these areas is that they comprise two components: a practice component and a written text which accompanies it. This is different from conventional doctoral submissions in that

Study area: Applied Linguistics

Title: Stories within stories: a narrative study of six international PhD researchers' experiences of doctoral learning in Australia

Chapter 1: Introduction
Background to the study
Focus of the study
Contribution of the study
Structure of the thesis

Chapter 2: Literature review
International doctoral students in Australia
Learning practices
Learning contexts
Scholarly Identity

Chapter 3: Methodology
Methodological Rationale
Implementation of the study
Phase One – Online survey and focus group
Phase Two – Longitudinal narrative study
From field texts to research texts

Chapter 4: Identity and learner autonomy in doctoral study
Introduction
Previous research
What the participants said
Discussion
Conclusion

Chapter 5: Doctoral students writing
Abstract
Introduction
Doctoral writing as a site of learning
Study context and participants
What writing experiences do the students encounter?
How do the students' writing experiences measure up?
Conclusion

Chapter 6: Student perspectives on doctoral pedagogy
Abstract
Introduction
Previous research
Background
Results
Discussion
Conclusion

Chapter 7: Six outsiders and a pseudo insider
Introduction
Background
Being an international doctoral student in Australia
Discussion
Conclusion

Chapter 8: More than just a brain
Abstract
Introduction
Emotions and the doctoral experience
Conceptual framework
Research design and methods
Emotion episodes in participants' narratives
Discussion
Conclusion

Chapter 9: Discussion
Major findings
Evaluation of the study
Implications of the study

Chapter 10: Conclusion
The affordances of narrative
Limitations of the study
Significance of the findings
Future research
Coda

Figure 2.6 A thesis by publication (Cotterall 2011).

Topic-based

Title: Ambivalent belonging

Chapters:

Introduction
1. Far from solid
2. Merged memories
3. Emotional geographies
4. Wandering words

Conclusion: Chora

Mixed simple traditional and topic-based

Title: UnstableActs: A practitioner's case study of the poetics of postdramatic theatre and intermediality

Chapters:

1. Introduction

2. Literature review

3. Methodology

4. A summary of the studies

5. The stylistic qualities of postdramatic theatre and intermediality

6. The poetics of postdramatic theatre: findings and conclusion

Figure 2.7 Examples of practice-based doctorates (Fenton 2007; van Niele 2005).

both pieces of work are evaluated as part of the process of doctoral examination. The texts that students write for these doctorates are often a mix of the thesis types described above. The chapter headings from two visual and performing arts doctoral texts are shown in Figure 2.7. The topic-based thesis *Ambivalent Belonging* (van Niele 2005) was a reflection on the student's experiences of being a migrant. She describes her chapters as a 'mapping of journeys' with each following a particular topic related to her overall theme. These topics are reflected in her chapter titles, such as Far from Sold and Merged Memories. There are no observable literature review or methodology chapters however in her thesis. The doctoral project *UnstableActs* (Fenton 2007) combines topic-based and simple traditional chapter headings. He has both literature review and methodology chapters which are typical of simple traditional theses. His final two chapter titles, however, reflect themes which emerged in his study rather than more traditional chapter titles, Discussion and Conclusion. In his study, Fenton explores the practice and poetics of postdramatic theatre, or what is elsewhere known as 'performance art'. His practice component was the development of a theatre piece, culminating in a final performance which is both described and theorized in his written text. Theses in these areas, further, are often on a continuum, from a text which makes it clear that it is accompanying a practice component to texts which are stand-alone and which make no or very little reference to the practice component of the submission (see Chapters 7 and 8 for further discussion of practice-based doctorates).

Obviously, then, not all doctoral theses are the same (Thompson 2016) and there are a number of ways in which students might write their thesis. The examples given here are not, of course, the only ways in which they can be presented. Anderson et al. (2020), for example, examined PhD theses in Education in Canadian universities and found a number of hybrid dissertations with students who had done a PhD by publication. These were 'hybrid simple/manuscript' and 'hybrid topic/manuscript' dissertations which, while organized in a simple IMRD or topic-based pattern, also contained work within their chapters that had been previously published, either in its entirety or in a modified version. Paltridge et al.'s (2012a, 2012b) examination of doctoral degrees in the visual and performing arts found a range of possibilities for the written text that is part of a doctoral submission in these areas of study. Among their data were very conventional doctoral texts with discrete components in a fixed order, and theses that were relatively unstructured. There was a tendency, however, for different thesis types and views of 'good research' to be favoured in particular institutions showing the importance of understanding disciplinary and institutional expectations when writing a thesis in a particular area of study at a particular academic institution, which leads us to a discussion of the context of thesis and dissertation writing and its importance for understanding why students' texts are written as they are.

The context of thesis and dissertation writing

It is important to consider the social and cultural context in which the thesis or dissertation is being produced as this will impact on what a student can say and do in their thesis, and how they will say it. This includes the kind of university the text is being written in. That is, it may be a comprehensive research university, it may be a university of technology or it may be a 'new' university where different sorts of work and different sorts of research projects are especially valued.

Another important issue is the kind of study area the thesis is written; that is, whether it is written in what Becher and Trowler (2001) call a 'hard' or a 'soft' discipline, a 'pure' or 'applied' discipline, or a 'convergent' or 'divergent' area of study. This has implications for the values, ideologies and research perspectives that are prioritized in the particular area/s of study. It may, for example, be the case that academic staff in the area of study share the same basic ideologies, judgements and values (a convergent area of study) or the research perspectives may be drawn from other areas of study (a divergent area of study). There is also the matter of how much variation there is as to what might be considered 'research' in the particular area of study. This all helps to place the thesis or dissertation in its particular academic setting as well as to bring to the fore the sets of values that hold in the area of study that might be shared by members of the disciplinary community (of not), but not openly expressed by them. Another matter is the research perspective and topic of the student's project and the extent to which this impacts on how the thesis or dissertation has been written. For example, it may be a quantitative, qualitative or a 'mixed method' study. For each of these research approaches, there are particular assumptions that underlie the use of them. This includes what sorts of claims can be made and what claims cannot.

Another important issue is the relationship between the readers and writers of doctoral theses and how this impacts on what is said in the text and how it is said. This relationship is often different from that of other academic texts such as research articles. Writers of doctoral theses, for example, are typically 'novices writing for experts', whereas writers of research articles are generally 'experts writing for experts'. Beyond this, students are sometimes unclear as to who the ultimate reader of their thesis is in the sense of who it is that will ultimately decide on whether their writing has reached the required standard for a doctoral thesis. In some cases, a student's supervisor may be one of their examiners, and in other cases they may not. If the supervisor is not one of the examiners, they will be a secondary reader of the thesis, not a primary one. This difference between 'primary' and 'secondary' readerships is important and is often not immediately obvious to students. In the case of thesis and dissertation writing, it is the primary reader that is the final judge as to the quality of the student's piece of work, rather than the secondary reader. As Kamler and Threadgold (1997: 53) have pointed out, a dominant, or 'primary', reader, within the academy, 'quite simply counts more than other readers' (such as friends, learning advisors and anyone else the student shows their text to). It is important, then, that students consider the expert 'all-powerful reader' of the thesis or dissertation who can either accept or reject the writing as being coherent and consistent with the conventions of the target discourse community (Johns 1990) and how they will (potentially) read their text. And, of course, there is often anxiety and stress in the thesis-writing process with students expected to be experts in their area and method of inquiry (Casanave 2019; Russell-Pinson and Harris 2019) but unsure of how they will display this.

Another issue is the background knowledge, values and understandings it is assumed thesis writers will share with their readers (their examiners), what is important to their readers, and what is not. This impacts on how much display of knowledge the text should contain, to what extent a student should 'show what they know', as well as what issues should be addressed in the text, what boundaries can be crossed and how this might be done. It is also important to consider general expectations and conventions for theses and dissertations, as well as the particular expectations, conventions and requirements of the particular area of study. This includes how a thesis or dissertation is typically organized and how this might vary for a particular research topic and kind of study. There are also institutional expectations and requirements that need to be met as well as the criteria that are used for the assessment of the student's thesis.

New technologies and thesis and dissertation writing

Technical developments, as Miller (2017) points out, are now enabling the production of PhDs that are much more multimodal than they once were. The Sousanis and Clemson PhDs referred to earlier are examples of this. Other examples are Orlow's (2002) PhD 'Housed memory' awarded by the University of the Arts, London which was a multi-screen video installation about a Holocaust archive at the Wiener Museum in London. The video component of Orlow's submission is an endless handheld tracking shot, 'in which the camera takes on the role of an historical witness and records – shelf by shelf – the contents of the archive' (Newman n.d. online). Karikis' (2006) PhD 'The acoustics of the self' from the Slade School of Fine Art, University College London is a further example of an alternate thesis type. Karikis' submission comprised a 400-minute audio-book and an illustrated text-book accompanied by CDs and a DVD containing four short films plus a written thesis. His doctoral project employs academic writing, music composition and art practice to explore notions of the 'self' through the study of voice and sound.

These texts contrast with traditional print-only dissertations which, in the view of Edminster and Moxley (2002), often do not acknowledge or address alternatives and resources that are taking place in the construction of knowledge. The use of hyperlinks, colour images, streaming video, animation and sound files in a PhD thesis, for example, extends 'the representational limits imposed by the single mode of text' that is often prevalent in doctoral dissertations (Edminster and Moxley 2002: 96) (see Chapter 10). Edminster and Moxley discuss this use of additional resources drawing on the notion of *remediation* (Bolter and Grusin 1999), that is, 'the process by which one medium is reformed and improved upon by another' (102). Beyond this, multimodal resources have, as Andrews and England (2012: 37) point out, 'led to new forms of transcription and representation of data and findings and the re-thinking of what counts as knowledge'.

Newer forms of the doctoral thesis, then, draw on a range of resources, such as images, video, animations, sound files and performance. Each of these resources has particular *affordances* (Gibson 1977; Jewitt et al. 2016) in thesis and dissertation writing, that is, what it is possible to represent and express through the particular resource. This meaning potential (van Leeuwen 2005) of the particular resource, or mode, further, is 'shaped by how the mode has been used, what it has been repeatedly used to mean and do, and the social conventions that inform its use' (Jewitt 2017: 26). As Bateman (2008: 1) argues, text nowadays 'is just one strand in a complex presentational form that seamlessly incorporates visual aspects "around", and sometimes even instead of, the text itself'. This is something that is increasingly being seen in thesis of dissertation writing, as we discuss in the final chapter of this book.

As Archer (2010) explains, different aspects of meaning are carried in different ways by different modes and they each have different weightings. These alternate modes may have a similarity, oppositional or a complementary relation with the written text. Or they may be completely independent of the text and tell the student's story in a completely different way. In Archer's (2010: 211) view, the choice of how to represent data or create an argument in alternate ways 'presents complex choices about conjunctions of meaning and form'. In addition, expressions of voice such as certainty or tentativeness, engagement with the reader and authorial distance can be expressed in different ways through the use of multimodal resources with, for example, the use of colour, detail and choice of image (Archer 2013). Academic argument, then, can move beyond writing in doctoral texts and, as we have seen in the earlier examples of alternate

PhD theses, can include comics, digital media and other multimodal resources (Huang and Archer 2017). This gives us a different, or rather extended, notion of 'text' from what has traditionally been the case in thesis and dissertation writing. In these new kinds of texts, multiple textual and visual resources can be brought together, with differing degrees of strength, each contributing in their way to the student's overall argument (Ravelli et al. 2013).

Conclusion

This chapter has presented theoretical matters which will be taken up further in the chapters of this book. The notion of genre emergence underlies Chapter 4 which examines the first doctoral theses which were submitted in English-medium universities, notably at Yale University, the University of Oxford, the University of Toronto and the University of Melbourne. The chapter then compares these early doctorates with submissions that have been made more recently in the same universities in the same, or parallel, areas of study, discussing the more recent theses in terms of genre change and continuity. Chapter 5 examines the 'new humanities' doctorate which might be seen as a challenge to the prototypical doctoral thesis in these areas of study. Practice-based and professional doctorates are discussed in Chapters 6, 7 and 8 as further examples of change and evolution in thesis and dissertation writing. These doctorates are very often multimodal and are examples of new technologies and their affordances being employed in thesis and dissertation writing. The thesis by publication is discussed in Chapter 9 as a further development in doctoral writing. Chapter 10 looks to the future in thesis and dissertation writing, considering what the 'PhD of the future' might look like and how it might extend and evolve from the doctoral theses that have preceded them.

Note

1   The University of Oxford doctorate is a DPhil rather than a PhD.

3

Investigating change and stability in doctoral theses and dissertations

Introduction

As long ago as 1985, Swales made the very important point that

> it is not only texts that we need to understand, but the roles texts have in their environments; the values, congruent and conflictive, placed on them by occupational, professional and disciplinary memberships; and the expectations those memberships have of the patternings of the genres they participate in.
>
> (Swales 1985: 219)

Swales (1993) also calls for greater contextualization of genres arguing that, when dealing with genres, 'we ignore investigating context of situation and contexts of culture at some peril' (p. 691), a view that is especially important for thesis and dissertation writing. As Johns (2016) pointed out, what is prototypical and conventional in a genre is not just in the text itself. It is also in elements of the situation of the text as well as in its language or tone. Gaining an understanding of the complexity of the writing situation and the influence it has on writers and texts, thus, is essential to successful academic writing. We should point out, however, that our understanding of 'text' is not limited solely to written texts but, as will be apparent in our discussion of variants to the doctoral thesis and dissertation in the chapters that follow, extends to include multimodal texts too (see also Ravelli et al. 2013).

These views have motivated much of our research into academic writing in which we have sought to understand not just what academic texts look like but also why they look like they do. Indeed, as Lillis (2008) pointed out, many studies of academic writing at her time of writing had focused largely on the written text, adopting what she called a 'textualist analytic lens'. She acknowledges, however, a growing recognition by the field of 'the need to focus on the context of writing, for understanding what is involved and at stake in academic writing' (p. 354). As Tardy (2012) puts it, we need to take 'into account the social worlds for and out of which a text is produced' (p. 39). Ethnographically oriented approaches provide a methodology that enable scholars of writing to investigate the complex relationships between texts and the contexts and practices which shape their production, reception and distribution (see Paltridge, Starfield and Tardy (2016) and Guillén-Galve and Bocanegra-Valle (2021) for discussions of ethnographically oriented academic writing research).

This chapter builds a case for *textography*, our chosen investigative approach, which uses ethnographic tools (Green and Bloome 1997), 'talk around text' (Lillis 2008), and other sources such as university policy documents and previously published research for our study of genre change and stability to enable us to access insiders' perspectives on the texts we are examining. Lillis (2008) and Lillis and Curry (2010: 121) discuss the analytic potential of talk around texts when they identify three dimensions of talk around text. While they point out that writing research has tended to take interview data in which writers talk about their texts as 'transparently meaningful', as simply portraying a writer's thoughts, they suggest that talk can also be seen as pointing to specific discourses about the writer's self, about writing, about knowledge production in specific contexts and so forth. Interviews can thus provide insight into the choices writers make from the options available to them and the ways in which they navigate generic expectations. When understood in this way, talk around text can provide us with broader and deeper understandings of the relationship between text and context in relation to academic writing.

As there have been relatively few studies examining the evolution of the doctoral genre over time, we begin by briefly examining approaches used in studies that have considered diachronic change in a related genre, the research article (RA), the majority of which use text-based methods. We then look at methods adopted to examine theses and dissertations in terms of their macrostructual evolution, that is, the overall organization and structure of the texts. This is followed by a discussion of textography as a research methodology and the specific approach taken in the studies reported on here.

Text-based approaches

Change in research articles

As a publicly accessible academic genre, the RA has been widely studied by applied linguists and writing scholars. The majority of the studies, particularly since the seminal work of John Swales (1981) on the structure of RA introductions in English, have examined the macrostructures of different sections of the RA across a range of disciplines. Swales (2019) has himself recently acknowledged the potential pedagogic value of such studies but has argued that, from a research perspective, they tend to be descriptive rather than interpretive or explanatory. He advocates 'going beyond the textual or transcriptual to interviewing producers and recipients, along with those who have gatekeeping or evaluating roles' (p. 77).

While synchronic studies of the RA have thus predominated, at the same time there have been a small but growing number of studies that have adopted diachronic perspectives on changes within the RA genre. As the RA has been used by scientists since the seventeenth century to communicate research findings with other scientists, genre analysts are able to study genre change and stability over a considerable period of time. Indeed, Swales (1990: 10) drew our attention to this when he commented, 'Like all living genres, the RA is continually evolving.' These studies are, by and large, all text based.

Historical studies such as Bazerman's (1988) study of the emergence of the genre of the experimental report in the *Philosophic Transactions of the Royal Society of London*, the first scientific journal in English, from its founding in 1665 until 1800, have been influential in this regard. While he is, for obvious reasons, unable to provide interview data, he nevertheless paints a picture of the contexts in which the RA emerged and developed into its current form. He describes how in the early years many of the experiments reported in the *Transactions* were demonstrated before the assembled body of the Royal Society; over time the written account came to replace the 'communal witnessing' of the experiment, leading to the RA as we know it today.

Bazerman examined all articles (about 1,000 altogether over 7,000 pages) in volumes 1, 5, 10, 15, 20, 25, 30, 35, 40, 50, 60, 70, 80 and 90 of the *Transactions*, a period of 135 years. All articles using the word 'experiment' either in the title or running text were then selected for closer examination. Only articles written by an experimenter reporting on new experiments were included, leaving about 100 articles to be analysed. In his analysis, Bazerman used a combination of descriptive content analysis and thematic analysis.

Atkinson's (1999) study of the *Philosophical Transactions of the Royal Society of London* from 1675 to 1975 covered some of the same ground as Bazerman's but extended the volumes examined into the late twentieth century. He selected volumes for examination at seven, fifty-year intervals from 1675 to 1975. His study can therefore be seen to provide what he calls a 'wide-angle' (p. xviii) perspective on the evolution of a set of scientific texts. His research approach differs from that of Bazerman in that he employs two independent methods of discourse analysis, namely rhetorical analysis, a qualitative approach and a form of register analysis known as multidimensional analysis (Biber 1988) which is quantitative. The rhetorical analysis revealed three major aspects of textual development across-time: changes in the author's presence or absence in the text; changes in the preferred reporting genres; and changes in the representation of the community of text users in the texts themselves over time. The register analysis revealed changes across several linguistic dimensions. Over the 300-year period of the study, the language became less informal and more informationally dense and nominalized; texts became less narrative and more impersonal, more decontextualized, less overtly persuasive and more abstract.

Banks (2008) tracked the development of certain linguistic features he deemed central to scientific writing in English with his primary focus being from the seventeenth century until the late twentieth century. His main corpus is constituted by research articles from 1700 to 1980, also taken from the *Philosophical Transactions*. The corpus consists of thirty articles in total, selected at twenty-year periods with two articles from each period, one from the physical sciences and one from the biological sciences. The selected features studied were the use of the passive voice, first-person pronouns, nominalizations and thematic structure. He identified changes in the usage of all of these features over the period under investigation as well as discipline-related differences.

In a further set of textually focused studies, Hyland and Jiang (2019) report on diachronically based research that draws on three computerized corpora of research articles from the same five journals, each of which had achieved the top ranking in their field, spaced at three periods over the past fifty years: 1965, 1985 and 2015. The journals were from four disciplines: applied linguistics, sociology, electrical engineering and biology. Six research articles were selected from each of the journals in each of the three designated years, leading to a total of 360 articles across the four fields. Hyland and Jiang make the interesting point that the RA is a genre 'traditionally exhibiting glacially slow variation' (p. 32). Their book length study focuses on changes in argument and organizational patterns including cohesion and coherence, citation patterns, lexical bundles and features of stance and engagement.

Li (2021) analysed a corpus of 2707 RA abstracts totalling 453,470 words published in four applied linguistics journals between 1990 and 2019 in terms of changes in the use of the first person. She divided the thirty-year period into three individual decades: 1990–9 (the 1990s), 2000–9 (the 2000s) and 2010–19 (the 2010s). No clear patterns seemed to emerge, possibly due to the fairly short timescale. While Li puts forward several interpretations for the changes in the use of the first person pronoun that she observed, she qualifies these with the statement, 'Such discussions have been merely speculations based on the writer's expertise. The writer's genuine motivations or intentions behind their rhetorical choice have not been examined systematically.' She goes on to recommend further study of factors underlying diachronic change, 'particularly from the ethnographic perspective' (p. 11).

Ayers (2008) examined changes occurring in abstracts accompanying full research articles in the scientific journal *Nature* over a fourteen-year period (1991–2005), through a detailed genre analysis of a small-scale corpus. A first study was carried out in 1993, further extended in 1997 and a third study was carried out in 2005. Over this time period, the short texts (up to eighty words) that accompanied the research articles in *Nature* and were known as 'headings' evolved into more conventional versions of the abstract (150 words) as we currently understand the part-genre. Ayers consulted the journal's executive editor and four specialists from different scientific fields to help her interpret her findings. She attributes the changes in the genre to technological developments such as online publication and a greater desire to communicate scientific findings to a broader readership.

In her study of the evolution of the research article, Pérez-Llantada (2013) compared a corpus of Elsevier's 'article of the future' enhanced online prototypes with a corpus of conventional research articles to examine the extent of genre change. She combined her comparative genre analysis of the two corpora with the findings of a ten-item survey that she emailed to the authors of the texts in both corpora in order to investigate their 'practices and perceptions regarding online RAs' (p. 230). Despite a relatively low response rate, the survey findings supported her conclusion that the genre of the RA in the online environment was 'stabilised for now'. In her recent monograph (Pérez-Llantada 2021), she expands her use of email surveys to solicit the perspectives on genre change and stability of 800 scientists either publishing in a number or highly reputable journals or taking part in innovative projects.

While Lin and Evans' (2012) detailed analysis of the principal macrostructures found in a sample of 433 empirical RAs published in 2007 across thirty-nine disciplines is not diachronic in nature, they found that although the 'standard' IMRD pattern is still one of the major structural patterns in empirical RAs, there are a number of other frequently used patterns of textual organization. Of particular relevance to our approach to the study of theses and dissertations is their recommendation that future studies, in addition to manual and corpus-based analyses of texts, 'employ interviews, surveys and case studies to elicit individual writers' ideas, views and experiences ... the motivations behind their choice of macro-structures and writing practices in their disciplines' (p. 158).

A study that has done this was carried out by Kuteeva and McGrath (2015) in which they combined genre analysis of 22 RAs in pure mathematics with semi-structured interviews with the lead authors of five of these articles. Probing the views of 'expert informants' or disciplinary insiders for insight into the reasons behind authors' rhetorical, organizational and lexico-grammatical choices has been adopted by several applied linguistic researchers as a research strategy over the last couple of decades (see e.g. Harwood 2006a, 2006b; Hyland 2000, 2004, 2005) in response to the criticisms of purely text-focused studies outlined above. This 'talk around text' approach (see above) may be of limited value when those interviewed are not the authors of the articles under study. Where Kuteeva and McGrath's study innovates is in their decision to interview authors of the actual studies that comprise part of their corpus and draw on the interview data to triangulate and enhance their own judgements as they built their understanding of the rhetorical structure of the RAs.

In the next section of this chapter, we examine studies that have looked at generic change in doctoral theses and dissertations before moving on to look at a number of studies that have utilized the more qualitative approaches recommended by Lin and Evans (2011) and adopted by Kuteeva and McGrath (2015) above.

Change in theses and dissertations

Over the last several decades, an increasing amount of attention has been paid to the PhD thesis as a genre worthy of study in its own right, particularly in regard to its organization and structure and, more specifically, to the macrostructure of the thesis as a whole and to certain of its components or part-genres. Early studies examined fairly small numbers of theses, using text analytic methods to describe and categorize the macrostructures of masters and doctoral theses and dissertations across a range of disciplines (see e.g. Bunton 2002; Dudley-Evans 1999; Paltridge 2002; Thompson 1999). Through these studies, four types of organizational pattern were identified, namely the traditional simple, the complex traditional, the topic based and the thesis by compilation or publication (see Chapter 4 for a discussion of thesis types). As discussed in Chapter 5, Starfield and Ravelli (2006) analysed the macrostructures of twenty sociology and history PhD theses from a single Australian university, eighteen of which were categorized as topic-based. These early studies were constrained by the inaccessibility of the theses which were only available in hard copy in the university library where the students had submitted their thesis. With the advent of electronic theses and dissertations, more recent studies have been able to build larger corpora and conduct both synchronic and diachronic studies of organizational patterns. These studies however remain entirely text based.

Anderson, Alexander and Saunders (2020) accessed the online repositories of five major Canadian research universities and compiled a corpus of 1,373 PhD dissertations submitted to Faculties of Education between 2008 and 2017. They analysed the global organizational patterns of the dissertation macrostructures and cross-referenced these patterns with each study's research perspective. In addition to the four thesis types previously identified, they found two new hybrid dissertation macrostructures. These are a *Hybrid TM* (topic/manuscript) organized in a standard topic-based structure but containing previously published sections within chapters or previously published chapters in their entirety or as modified versions of previously published work and a *Hybrid SM* (simple/manuscript) organized in a standard IMRD sequence but containing previously published sections within chapters or previously published chapters in their entirety or as modified versions of previously published work. As the number of dissertations in these two categories was fairly low (below thirty in each instance) and almost all came from the same university, more research is certainly needed to see how widespread this development might be. In terms of the research perspectives employed, their findings indicate that 66 per cent of the PhD dissertations they examined could be classified as qualitative.

In a related study, Anderson, Saunders and Alexander (2022) extended their examination of their corpus of 1,373 PhD dissertations submitted to Faculties of Education at five major Canadian research universities between 2008 and 2017. They focused specifically on the 184 manuscript-style and 131 topic-based dissertations in the corpus, adopting a content analytic approach, comparing word counts, the number of chapters, authorship status and the research designs of the dissertations. Their major findings were that the manuscript-style dissertations were on average shorter than the topic-based dissertations and were largely co-authored, while the topic-based dissertations were entirely single authored. In addition, quantitative and mixed-method designs were mainly multi-authored, whereas qualitative dissertations tended to be single authored.

In a diachronically focused study, Anderson and Okuda (2021) compiled a corpus of 1,254 doctoral dissertations from a single Canadian research university spanning a fifty-two-year period from 1966 to 2018. In comparison with Anderson et al.'s studies discussed above, this approach allowed the authors to consider genre change over a lengthier period. Their corpus included 277 EdDs and 977 PhDs as, prior to 1993, the EdD had been the primary doctoral qualification in Education on offer at the particular university. From 1993, the EdD became more practice focused and the study excluded EdDs submitted after this date. The authors once again drew on genre and content analysis to analyse the dissertations. The overall results show a decline over time of the simple traditional macrostructure and an increase in topic-based dissertations. Until 1992, however, 88 per cent of all dissertations were in the traditional-simple format. By the mid-2000s, manuscript-style dissertations replaced topic-based dissertations as the second most common format. They also observed a growing occurrence of co-authorship within the manuscript-style dissertations from the turn of the century.

Dong (1998) adopted a somewhat different approach and surveyed 137 masters and doctoral students and thirty-two professors at two south-eastern US research institutions about their perceptions of dissertation writing. Her study compares student and supervisor uptake of the traditional five-chapter dissertation with that of the article compilation (manuscript) dissertation. Responses revealed that overall, 38 per cent of the graduate students were writing in the article-compilation format, although there were differences at the institutional level and in terms of whether the students spoke English as an additional language.

In a recent study looking at genre emergence, Paltridge and Starfield (2020b) analysed a corpus of 100 PhD theses, consisting of twenty of the earliest doctorates submitted to four leading English-medium universities in the United States, Canada, the UK and Australia and compared the overall organizational patterns of these early dissertations with more recent dissertations from the same universities (see Chapter 4 for discussion of this study).

Textography

While the diachronic studies reported on above locate the changes and stabilities they observe over time within the specific sociorhetorical contexts in which they arise, the evidence they provide is, as noted earlier, in some cases for obvious reasons, largely dependent on the authors' interpretations. The contextual understandings they provide are somewhat thinly sketched and largely gleaned from their reading of historical documents or rather perfunctorily addressed.

Some authors, like Anderson et al. (2020), who conducted the entirely text-based examinations of dissertation macrostructures described above, have suggested that more contextualized understandings such as 'a textographic approach … that integrated interviews with writers and supervisors could help unravel why [they] saw macrostructure clusters for the hybrid dissertations, for example' (p. 10).

Textography (Swales 2018) is a research method which combines elements of text analysis with ethnographic techniques such as interviews, observations, document analysis and other data sources. The analysis thus goes 'beyond the text' (Freedman 1999) to investigate the ways in which language is used in specific writing contexts and the reasons for it. The term 'textography' was first coined by Swales (1998; Swales and Luebs 1995) to describe an investigative approach that aims to get an inside view of the worlds in which texts are written, why texts are written as they are and the values that underlie the texts that have been written. A particular goal of a textography is to examine the 'situatedness' of written texts (Swales 1998). A textography, thus, aims to explore the context in which a text is produced in order to gain an understanding of why the text is written as it is. This examination of context includes consideration of the role and purpose of the text, the audience for the text, expectations of the particular discourse community and the text's relationship with other texts. It, thus, aims to get an inside view of the worlds in which texts are written, what guides the writing and the values that underlie the texts that have been written. It may also consider texts that surround the text in terms of the chain of genres and networks (Devitt 2004; Swales 2004; Tardy 2003) of which it is a part.

A textography, then, is more than a traditional text analysis yet less than a full-blown ethnography. Its prime focus of interest is the text and it aims to develop 'ethnographically sensitive text analytic tools which enable researchers to bring the text back into frame' (Lillis and Scott 2007: 22). It does not necessarily involve the sustained engagement over a period of time with the research site that one would expect of ethnography. Rather, it draws on a range of ethnographic techniques and combines these with text analysis, with the aim of understanding both the form and formation of the texts that people write.

Swales (2018) carried out a textography of the texts produced in a university building that housed not only the English language centre in which he worked at the time but also the Computer Centre and the university Herbarium. In addition to examining these texts he gathered observational data, analysed documents and correspondence, and conducted text-based interviews with employees on each floor of the building. He then compiled textual life histories of seven of the people who worked in the building, including himself. He found that on each floor of his building people wrote quite different texts, even though they were all working at the same institution. He also found the writers' professional and academic histories and their life commitments were an important influence on what they wrote and how they wrote it.

Subsequently, several studies have adopted textographic approaches to examine thesis and dissertation writing. Paltridge (2004) employed textography to examine the exegeses that art and design students write as part of their master's degrees at a New Zealand university. An exegesis is a written text that accompanies a visual project submitted as the research component of the student's degree. These texts are similar in some ways to the thesis genre, but in many ways are also quite different. A genre analysis of the exegeses was combined with an examination of texts that surrounded the exegeses, such as the postgraduate student handbook, the guide to examiners, examiners' reports and the annual report on the master's degree. Interviews were also carried out with students, advisors and examiners. This was done in order to explore the particular nature and character of the students' texts, the values that underlay the texts and the role the texts played in the particular academic setting, that is, to examine the texts, role and context of the students' texts (Johns 1997).

Paltridge, Starfield, Ravelli and Tuckwell (2012a) (see also Paltridge et al. 2012b; Ravelli et al. 2013; Starfield et al. 2012) employed textography in their study of texts that visual and performing arts doctoral students write as part of the submission requirements for their doctoral degrees. Data collected for their study included a nation-wide survey, thirty-six dissertations, thirty-six supervisor questionnaires, fifteen student and fifteen supervisor interviews, university prospectuses, information given to students in relation to their candidature, published studies on doctoral research and examination in these fields of study, in-house art school publications, discussion papers, and attendance at roundtable discussions and exhibition openings. Their study found that there was a range of ways in which students could write their texts as well as reasons for this variability, some of which were institutional, and some of which were due to the influence of key figures in the field, rather than conventions of the particular disciplines. The analysis of the macrostructures of the thirty-six dissertations in their corpus identified eighteen topic-based and seventeen traditional-simple categories with one traditional-complex thesis. They found that the standard IMRD structure, however, was often reconceptualized to better represent the research topic and setting as well as the creative decisions and agency of the doctoral writers.

Seloni (2014) conducted a textographic analysis of a Colombian art historian's thesis writing for his MA degree in visual culture at a North American university. She collected data from multiple sources including his multimodal drafts, six semi-structured interviews, email exchanges, her own researcher journal and different types of written artefacts produced in the process of his thesis writing. She triangulated these data sources to understand Jacob's (the student) choices as he developed the 'non-conventional macrostructure' (p. 86) for his thesis.

In her doctoral dissertation, 'Multimodal meaning making and the doctoral dissertation – An exploration of academic forms', Estima (2020) examined four successfully defended multimodal dissertations and included interviews with the authors and their supervisors as to their experiences of producing their dissertations. She also examined each of the dissertations to determine what multimodal resources were used and for what purpose and collected university dissertation guidelines and requirements to inform her analysis. Her thesis is itself multimodal in that some of the interview data is presented multimodally in embedded video format and the thesis is available in PDF and online formats.

For her doctoral dissertation, Panteledis (2013) investigated the genre ecology of doctoral dissertation writing in the social sciences and humanities at a North American university in order to understand how various stakeholders understood the norms and expectations of the dissertation genre and how it might be evolving. She was particularly interested in how the advent of electronic publication of theses and dissertations might be impacting on genre evolution. She conducted a focus group with six students who were working on their dissertations and interviewed five faculty members interested in genre and dissertation writing. She used textual genre analysis to analyse fourteen award-winning dissertations to compare their uptake of genre conventions and consulted graduate handbooks, award descriptions and listserv conversations.

More recently, Amell (2022) adopted a textographic methodology in her doctoral research into unconventional doctoral dissertations. She collected and examined seventy-one dissertations, fifty-one of which were considered to be unconventional in some regard. She collected additional data through an online questionnaire, receiving seventy responses from participants in twelve countries and recruited nine of the respondents for unstructured interviews about their experiences of writing or supervising unconventional dissertations. In addition, she collected university guidelines and policies on dissertations from thirty-eight Canadian universities as well as other texts such as blogposts and Twitter posts that mentioned dissertation writing. Her use of textography allowed her to explore with participants how they engaged with the dissertation genre and better understand the decisions they made in terms of the expectations within their specific contexts of production and reception rather than analysing the texts in isolation.

There is thus a developing interest in adopting more contextualized approaches to study genre change in doctoral theses and dissertations. As textography aims to narrow the gap between text and context in its examination of academic writing (Lillis 2008; Sizer 2021), it is a 'step away' from more traditional textual analysis in that it explores situated writing practices from insiders' perspectives, allowing us to provide contextualized accounts of a discipline's texts and practices. In the study we report on here, our textographic approach has allowed us to combine our initial diachronic view of the development of the doctoral thesis with synchronic perspectives on the shape and form of recent theses and dissertations which are in turn informed by the perspectives of the creators of some of the texts and those who supervised their production in four distinct geographical locations.

Data collected for the book

In this section, we describe the various data sources that we collected for our textographic study of change and continuity in doctoral theses.

Theses

For the first phase of the study reported on in this book, we compared the first doctoral theses awarded in the English-speaking world, in this case at Yale University, Oxford University, the University of Toronto and the University of Melbourne, with theses awarded more recently at the same universities in the same, or similar, areas of study. We collected 100 doctoral theses for this stage of the study. The theses were in the areas of Science and the Humanities. Our reason for doing this was to gain a benchmark for genre change in terms of thesis types across these two broad areas of study. The theses examined in the later stages of the study were in the Humanities and Social Sciences, the overarching interest of the book, and were much broader in terms of university and type of doctorate than the first stage of the study. They were, specifically, new humanities doctorates, practice-based doctorates, professional doctorates and doctorates by publication awarded in the United States, the UK, Canada and Australia. For this later data set, we collected twenty new humanities doctorates (ten history and ten sociology theses), forty professional doctorates (all Doctor of Education theses), eighty practice-based doctorates (forty in music and forty in the visual arts), and hundred doctorates by publication. It is important to note that in the case of the practice-based doctorates, the term 'thesis' encompasses both the written and creative components of the thesis. Details of the universities from which the theses were collected and specific information on each corpus can be found in the later chapters of the book.

Interviews

As Sizer (2021) points out, interviews are a frequently used method in textographic research as they 'present opportunities for dialogue and discussion of texts, and the authors' voice to be heard rather than monologic reports from researchers about what authors have written' (p. 46). We interviewed nineteen students and four supervisors. All interviews were conducted post submission of the students' thesis. Interviewees were asked whether they wished to remain anonymous which is why, in some of the chapters, specific texts are discussed and the authors identified and in others they are not. Supervisors were, however, not asked to comment on specific theses but on their experiences of supervising the particular thesis type more broadly. Prior to publication, we shared the sections of the book in which they were cited with our interviewees to seek their permission to cite specific interview data.

Our interviews were semi-structured and followed the questions shown in Appendix A. Space was allowed in the interviews, however, to ask about specific matters that had come to our attention in the textual analysis of the theses which we wished to follow up on in the interviews. Interviews were conducted over Zoom and were up to an hour long in most instances. Interview data allowed us to paint a richer picture of the contexts in which the students had produced their theses and dissertations, explore motivations for the choices they had made in relation to structure, organization and presentation of their text as well as develop a deeper understanding of the expectations and concerns of supervisors.

We found contacting recently graduated students more challenging than we had anticipated. That our data collection period coincided with the Covid-19 pandemic may have been a factor in some potential interviewees not responding to our invitations. We were however surprised to find that some of the student authors whom we had hoped to talk to either had no recent online presence or had no online presence whatsoever which meant they were not employed in any academic institutions and could not be contacted. Some of the concerns we report on in Chapter 10 in regard to the future of the PhD relate to the scarcity of academic positions in the humanities and social sciences and this may account for some of the challenges we experienced. High-profile graduates in the musical and visual arts with burgeoning professional careers also proved difficult to access. Some of the supervisors whom we approached had retired and did not wish to take part in the study. That said, the students and supervisors who agreed to take part in the study gave willingly of their time and were genuinely interested in our project and we are most grateful to them.

University guidelines and policies

In addition, we examined university policies and guidelines for the completion and award of the degrees in each of these countries to gain institutional and disciplinary perspectives on generic requirements for each of the doctorate types we examined. We also read published accounts of students' and supervisors' experiences of working on these degrees.

Conclusion

While, as discussed above, most approaches to investigating genre change in research articles and theses and dissertations have adopted text-based methods and been diachronic in nature, recent studies have begun to explore the wider contexts of production and reception of these texts drawing on participant interviews that enable thicker understandings of the situated nature of doctoral writing. Our study continues this latter trajectory.

4

The evolution of thesis and dissertation types

Doctoral degrees have been offered for over 200 years and, in English medium universities, since the 1860s. In this chapter, we examine the emergence of the doctoral thesis/dissertation as a research genre and trace its development over time. We do this by examining the first doctorates that were awarded in English-medium universities and then by comparing these theses and dissertations with doctorates that have been awarded more recently at the same universities in parallel areas of study. Our aim in doing this is to see to what extent doctoral theses have changed over this time period and in what ways (or if) they have remained constant. We are doing this not just to understand where the doctoral thesis has come from but also in what ways it has evolved or emerged (Allori et al. 2014; Miller 2016) as the genre it is today (see Chapter 2). Change in other genres, such as the research article (see Chapter 3), has been examined by a number of researchers (see e.g. Atkinson 1999; Bazerman 1988; Berkenkotter and Huckin 1995; Luzón and Pérez-Llantada 2019; Pérez-Llantada 2013). Such an analysis has not, however, been undertaken in relation to the doctoral thesis, the focus of this chapter. Our focus in this chapter is on thesis types, that is, the macrostructures of doctoral theses and how they have changed over time. We examine theses in both science and the humanities, the two broad areas in which doctorates were first awarded. Our aim in doing this is to create a baseline for the book where the focus, after this chapter, is on social sciences and humanities theses.

Thesis and dissertation types

Anderson, Saunders and Alexander (2022) provide a review of thesis types and their typical macrostructures. Figure 4.1 is a summary of thesis types found in their and other studies of thesis types, that is, traditional simple and topic-based

Thesis type	
Traditional: simple	Reports on a single study
Traditional: complex	Reports on more than a single study
Topic-based	Reports on a number of sub-topics
PhD by publication	Comprised of a number of already published, accepted, or publishable research articles or book chapters

Figure 4.1 Summary of thesis types (based on Paltridge 2002).

theses which report on a single study and traditional complex theses and PhDs by publication which report on two or more studies. Typical sections of each of these thesis types are shown in Figure 4.2.

Anderson, Saunders and Alexander's (2022) study was based on 1,373 doctoral theses submitted at five Canadian universities. They found that some sections of the theses occured separately, but this was not always the case. Thus, a traditional simple thesis may often (although not always) have a separate literature review chapter and have more than one results chapter, especially when the thesis is based on a qualitative methodology. Traditional complex theses, they found, sometimes contain a separate literature review chapter but on occasion the literature review section may be found in the individual studies contained in the thesis. They describe the PhD by publication as commencing with an Introduction section followed by each of the published or publishable manuscripts followed by a Conclusion. Methods, Results, Discussion and Conclusions sections are typically contained in each of the manuscript chapters, but they may be complemented by broader Literature review, Methodology, Discussion and Conclusions chapters as well, as in the PhD by publication shown in Figure 2.6 in the Chapter 2 of this book. Topic-based theses may or may not contain a methods chapter, even though they typically report on empirical studies.

Paltridge et al.'s (2012b) examination of doctoral degrees in the visual and performing arts found there was a range of organizational possibilities for the written text that is part of a doctoral submission in these areas of study, each at different points on a continuum. Among their data were very conventional doctoral texts with discrete components in a fixed order, and theses that were relatively unstructured. Notwithstanding, all of the theses had met the expected

Traditional: simple

Introduction
Literature review
Materials and methods
Results
Discussion
Conclusions

Traditional: complex

Introduction
Background to the study and review
of the literature
(Background theory)
(General methods)
Study 1
   Introduction
   Methods
   Results
   Discussion and conclusions
Study 2
   Introduction
   Methods
   Results
   Discussion and conclusions
Study 3, etc.
   Introduction
   Methods
   Results
   Discussion and conclusions
Discussion
Conclusions

Topic-based

Introduction
Topic 1
Topic 2
Topic 3, etc.
Conclusions

PhD by publication

Introduction
Background to the study
Research article 1
   Introduction
   Literature review
   Materials and methods
   Results
   Discussion
   Conclusions
Research article 2
   Introduction
   Literature review
   Materials and methods
   Results
   Discussion
   Conclusions
Research article 3, etc.
   Introduction
   Literature review
   Materials and methods
   Results
   Discussion
   Conclusions
Discussion
Conclusions

Figure 4.2 Typical sections of thesis types (Paltridge 2002: 135).

requirements for PhDs such as contribution to knowledge and an awareness of previous research, although at times these were presented in less than conventional ways. This research highlights how genre change (Berkenkotter 2007; Devitt 2004) can be understood as the 'stabilized for now' outcome of complex institutional negotiations – the centripetal forces for unification and hierarchy interacting dynamically with the centrifugal forces for change

(Bakhtin 1981) that play out through the academy as communities and their members position themselves within new contexts of production, reception and assessment.

In a study of twenty sociology and history PhDs, Starfield and Ravelli (2006) identified a cluster of 'new humanities' theses that could be seen to challenge the conventional thesis in these disciplines. At the time, they questioned whether the changes they observed at the macrostructural level and in terms of the presentation of the researcher's identity constituted a passing 'fad' or were indications of more longer-term change (see Chapter 5 for further discussion of new humanities theses). Anderson, Alexander and Saunders' (2020) study of PhDs in Canada found many dissertations which followed the thesis and dissertation types outlined above but also a number of hybrid dissertations. These were 'hybrid simple/manuscript' and 'hybrid topic/manuscript' dissertations which, while organized in a simple IMRD pattern, also contained work within their chapters that had been previously published, either in its entirety or in a modified version.

The PhD by publication is relatively new in some areas of study. This version of the genre shares features of both research articles and more conventional features of the doctoral thesis. This was seen in Dong's (1998) study of doctoral dissertations based on a compilation of publishable research articles. She found these to be quite different from other sorts of doctoral dissertations. The research article chapters in the dissertations were more concise than typical dissertation chapters with less of the 'display of knowledge' that is often found in a doctoral dissertation. Further, in terms of audience, they were written more as 'experts writing for experts' than novices 'writing for admission to the academy'. In this sense, theses by publication are quite different from the 'traditional: complex' type thesis described above (see Chapter 9 where the PhD by publication is discussed in more detail).

Data collected

In order to consider changes in time in terms of thesis types over time, we collected examples of the earliest and most recent doctoral theses from Yale University, the University of Oxford, the University of Toronto and the University of Melbourne, the first universities in each of their respective countries to award doctoral degrees. In order to decide exactly what and how much data to collect, previous studies of a similar kind were examined to identify what data had been collected and the period/s of time over which they were collected. The two key studies examined were Evans et al.'s (2003) examination of PhDs in Australia and Simpson's (2009) review of the development of the PhD in Britain. The Evans et al. study commenced with PhDs awarded in 1948 and the Simpson study examined PhDs awarded since 1917. After this, both studies looked at PhDs in ten-year blocks. This was considered for the current study but was not adopted given that the commencement date for the award of PhDs in each country was different meaning that there would be uneven sets of PhDs which would make comparisons across the data sets difficult. Instead, it was decided to collect the first doctoral theses that were awarded in each of the countries and a set of theses awarded more recently at the same universities in the same, or parallel, areas of study. The reason for the choice of 'parallel' rather than the same areas of study is that, in some cases, it was difficult to determine the disciplinary area of the early PhDs whereas this was always clear in the recent theses. Dobson (2012) reports similar difficulties in classifying doctoral theses; finding the award of PhDs in terms of faculties, disciplines and fields of study has changed over time. For example, one of the first PhDs awarded at Oxford was in the area of 'Science' whereas nowadays Science is broken up into many different sub-areas. In a case such as this, the recent area of study was chosen on the basis of the sub-area that the early PhD seemed to most closely fit in to.

Each of the university's library websites were searched in order to identify the theses to include in the study. Some of the North American theses were obtained through the ProQuest Dissertations and Theses Portal. The British Library Electronic Digital Thesis Online Service (EThOS) was also helpful for identifying possible theses to include in the study. Early PhDs, however, were especially difficult to locate and inquiries were sent to university librarians for help with this as well as for assistance in obtaining copies of the theses. Library records were, however, sometimes incomplete, some of the earliest doctoral theses were not in the university libraries and a thesis that was listed as a PhD in a library catalogue sometimes turned out to be a master's thesis. Evans et al. (2003) and Simpson (2009) report having similar problems in their collection of doctoral theses, as does Herman (2017) in a recent study of the development of doctoral education in South Africa. In addition, in one university early PhDs were not available for view or for purchase even though they were listed in the university's catalogue. One of the universities, further, had an embargo on many of their recent PhDs before they could be accessed, or the thesis could only be accessed by the university's staff and students. In addition, not all the theses and dissertations were in digital form so hard copies had to be requested from the particular university library. This was particularly the case with the early theses where, if they were available, a digital copy had to be made. One university charged a very high fee for these digitized copies while others provided them for free.

The earliest PhDs collected from Yale University were in the areas of Astronomy and History. The recently awarded PhDs from Yale collected for the study were also in Astronomy and History. The early PhDs from Oxford University were in the areas of Science and Literature with the recent PhDs from Oxford in the areas of Microbiology and English. The early PhDs from the University of Toronto were in Physics, Biomedical Sciences and Geography and the recent PhDs in Physics and Geography. The early PhDs collected from the University of Melbourne were in Chemistry, Biology/Biochemistry, Literature and Physics. The recent PhDs from the University of Melbourne were in Medicine and Literature. An attempt was made, thus, to have a balance of areas of study in Science and the Humanities in order to see if there were similarities or differences across these two very broad groupings of study.

While access to early theses made it difficult to collect a large data set in terms of even numbers of early doctoral theses, this was less of a problem with recently awarded PhDs where a greater number of theses were collected from each of the universities. Thus, while it was possible to collect five early PhDs from each of the institutions, we were able to collect more recent PhDs, ten from each of the two subject areas chosen for each of the universities, a total of hundred PhDs in all. It would, of course, have been preferable to have larger set of early PhDs in the data set to balance the number of recent PhDs. This, however, was not possible due to the difficulty, and in one case the cost, of obtaining early doctoral theses.

Analysis of the data

As discussed above, the data for the study were examples of the earliest doctorates awarded at Yale University, the University of Oxford, the University of Toronto and the University of Melbourne, as well as doctorates awarded in the same universities more recently in either the same or parallel areas of study. The early theses were analysed to see to what extent they fitted with the research into thesis types described above, particularly, traditional simple, traditional complex, topic-based thesis types and theses by publication. These early theses were then compared with the more recent theses and dissertations drawing on the same framework for analysis as was applied to the early theses. This analysis was then considered in relation to the concepts of prototype, family resemblances (see Chapter 2), and discussions of choice and constraint in academic writing (Devitt 2004; Swales 2004).

Findings

Early PhDs at Yale

The first PhD that was available from Yale was the dissertation by Margaretta Palmer in the area of Astronomy titled 'Determination of the orbit of the comet 1847 VI' (Palmer 1894), published in the same year in the *Transactions of the Astronomical Observatory* at Yale University. Palmer's dissertation was twenty pages long. The Table of Contents for Palmer's PhD is shown in Figure 4.3. Her dissertation commenced with an Introduction which was followed by further sections which discussed the history of the comet she was investigating, then her calculation of the orbit of the comet. On the final two pages of her dissertation, she reports on her results and discusses them, although not in relation to the earlier research she had cited. Her dissertation could be described as a very early traditional simple dissertation with an introduction, review of previous research, outline of her method of analysis, and a results section but without a discussion section in which she compares her results with those of previous research. Her thesis was typed, as opposed to Larson's (1910) PhD which was hand-written.

Determination of the Orbit of the Comet 1847 VI

1. Introduction
2. History and discovery of the comet
3. Computation of the ephemeris
4. Determination of the places of the companion-stars
5. Computation of the ephemeris with the observations
6. Determination of the normal places
7. Computation of the perturbations
8. Formations of the equations of condition
9. Determination of the elements and discussion of the results

---

Figure 4.3 Table of Contents for Palmer's (1894) PhD from Yale University.

Larson's (1910) PhD in the area of Astronomy, 'A computation of the orbit of E3062', described the calculation of the orbit of a star. The dissertation was ninety-five pages long and did not include a contents page. The first two pages of the dissertation listed the sources that were drawn on for the study, twenty in all. The next three pages gave references to the measures used in the study. The dissertation continues with an outline of the methods of calculation that were used, and the results of the study, titled 'Observations'. A section then follows titled 'Insights and reflections' which discusses the results but not in relation to previous research on the topic. The dissertation contains fifty-seven pages of data analysis in the form of calculations presented in table form with commentaries on the calculations dispersed amongst the tables. The dissertation concludes with five pages of 'Remarks'. Larson's dissertation could also be seen an early version of a traditional simple dissertation but without literature review or discussion sections in the way that is expected of a doctoral dissertation today. The early Astronomy dissertations, then, while containing the fundamentals of what would be expected of a research report, presented them in ways that are very different from and not as extensive as present-day traditional simple dissertations.

The early History dissertations from Yale were similar to each other in that they were all topic based which is similar to monograph-style History PhDs today (see Chapter 5). In contrast with the Astronomy dissertations, however, there was constant reference to previous research in the History dissertations. There was, however, no methodology section in the early History dissertations which is in contrast to many current History PhDs which have a 'historiography' section in them (see Chapter 5). The early History PhDs, further, had no discussion chapters. Beyond this, none of the early Yale dissertations contained an abstract, or lists of tables or figures, and not all contained a table of contents. One of the History PhDs was seventy pages while the other two were much longer, 383 and 390 pages long. In two of the early History PhDs, the bibliography was presented before the main text of the dissertation and in the other it followed the main text.

Recent PhDs at Yale

The recent Yale PhDs in the area of Astronomy were all 'traditional complex' dissertations and reported, in every case, on three separate but related studies. Powell's (2019) dissertation titled 'The environments of accreting supermassive black holes', for example, reports on investigations of black holes in terms of colour-mass, halo occupations and environments. Each of the studies draws on different data sets, describes the methods employed, results of the analysis and discusses the results in relation to previous research. The Table of Contents from Powell's dissertation is shown in Figure 4.4. This dissertation is typical of traditional complex dissertations in that the chapters which present the separate studies each contain data, analysis, results and discussion subsections making the chapters stand alone as research studies while still remaining within the overall topic of the dissertation. The chapter titles for these studies reflect the focus of the chapter as well as sub-themes within the broader focus of the dissertation.

While all the Astronomy dissertations were written in the same academic department, they each had different supervisors showing an obvious departmental preference for 'traditional complex' dissertations in this department. When compared with the early PhDs in Astronomy at Yale, the recent dissertations are much more formalized and in line with current expectations for doctoral

---

The Environments of Accreting Supermassive Black Holes

1 **Introduction**
　1.1 Active Galactic Nuclei
　1.2 Black Hole-Galaxy Co-evolution
　1.3 AGN in a Cosmological Context via Clustering
　1.4 X-ray+Multiwavelength AGN Surveys
　1.5 Thesis Overview

2 **Color-Mass and Morphology at z ~ 1**
　2.1 Data
　2.2 Morphological Analysis
　2.3 Color-Mass and Morphology
　2.4 Summary

3 **Test Cases for A G N Feedback in Two Nearby AGN**
　3.1 The Close AGN Reference Survey
　3.2 Observations and Data Reduction
　3.3 Data Analysis
　3.4 Discussion
　3.5 Summary and Conclusions

4 **Halo Occupation Statistics of Local AGN**
　4.1 Data
　4.2 Method
　4.3 Results
　4.4 Discussion
　4.5 Summary

5 **Environments of X-ray Luminous Quasars**
　5.1 Data
　5.2 Clustering Methodology
　5.3 Halo Mass Estimation
　5.4 Results
　5.5 Discussion
　5.6 Summary

6 **Conclusions**
　6.1 Summary
　6.2 Future Work
　6.3 Comparison to GOODS Morphology in the Literature

Bibliography

Figure 4.4 Table of Contents from an Astronomy traditional complex dissertation (Powell 2019).

writing. Notwithstanding, both the early and the recent dissertations make a substantive and original contribution to knowledge, essential requirements for doctoral dissertations (Holbrook et al. 2004).

The recent History PhDs at Yale were all topic based, the same as the early History PhDs described above; that is, the dissertations commenced with an introductory chapter which was then followed by a series of chapters which address the sub-topics being investigated and have titles which are reflective of these sub-topics. The Table of Contents from Decker's (2017) dissertation 'Gender, religious difference, and the notarial economy in medieval Catalonia' is shown in Figure 4.5. After the Introduction, the dissertation is broken into two parts which, between them, contain six topic-based chapters. The dissertation ends with a Conclusion.

There are, then, both differences and similarities between the early and recent Yale dissertations. The early Astronomy dissertations reported on a single empirical study, whereas the recent Astronomy dissertations, in each case, reported on three empirical studies. The recent Astronomy dissertations all followed the same organizational structure, whereas the early Astronomy dissertations, while containing all of the components that would be expected from a dissertation based on an empirical study, did this in a less easily recognizable way. The early Astronomy dissertations, further, were shorter

---

Gender, Religious Difference, and the Notarial Economy in Medieval Catalonia

Introduction: A Tale of Three Cities
Part I: Home Economics – Marriage, Kinship, and Money
        Chapter 1: The Economics of Marriage
        Chapter 2: The Ties of Blood and Money
Part II: Women's Labor in the Notarial Economy
        Chapter 3: Women's Work in Catalan Credit Markets
        Chapter 4: Women and Social Networks in Catalan Credit Markets
        Chapter 5: Women's Work in Commerce, Production, and Domestic Service
        Chapter 6: Gendered Landscapes in Urban Real Estate Markets
Conclusion
Appendix 1: Summary Statistics
Appendix 2: List of Professions

Figure 4.5 Table of Contents from a topic-based History dissertation (Decker 2017).

than the recent Astronomy dissertations and drew on many fewer sources than the recent dissertations. The early and the recent History dissertations were all topic-based, as are most current History PhDs (see Chapter 5), showing that this preference for organizing the dissertations has not changed since the earliest days. The recent History dissertations were between 117 and 648 pages long. They, thus, varied in length, as did the early History dissertations. In every case, however, the recent History dissertations drew on many more sources than the early History dissertations which is perhaps not surprising given the access current students have to academic resources compared to students writing in the early days on the PhD.

Early DPhils at Oxford

The early DPhils at the University of Oxford were in the areas of Literature and Science. The DPhil by Eleanor Simpson (1922) titled 'The prose works of John Donne' is topic based as is the other early Literature DPhil in the data set by Leon Roth (1922) 'A critical discussion of the sources of Spinoza with special reference to Maimonides and Descartes'. Simpson's thesis was made up of twelve chapters plus four appendices, the final chapter titled 'List of books consulted'. Roth's thesis was only six chapters but with substantial subsections within them. An Appendix contained the main texts Roth had examined in his study.

The early Science DPhils at Oxford, like the early Yale Astronomy PhDs, each reported on a single study. The early Science DPhils, like the early Literature DPhils, could also be described as being topic-based but with the inclusion of a results chapter in every case. The Table of Contents of Ayres' (1923) thesis 'Ionisation by electrons travelling with small velocities in various gases' is shown in Figure 4.6 as an illustration of this. The thesis is in five sections. There are no literature review or methodology chapters with an analysis of the results of the study being presented as the final chapter of the thesis.

The other two early Science DPhils in the data set were similarly topic-based, both four-chapter theses. One of the theses was hand-written. The other theses were type-written but with hand-written symbols placed within the text.

Recent DPhils at Oxford

The recent Oxford DPhils were in the areas of English and Microbiology. The recent English DPhils were, like the early Literature DPhils at Oxford, also topic-based. The Table of Contents from Clucas' (2014) thesis 'Romantic reclusion

---

Ionisation by Electrons Travelling with Small Velocities in Various Gases

Section I.   The ionisation of air, hydrogen and nitrogen by x-rays from polonium
Section II.   The ionisation by collision of hydrogen, nitrogen and argon using ultra-violet light
Section III. The ionisation by collision of helium, using ultra-violet light
Section IV.   Considerations arising out of the behaviour of helium
Section V.   Analysis of results

Figure 4.6 Table of Contents of Ayres' (1923) topic-based thesis.

in the works of Cowper and Wordsworth' shown in Figure 4.7 is an example of this. The thesis is made up of an Introduction, four topic-based chapters ('Creative Reclusion', 'Medical Reclusion', 'Political Reclusion', and 'Natural Reclusion') and a Conclusion. As with most topic-based theses, there are no separate literature review, methodology, results or discussion chapters in the thesis. Clucas' description of Chapters 1–4 shows that they each investigate a particular theme, for example, by saying 'Chapter Two explores …' and 'Chapter Three examines …' (p. 2). This is not apparent however in his chapter headings (or subheadings).

The recent Microbiology DPhils at Oxford ranged from reporting on a single study as in Allen's (2014) 'The structure, function and specificity of the Rhodobacter sphaeroides membrane-associated chemotaxis array', through to five studies as in Barros' (2012) 'Transcriptional regulation by non-coding RNAs in *Saccharomyces cerevisiae*'. Apart from Allen's DPhil, all the Microbiology theses were traditional complex in their organization, ranging from reporting on three studies to five studies. Each of the traditional complex theses contained an Introduction–Methods–Results–Discussion structure within the chapters that reported on the separate studies, although one of the Microbiology theses (Mestek 2011) placed the Methods section of the chapter after the Discussion in each case, as is increasingly common in published research articles in the sciences more broadly (Lin and Evans 2012).

What we see then is that a preference for topic-based theses has continued in the area of English at Oxford from its earliest theses through to the present day. In the case of Science, however, we now see a preference for multiple studies in more recent DPhils, in a traditional complex format, as is the case with the current Astronomy PhDs at Yale.

Romantic Reclusion in the Works of Cowper and Wordsworth

Introduction
    'Community is made of what retreats from it': The theory of reclusion
    'No need to inquire outside yourself': Critics of sociability
    'The world is too much with us': Reclusion as dissent
    'Far from the madding crowd's ignoble strife': Political retirement literature
    'A pure form of Society': The reclusive revolution

1. **Creative Reclusion**
    Poetic exiles and hermeneutic hermits
    'What dost thou in this world?': Miltonic precedents
    'His genius fed on manna': Cowper's Milton
    Milton as Wordsworth's 'great Predecessor'
    'A wretched exile's song': Cowper and the plain style
    'Farewell! – farewell, Popinjay!': Wordsworth's linguistic solitude

2. **Medical Reclusion**
    'Honest melancholy'
    Cowper at 'The College': Reclusion as a cure for melancholy
    Pathological Selfhood: Cowper's confessional personae
    'Having two natures in me': Wordsworth's melancholy exiles

3. **Political Reclusion**
    Men in the moon: eighteenth-century historiography
    'His warfare is within': Cowper's response to the Machiavellian moment
    'Let us look to ourselves': lessons from the French Revolution

4. **Natural Reclusion**
    'Books in the running brooks': Morality from nature
    'Retired behind his own creation': Cowper's natural Calvinism
    'An active principle alive in all things': Wordsworth's natural reclusion

Conclusion
Bibliography
Note to Texts

Figure 4.7 Table of Contents from an English topic-based dissertation (Clucas 2014).

Early PhDs at the University of Toronto

The early PhDs at the University of Toronto were in the areas of Physics, Biomedical Sciences and Geography. McLennan's (1900) PhD in Physics, 'Electrical Conductivity in gases transversed by cathode rays', was published in the *Philosophical Transactions of the Royal Society of London*, also in 1900, and is twenty-eight pages long. It reports on three related experiments. The methods for the experiments are explained after the results of the experiments have been presented. The thesis continues with sections which further discuss the results of the experiments and concludes with a section titled 'Summary of results'. His PhD could be described as a traditional complex type thesis in that it reports on several studies. It does not, however, follow what would nowadays be considered a typical form for a traditional complex thesis in that the studies are not presented in stand-alone form within the thesis, with the methods presented separate from each of the studies rather than within them.

A thesis titled 'The structure, micro-chemistry and development of nerve cells, with special reference to their nuclein compounds' in the area of Biomedical Sciences was also submitted in 1900 (Scott 1900). It was published in the *Transactions of the Canadian Institute* and was thirty-four pages long. The first two sections of the thesis provide background to the study. Methodological matters and results are then combined in two further sections. The PhD could be described as a traditional simple thesis as it reports on a single study, although the sections of the study do not neatly parallel that of a conventional IMRD format.

Parks' (1900) thesis in the area of Geography, 'The Huronian of the basin of the Moose river', was thirty pages long, a similar length to the other PhDs at the University of Toronto submitted in 1900 referred to above. His thesis was published in *University of Toronto Studies* in the same year and was re-published in 2015 by Book on Demand Ltd suggesting a continued interest in Parks' work. The thesis commences with an introduction which is followed by three topic-based sections and a Summary. Parks' PhD is a clear example of a topic-based thesis. The Table of Contents for Parks' thesis is shown in Figure 4.8.

The Huronian of the Basin of the Moose River

I.   Schists of eruptive origin
II. Schists of fragmental origin
III. Schists of doubtful or variable origin

Summary

Figure 4.8 Contents of Parks' (1900) topic-based thesis.

Recent PhDs at the University of Toronto

The recent PhDs at the University of Toronto were in the areas of Physics and Geography. The Physics PhDs showed no preference for a particular thesis type. One of the theses was by publication being based on two already-published articles, one thesis was topic-based, two were traditional simple and six were traditional complex in that they reported on more than a single study, from three to five, and contained sections which outlined the methodology, results and a discussion of each of the studies. Gao's (2019) thesis 'D-brane Chan-Paton factors and orientifolds' is interesting however in that, even though it reports on more than a single study, its presentation is topic-based rather than traditional complex. Figure 4.9 shows the chapter titles of his thesis. While Gao's thesis contains the essential components of a doctoral thesis, a review of relevant literature, an outline of methods employed, presentation of results of each of the studies and a discussion of results in relation to previous research, this is not immediately obvious in his chapter titles nor in the use of subsections within the chapters.

The recent Geography PhDs at the University of Toronto also showed no preference for a particular thesis type. One of the PhDs was a thesis by publication, one was topic-based, three were traditional simple theses and five were traditional complex theses. Webb's (2019) topic-based thesis, as with the Physics topic-based thesis described above, did not have a separate methodology chapter but described his methodology and recruitment of participants in a section titled 'Methodology, methods and profile of participants' in the Introduction. The Table of Contents of Webb's thesis is shown in Figure 4.10. The individual studies in Wessel's (2019) thesis by publication were structured as stand-alone research articles with an Abstract at the beginning of the chapter, followed by

---

D-brane Chan-Paton Factors and Orientifolds

1. Introduction
2. Review of D-branes and Orientifolds
3. Worldsheet Parity and Chan-Paton Factors
4. Orientifolds and K-theory
5. D-branes in Orientifolds of Linear Sigma Models
6. Conclusion

Figure 4.9 Contents of Gao's (2019) topic-based thesis.

Liberating the Family: Education, Aspiration and Resistance Among South African University Students

Chapter 1. The Long History of Education, Reproduction and Resistance in South Africa

Chapter 2. 'This country beyond the township': Understanding Aspiration Among Working Class Youth in Higher Education

Chapter 3. *Asinamali:* #FeesMustFall, Debt and the Right to Education

Chapter 4. The Tithes of Education: Youth, Family and Paying the 'Black Tax'

Chapter 5. #FeesMustFall, Citizenship and the Contradictory Functions of Higher Education in South Africa

Conclusion

Figure 4.10 Contents of Webb's (2019) topic-based thesis.

standard research article sections, Introduction, Literature Review, Methods and Data, Results, and Discussion. Unlike recent Physics PhDs at Yale and Oxford, then, there was no preference for thesis types in the recent Physics or Geography PhDs at the University of Toronto as there were traditional simple, traditional complex, topic-based and theses by publication in both areas of study. Of the ten Toronto Geography PhDs, six were in Human Geography and four in Physical Geography. There were examples of traditional simple and traditional complex thesis types in both Human and Physical Geography, as well as a topic-based thesis in Human Geography and a thesis by publication in Physical Geography.

Early PhDs at the University of Melbourne

Each of the early PhDs at the University of Melbourne was awarded in the same year, 1948. They were in areas of Chemistry, Biochemistry, Physics and Literature. The early PhDs contained examples of traditional simple, traditional complex, topic-based theses and a thesis by publication. The topic-based Biochemistry PhD (Stone 1948) was a review of the literature and, unlike the other Science PhDs in the data set, did not have an empirical research component. Wolff's (1948) topic-based Literature PhD also did not have an empirical component and was based on a reading of previously published literature on her topic. The thesis by publication (Culvenor 1948) in the area of Chemistry contained three articles that had already been published, two in the *Journal of the Chemical Society* and one in the *Journal of Australian Scientific Research.*

Recent PhDs at the University of Melbourne

The recent PhDs at the University of Melbourne were in the areas of Medicine and Literature. The Medicine PhDs comprised four theses by publication and six traditional complex theses. There were no traditional simple or topic-based theses amongst the Medicine theses. The theses by publication were made up of two to four published, or about to be published, research articles presented as individual chapters. The traditional complex theses contained from two to four studies. There is, then, in Medicine at the University of Melbourne a strong preference for multiple studies in doctoral theses, whether they be written as a thesis by publication or a traditional complex thesis.

The recent Literature PhDs at the University of Melbourne were all topic-based. Figure 4.11 shows the Table of Contents of Cerfeda's (2019) thesis 'The performance of perversion in Kafka's literature and its adaptations'. Unusual for the Literature PhDs, his thesis contained a section titled Methodology in Chapter 1 in which Cerfeda outlines the works the study is based on as well as recordings and performances of Kafka's work that he observed. He then outlines the theoretical position he takes on his study material (poststructuralism) and makes a case for this choice of theory.

The findings of the study reveal trends in thesis types both within and across the disciplines and universities that were the focus of the study. Traditional-type theses occurred in Science doctorates in each of the universities' early doctorates although at times in less recognizable forms compared with how these types of theses are written today, and in most cases the theses reported on a single study. Yale and Oxford showed a preference for traditional complex theses in the recent Science doctorates while the University of Toronto showed no

---

The Performance of Perversion in Kafka's Literature and its Adaptations

Introduction
Chapter One: Overview
Chapter Two: Performing the perverse self
Chapter Three: The performance of gender and its perversion
Chapter Four: The perversion of humanity
Chapter Five: Punishment and law: The perversion of justice
Conclusion

Figure 4.11 Contents of Cerfeda's (2019) topic-based thesis.

preferences for a particular thesis type in their recent PhDs. The University of Melbourne favoured traditional complex theses and theses by publication in the recent Medicine doctorates. The thesis by publication by Culvenor (1948) at the Melbourne University of Melbourne, the only thesis by publication in the early Melbourne corpus, is of particular note, however, in that it was one of the first PhDs to be awarded at that university and is a thesis type that continues through to this day. In addition, the early Physics and Biomedical Sciences PhDs at the University of Toronto in the data set were published in their entirety in academic journals, even though they were not what could be termed theses by publication.

All of the universities awarded topic-based theses in the Humanities doctorates in their earliest days. There was, further, a continued preference for topic-based theses in the Humanities areas that were examined in the study. There were no Humanities theses by publication in the data set although there was early evidence of the publication of Humanities doctoral research (e.g. Simpson 1924) as well as more recent examples of this such as Pilz's (1998) Literature PhD at the University of Melbourne being re-published as a book (Pilz 2004).

Conclusion

The study outlined in this chapter aimed to explore how doctoral theses and dissertations have evolved since their earliest days in relation to how they are typically written now. We found that while there has been some continuity in how doctoral theses have been written since their earliest days, there has also been some change. Continuity can most clearly be seen in the Humanities theses in that they were all topic-based. That is, the chapters of the theses all followed an organizational structure based on sub-themes that emerged in the particular studies. Change, however, was very clear in the Science theses in that none of the early theses followed an IMRD structure even though the components of this structure were present in most of the texts. It is not possible to determine, from the data that were collected, exactly when the IMRD structure, whether of a traditional simple or traditional complex thesis, became the standard format for doctorates which report on empirical studies but is very clear that this has become the case. What we have seen, then, is a case of both genre change, especially with regard to Science-based PhDs. Following Miller's (2016) discussion of genre evolution, our findings show diachronic change where genre features are inherited from earlier exemplars of the dissertation genre. An example this is the more transparent ways in which research methods are presented in current

Science theses and dissertations compared with early PhDs in this area where they were present but not so clearly outlined. And, as discussed in Chapter 2, the notions of prototype and family resemblances enable us to see how early examples of PhDs which were not written a way that would be expected today still remain examples of the doctoral dissertation when considered from this perspective.

Atkinson (1999) provides a parallel example of genre change in a study which examines the development of the conventional form of research articles in the *Philosophical Transactions of the Royal Society of London* from 1675 to 1975. As mentioned in Chapter 2, he found that reports on research in *Philosophical Transactions* in the seventeenth and eighteenth centuries were in the form of 'polite letters' and from this they evolved so that by the nineteenth century the reports were clearly marked by section titles and headings, and with increasingly developed descriptions of the methods employed in the studies being reported on. By the twentieth century the research articles were closer to what today is considered the basic form for a research article, the IMRD format. Not all of the earlier articles, however, were based on empirical research, whereas by the twentieth century they nearly always reported on experimental studies and, increasingly, more than a single study. A similar development can be seen in Science-based doctoral theses, as has been outlined in this chapter.

A possible reason for the shift to a more conventional IMRD form and variations on it in Science-based doctoral theses could be the increased pressure to publish for doctoral students (Badenhorst and Xu 2016; Curry 2016), either by themselves or with their supervisor/s. This is especially the case in programmes where successful publication is a requirement for the award of the degree (see Barbero 2008; Li 2016). Publication, for science students, is most typically in the form of IMRD research articles which are reflective of the largely standardized form of their doctoral theses, whether they be simple or complex traditional type theses. Many research articles in the humanities, however, are not empirical in the same way and, as a consequence, the IMRD article is not typically found in humanities publications (Lin and Evans 2012). Thus, if humanities students are writing their theses with a view to future publication, they do not normally have an IMRD organizational pattern in mind and it is not reflected in their theses. Changes in epistemologies and ontologies over time, and what 'counts' as knowledge in these two broad areas of study, could also be forces behind the different thesis formats in each of these areas of study. The emergence of new disciplinary areas within each of these two areas, further, could see them inheriting (Hudson 2015) writing styles and conventions from the broader field from which they came. And, of course, thesis writing instruction which typically focuses on an IMRD format could also be encouraging this kind of writing, at least in the area of Science-based theses.

So while shifts were seen in several of the disciplinary areas that we examined, there was also, in some cases, a preference for a particular thesis type at particular universities in some of the areas of study. There are, of course, limitations to the study we have discussed in this chapter. One of these is the sample size, especially in relation to the number of early PhDs we were able to obtain for our study. Another limitation is the disciplinary areas we chose for the recent PhDs. Doctorates in other disciplinary areas may be quite different in terms of genre expectations, even within the same broad study groupings of Science and the Humanities. It is, further, not possible to generalize our results to the same disciplinary areas in universities other than the ones we examined. Further research on this topic, thus, needs to employ a larger sample size and examine more disciplinary areas than we have in our study and in a wider range of universities.

Notwithstanding, our findings have important implications for the teaching and supervision of thesis and dissertation writing. There are, for example, a number of different ways in which doctoral theses can be presented. It does not seem however that, in every case, these options are always open to students. A student undertaking a PhD at Yale in Astronomy, for example, seems to be expected to carry out a study which is made up of three separate but related studies and present their dissertation in a traditional complex format. This does not mean, however, that PhDs in Astronomy at other universities will necessarily be the same. In addition, while there are further ways in which doctoral theses are now being presented (see the Sousanis (2014), Carson (2017) and Harron (2016) PhDs referred to in Chapter 2), these seem to be mostly only appearing in certain areas of study. Thus, while doctoral theses, as with all genres, are dynamic and open to change, there are both choices and constraints (Devitt 2004) in terms of how they can be written. It is not a case, then, of 'anything goes'. As Devitt (2004: 86) explains, conformity among genre users 'is a fact of genre, for genres provide an expected way of acting'. Choice and constraint, thus, need to be understood within the disciplinary context and expectations of the institution in which the thesis is being written (Pantelides 2013). Both writing teachers and supervisors need to be aware of this so that they can advise their students accordingly in the writing of their theses and dissertations.

Paré (2019), in a discussion of the 'doctorate of the future', argues that the PhD is likely to undergo even more change than has been seen in this chapter.

He argues that doctoral education needs to 'serve students as they move into their futures, not prepare them for the scholarly forms and practices of the past' (p. 83). We, therefore, need studies which examine what 'scholarly forms and practices' are now being accepted for PhDs. The Canadian Association for Graduate Studies (Porter et al. 2018), for example, suggests doctoral theses might include material written for non-academic audiences such as reports, policy papers, op-ed pieces and museum curation material. Doctoral theses could also present material in the form of YouTube videos, teaching curricula and blueprints or site designs. PhDs, further, do not necessarily need to be written in what might be termed traditional academic English. Stewart's (2016) PhD 'Indigenous architecture through indigenous knowledge' discussed in Chapter 2 is an example of this. And the doctoral thesis does not always need to be written in a language of the academy. An example of this is Roxana Quispe Collantes's (2019) PhD awarded by the University of San Marcos in Lima which examined poetry written in Quechua, the language of the Incas, which is still spoken by millions of people in the Andes. She wrote and defended her thesis (answering questions from examiners) entirely in the native language, the first time in the university's 468-year history that this had been done. The question then is, to what extent are these new forms and practices being accepted for PhDs as well as what will the 'dissertation of the future' look like and in what ways will it be different from what students are writing today?

5

The 'new humanities' PhD

Introduction

When Bob Hodge coined the term 'new humanities' in the mid-1990s to refer to the outcomes of the epistemological upheavals occasioned by the postmodern turn in the social sciences and the humanities, he identified a 'Kuhnian' paradigm revolution (see also Chapter 10) in the traditional organization of academic disciplines in the social sciences and humanities. This 'revolution', Hodge argued, affected not only claims as to what constituted knowledge within academic fields of study but the production of both new scholars and their texts. Hodge's (1995) provocative paper, 'Monstrous knowledge: Doing PhDs in the new humanities', specifically focused on the urgent need for thesis and dissertation examiners and supervisors to understand and respond to the exigencies of what he saw as texts that 'break[s] with the modernist values of realism, transparency of text, linear logic, purity of genres' (p. 38).

Hodge identified doctoral theses influenced by postmodernism as being of the 'new' humanities; he was particularly concerned that these theses might be read by examiners and supervisors through the lens of the 'old' humanities and be judged negatively. For Hodge, the 'central characteristic' of these PhD theses was that they eschewed identification with the traditional disciplines of, for example, sociology or history. Hodge argued forcefully for the emergence of a new disciplinary configuration of discourses and epistemic values within new boundaries. New humanities theses were 'innovative, transdisciplinary, critical' (p. 38); they were self-reflexive, performative and creative. They drew on a body of postmodernist thought influenced by the work of theorists such as Foucault, Derrida, Lyotard, Said and others.

Hodge's conclusion that it was 'likely that a reasonably high proportion of doctorates in the humanities and social sciences commenced or completed over the next five years will be broadly in the "New Humanities" areas' (p. 39) was borne out to an extent by the findings of a small-scale study of a corpus of twenty PhD theses comprising ten each from the Schools of Sociology and History at one Australian university carried out in the early 2000s. Starfield and Ravelli (2006) identified several of the theses in their corpus as embodying characteristics of the 'new humanities' as described by Hodge. They posed the question as to whether aspects of the title pages, tables of content and introduction chapters that appeared to challenge convention through the use of the first person, reflexive presentations of the authorial self, playful metaphorical thesis titles, marked choices of fonts and other typographic features were suggestive of more fundamental changes in thesis writing, disciplinary alignment and the presentation of the researcher/writer's identity or were a mere 'blip' on the disciplinary horizon. They also asked whether the New Humanities thesis might be becoming the default genre for student writers adapting to new rhetorical expectations of the postmodern thesis in these two disciplines.

Studies of the genres of academic writing, primarily of the research article and the doctoral thesis, have also identified Introductions as key rhetorical sites in which the author presents a series of arguments that create a research space for their study (Swales 1990) or a research warrant (Hood 2010), by aligning themselves with or distinguishing themselves from previous research traditions and identifying a niche or gap that their study will fill. Genette (1997) coined the term 'paratext' to describe the ways apparently insignificant elements of a text reveal aspects of writer identity and positioning. The paratext comprises the initial components of a text 'a heterogeneous group of practices and discourses' according to Genette (p. 2) that act as a threshold or entry point to the text and work to control how the text will be received by the reader. As the bulk of the Introductions in our study sit outside of the numbered chapter structure, they can be considered part of the paratext. Title pages, Tables of Contents and thesis introductions can function as key sites in which student writers negotiate their researcher identity with and present their topic to their readers who are also their thesis supervisors and examiners.

Almost twenty years later, we have returned to this topic to investigate the extent to which the identified features are present in more recent sociology and history PhD theses. We have collected a corpus of twenty recently submitted PhD theses from these same disciplinary fields and describe below how we have compiled this corpus. While we primarily look at the theses' macrostructures and introductions as in the previous study, we extend our examination of the writers' presentation of self to other sections of the thesis. While the 2006 study was entirely text based, our discussion of the new corpus includes data from interviews with four of the students whose theses we examine. Prior to this, however, we discuss key features of the new humanities theses identified in the 2006 study.

Features of the new humanities theses in the 2006 study

Geertz (1980) used the phrase 'blurred genres' to evoke the gradual blurring of clear boundaries between the social sciences and the humanities under the growing influence of postmodernism which led to what Hodge called the new humanities. The title of Starfield and Ravelli's (2006) paper began with a quote from the introduction to one of the sociology theses in the corpus which echoed this reconfiguration of the social sciences: 'The writing of this thesis was a process that I could not explore with the positivistic detachment of the classical sociologist' (Fiedler 2000: 10). The sentence not only captured the self-reflexivity of the new humanities thesis and the methodological rupture with more conventional positivist approaches to sociology, it also foregrounded the act of writing, positioning the author at the centre of the construction of the thesis itself. In addition to Hodge, theorists such as Richardson (2000) had argued that writing should be understood as a 'method of inquiry'; she called on qualitative researchers to 'eschew the questionable metanarrative of scientific objectivity' and embrace reflexivity, arguing that they would 'still have plenty to say as situated speakers, subjectivities engaged in knowing/telling about the world as they perceive it' (p. 518). Concerns with portraying writer subjectivity and situatedness led to what was called the 'crisis of representation', an interrogation of the role of the researcher and how their presence in the research field was to be accounted for (Marcus and Fischer 1986).

Reflexivity is 'the processes of critical self-reflection on one's biases, theoretical predispositions, preferences, and so forth' that acknowledge that 'the inquirer is part of the setting, context, and social phenomenon he or she seeks to understand' (Schwandt 2015: 268). Schwandt also emphasizes that reflexivity can be a 'very important procedure for establishing the *validity* [author emphasis] of accounts of social phenomena' (p. 268). Starfield and Ravelli coined the term 'reflexive I' to capture a distinctive use of the first person in several of the theses in their corpus such as in the quote from the title of their paper cited above which helped them identify the theses they saw as pertaining to the new humanities.

While all but two of the original twenty theses adopted a topic-based macrostructure, Starfield and Ravelli (2006) argued that this description failed to distinguish the more conventional sociology and history theses from those that seemed to embrace aspects of the new humanities. They suggested that it would be helpful to locate the twenty theses on a continuum with 'some being clearly traditional in terms of their macrostructure, layout, title choices, typography and absence of I' (p. 235). The traditional theses included the two complex traditional sociology theses in the corpus, three of the history theses and one of the topic-based sociology theses and were thus located within either the traditional humanities (history) or social sciences (sociology). Six of the remaining theses, through a combination of the features identified above, in particular the discursive construction of a reflexive, embodied authorial self, were seen to pertain to the new humanities. The remaining theses did make some use of the first person in the introduction chapter but this tended to be used to organize the discourse, as, for example, in Wilson (2000: 7), 'In the first part, I analyse and discuss the relationship between some contemporary, pessimistic sociological views about work and earlier classical sociological statements about work and modernisation'.

Figure 5.1 shows the first page of the Table of Contents from a thesis titled 'Being *somewhere*: Young homeless people in inner-city Sydney' (Robinson 2002, italics in original) submitted to the School of Sociology. The macrostructure is topic-based but a closer examination reveals the characteristics that enabled Starfield and Ravelli to identify it as belonging to the new humanities and that might have unsettled the 'modernist' examiner imagined by Hodge. The title itself with its word play on being homeless and yet being *somewhere*; the use of the gerund 'being' in the title as well as in several of the chapter titles (grieving home, sensing the other); the absence of conventional chapter headings such as literature review or methodology; slightly enigmatic, alliterative titles such as 'the catch of the surrendering self', all suggest a hyper-awareness of language as well as a playfulness with words and meanings. None of these are trivial choices; all are deliberate and have been accepted by the thesis examiners.

As with all but two of the theses in the 2006 corpus, Robinson's Introduction sits outside of the chapter structure, overviewing the entire thesis and introducing the author through a brief personal narrative of the origin of her research and of the genesis of the thesis. Despite the fairly unconventional chapter headings and sub-heading in the Table of Contents, the Introduction has a sub-heading 'The chapters' which contains the expected preview of the thesis structure and main argument, clearly signalling to the reader that this is a thesis. Just prior to the heading, three research questions are laid out, again reminding us that we are reading a thesis and not a personal story of homelessness. Similarly, while there

Abstract
  Acknowledgements
  Table of contents
Introduction: Being *somewhere*
  Moving towards *somewhere*
  Young homeless people in inner-city Sydney
  Inhabiting the field of homelessness: Thinking conjuncture
  The chapters
Chapter One: House and home: The 'problem' of homelessness
  The problem of the 'problem': Homed or homeless?
  Broader literature and the 'problem' of homelessness
  Homes or houses?
  Subjective or objective?
  Social policy and homelessness
Chapter Two: 'Getting back into place': Researching homelessness through the framework of place relations
  Home
  Bourdieu and Casey: Getting back into place
  Bourdieu: The discordant habitus
  Casey: Phenomenology and 'getting back into place'
Chapter Three: Sensing the other: The catch of the surrendering self
  Becoming part of the field of homelessness
    i Reflexivity and the location of the subject
    ii Outreach: An introduction to the field
    iii Surrender and catch
  Conducting Research
    i Setting up: Introductions, ethics and limitations
    ii In-depth interviewing and participant observation
  Moving towards the catch: Analysis of interview data
Chapter Four: Grieving home
  Relating to place through grief: Participant observation and working with young homeless people
  Places of grief: 'Home'
  Sue
  Ben
  Crystal
  Surfacing through grief?
  Places for grieving
Chapter Five: Spatial hauntings: Found place
  Haunting place
  Found places and homeplaces
  The search for boundaries: Marking out a specific place

Figure 5.1 Table of Contents topic-based new humanities thesis (Robinson 2002).

is no obvious literature review chapter, Chapter 2 has the name of well-known sociologist, Pierre Bourdieu, as a sub-heading, together with a reference to 'habitus' one of his key concepts, and the word 'framework' occurs in the chapter title indicating that the theoretical framework is developed in this chapter. Chapter 3 does not call itself 'methodology'; however, 'conducting research' and a lexis associated with research methods is used in the chapter sub-headings: 'ethics and limitations'; 'in-depth interviewing and participant observation'; 'analysis of interview data'. A sub-subheading, 'reflexivity and the location of the subject', clearly locates the thesis and the researcher/writer as being within the postmodern turn with its concerns for subjectivity, reflexivity and articulating the author's positionality.

Robinson's introduction to her study of youth homelessness opens with a personal meditation on growing up in Tasmania and the sense of place this occasioned, leading the reader through an account of the genesis of her thesis topic. She gradually weaves in references to her academic life linking these closely however to her autobiographical story. The poetic, personal tenor of these early pages contrasts with the traditional impersonal, academic tenor of much academic writing:

> Perhaps it is a function of growing up in the stunning environment and protective gaze of a smaller town that has made me more aware of the importance of place. Perhaps too, a growing sense of being remote and then some living and travel 'overseas' has forced a continual reimagining of where I am in the world and where I am in relation to what I think too though, in a time of such movement, indeed around the globe, what continues to shine in my head are images of mountains, of still tarns, of bright fagus (deciduous beech) and then of trees, trees and ocean, a wheeling sea eagle and then of a dog at the gate, of a house rubbing shoulders with peppermint gum. Of home.
>
> My own interests in tracing more strongly the contours or rhumb lines of my own connections (perhaps because now they feel more under threat) has [sic] brought me towards a growing phenomenon and academic area of interest: 'youth homelessness'. Even as I think more carefully about my own homeplace, I become more and more conscious, obsessed even, with my growing awareness of a shifting population of young and old people through this new city in which I am desperately trying to carve a sense of permanence, a sense of place, myself.
>
> (Robinson 2002: 1–2)

Several other new humanities theses shared this concern with 'foregrounding rather than eliding the researcher's role in the academic process' (Ravelli 2019: 346), frequently in the introduction chapter.

Less poetically perhaps, Fiedler, whose thesis 'Beyond Pinochet: Class, power and desire in Pinochet's Chile' (2000) provided the title for the 2006 paper, articulated his desire to be free of what he perceived as the constraining forces of classical sociology in terms of writing and self-representation:

> The writing of this thesis was a process that I could not explore with the positivistic detachment of the classical sociologist. After all I was affected by the repression, the exile and the mutations within Chilean society as much as anyone else in the country. As an activist of the Chilean left, I was an active participant in that collective constitution of the political opposition and protest movement that challenged the regime in the early 80s. For the same reason I could not write a thesis about others' displacement and subjectivity without talking about my own.
>
> (Fiedler 2000: 10)

Fewer of the history theses showed evidence of the disruptive forces of postmodernism with only two being located by Starfield and Ravelli in the new humanities. '"Saving the Aborigines": The White Woman's Crusade' (Holland 1998) contains elements of a personal narrative in its introduction, presenting the origin of the study as a mystery that needs to be unravelled, but this personal voice was much less common in the history corpus:

> Reading about this incident in the initial stages of research for my doctoral thesis left an indelible impression on me. I wondered why someone like Mary Bennett and the papers she had collected were considered such a threat to the state as to be hastily and somewhat furtively banished, ensuring the death of her legacy as well. I had not intended to focus particularly on her, indeed I came across the details of this event in the papers of Jessie Street. But she was becoming more and more central as I tried to trace white women's relationship to questions of race, and more particularly to Aborigines and Aboriginal issues. … It was in this context that I became more intrigued by these white women's campaigns, about the contemporary feminist analysis and the relationship between the two.
>
> (Holland 1998: 1–2)

Wessell's (1999) thesis 'history making/*making history* – traversing the boundaries between contesting and commemorating Australia day and Columbus day', although lacking the personal narrative described above, offers evidence of a consciously designed new humanities thesis. The Introduction reveals that the thesis, while clearly aligned with history and historiography, locates itself explicitly within the field of cultural studies, itself closely associated with postmodernism. The thesis can thus be seen to constitute a challenge to more traditional historiographical writing and an examination of the typographical innovations of the title page and Table of Contents reinforces this challenge to what the reader of a doctoral thesis might expect.

If we contrast Wessell's title page (Figure 5.2) and Table of Contents (Figure 5.3) with that of another history thesis from the 2006 corpus (see Figure 5.4), the extent to which her choices differentiate her work is highlighted. The Table of Contents of Scharen's (2000) thesis 'Famine and prophecy: General

history making
making histories:

traversing the boundaries between contesting and
commemorating australia day and columbus day

A THESIS SUBMITTED FOR THE DEGREE OF DOCTOR OF PHILOSOPHY IN HISTORY
UNIVERSITY OF NEW SOUTH WALES
1999

Figure 5.2 Title page new humanities thesis (Wessell 1999).

contents

acknowledgments		iv
introduction	speculating about commemorating	1
chapter 1	a mongrel history: mixing history and theory, australia and the u.s.	21
chapter 2	contested voices presenting colonial pasts: the bicentenary and the quincentenary	79
chapter 3	engaging the popular in modernity and the nation: audiences and events in the 19th century	153
chapter 4	parts of the whole: ethnicity and the time of the nation	207
chapter 5	re-enacting invasions/replicating the past: re-presenting the first fleet and spanish caravels	262
chapter 6	the future of the past: commemorating in the classroom	307
epilogue		359
selected bibliography		366

Figure 5.3 Table of Contents topic-based new humanities thesis (Wessell 1999).

Famine and Prophecy: General Sir Arthur Cotton and the Poverty of India, 1844-4

Introduction: Necessity and Famine
    Glossary
Chapter 1: Droughts, Famines and the Famine Policy, 1860–1900
    List of Famines, with Remarks on the Famines
Chapter 2: The Engineer's Daring, 1844–53
Chapter 3: The Roots of Prophecy, 1854–65
Chapter 4: Life and Death, 1866–78
Chapter 5: Judgment by Rule, 1878–79
Chapter 6: At the End of the Debate, 1878–80
Chapter 7: In the Shadow of the Granary, 1879–84
    Map: The Madras Presidency, Northern Section
Conclusion: Awaiting Famine
Appendices:
    I Statements of the Irrigation Imperative in India
    II The Debate between Cautley and Cotton
    III Table: Expenditure on Public Works in India
Bibliography

Figure 5.4 Table of Contents history thesis (Scharen 2000).

Sir Arthur Cotton and the poverty of India, 1844–84' looks much more like a traditional monograph and adopts a chronological structure and organization.

Wessell's title page (see Figure 5.2), however, playfully challenges a number of layout conventions: it does away with capital letters, it uses shading in the title to contrast the title and subtitle and draws on typographic resources, inserting a rule to separate the first two components of the title, 'history making/*making histories*' (italics in original), in order to evoke the idea of boundaries referred to in the subtitle. The title of the thesis itself engages in postmodern word play: 'history making/*making* history' emphasizing the discursively constructed nature of historical events. Several gerunds can be found in the title and subtitle (e.g. contesting and commemorating) and seem to signify an identification by the author with postmodern qualitative research writing in which meaning is not fixed and static as nominalizations such as contestation and commemoration might suggest but rather an active process involving human agents.

Wessell also makes use of the first person through the introduction, displaying a strong authorial voice to align herself with alternative views of the practice of history:

> In constructing their survey about the presence of the past in the everyday lives of Americans, David Thelen and Roy Rosenzweig favoured the term popular historymaking, for the way it implied that people play an active role in using and understanding the past. In a similar way, I hope to be able to broaden the practice of history beyond a description of how scholars approach the past, to acknowledge the way different groups and processes are central to the shaping and construction of cultural expression and reception.
> (Wessell 1999: 7–8)

The theses discussed above as representative of the new humanities have in common that they draw on a body of theory associated with the key postmodernist thinkers identified by Hodge such as Derrida, Foucault, Said and other philosophers and social and cultural theorists such as Bourdieu, Butler, Deleuze and Guattari. Aligning themselves with these theorists, who radically challenged existing knowledge paradigms, may have prompted the student writers to consider challenges to the dominant thesis genres as we saw, particularly in Wessell's thesis and to an extent in Robinson's and Fiedler's.

Compiling the 2020 corpus

In Starfield and Ravelli's (2006) study, the thesis corpus was compiled from a list of recently completely PhD theses supplied by the Schools of Sociology and History at the University of New South Wales (UNSW) in Australia. They then worked backwards from the most recently submitted thesis on each list until they were able to locate ten theses from sociology and from history respectively. The theses in the history corpus were completed between 1998 and 2001 and the sociology theses between 1999 and 2002. A sociology thesis was then one which had been submitted by students enrolled in the School of Sociology and supervised by members of the school and, similarly, a history PhD was submitted by students from the School of History and supervised by historians who were members of that school.

In the intervening period, institutional restructuring largely due to financial pressures has meant that sociology and history no longer exist as separate schools at the University of New South Wales. They have been subsumed into two larger entities, respectively called the School of Social Sciences and the School of Humanities and Languages. This development has made the identification of recent theses in the two disciplinary areas much less straightforward than in the earlier study.

The School of Social Sciences is an amalgamation of the former schools of sociology, social sciences and policy, social work, development studies, and political science and international relations, while Humanities and Languages comprises history, philosophy, linguistics, several modern languages as well as the environmental humanities, women's studies and Latin American and Asian studies. Our compilation of a corpus that most closely approximated the earlier sociology and history corpus is described below.

In the early 2000s, when Starfield and Ravelli carried out their study, all theses were submitted in hard copy and stored in the library basement; by early 2021, when the new corpus was compiled, all thesis submission had become digital. Our new corpus was thus compiled using the university's online repository, *UNSWorks* https://unsworks.unsw.edu.au/home using the search terms sociology and history, limiting the search to PhD theses and the search dates to between 2014 and 2020.

In the case of sociology, 192 theses were initially identified and these were individually searched to eliminate theses from outside of the School of Social Sciences. Theses that clearly identified themselves through their titles and key words as being affiliated to social policy studies, social work, political sciences and international relations, criminology and development studies were eliminated. We cross-checked the names of supervisors listed on *UNSWorks* with those listed on the School of Social Sciences website as being affiliated with the school's sociology and anthropology strand to establish that the theses we selected could be seen as sociology theses and where a supervisor was listed in another strand such as international relations, we disregarded those theses. Working backwards from the most recent of the remaining theses we were able to select ten theses for our sociology corpus submitted between 2014 and 2019. We further searched each thesis for the terms sociology and sociological to confirm that the authors identified with the field of sociology or saw their study as making a sociological contribution.

When compiling our history corpus of ten recent PhD theses, we searched the *UNSWorks* site for history PhD theses submitted from 2014 to 2020 in the School of Humanities and Languages which produced a total of 171 theses. Each thesis was then individually searched for evidence of its identity as a 'history' thesis. Particular attention was paid to the title, keywords and to whether the supervisors identified as part of the history strand on the school website, and to explicit reference to 'historiography' and 'history' in the introduction chapter and remainder of the thesis. In addition, all but one of the ten theses include either dates or a reference to a historical era or period in its title, which provided further confirmation that the thesis was a 'history' thesis. Theses from areas such as the environmental humanities and area studies were eliminated. Using these criteria and working backwards from 2020, we were able to identify ten PhD theses submitted to the School of Humanities and Languages between 2015 and 2019.

In the next section of this chapter, we examine the new corpus and consider the extent to which 'new humanities' characteristics identified above can still be found in the theses we have identified as from sociology and history, at the same university, a decade and a half later.

Sociology theses: A degree of disruption

The ten sociology theses that constitute our new corpus all appear to contain elements that would identify them as pertaining to the new humanities. At the same time, the majority of authors clearly position their studies as located within the field of sociology and see their work as contributing to further developing the field. They directly refer to sociology as a discipline or use terms such as sociological, social theory or occasionally social sciences, for example, 'My dissertation is another such contribution, albeit with a sociological focus on contemporary narratives of circumcision' (Carlin 2016: 187) and 'another lynchpin of my thesis is its return to the sociological canon' (Dalziell 2018: 17).

The postmodern theorists that Hodge identified are still widely cited but newer theorists and new theories are present too. Theorists such as Barad, Butler, Berlant, Ahmed, working in fields such as posthumanism, new materialism, emotion and affect are cited while deconstructionist, psychoanalytic and Foucauldian analyses are still prominent as is the work of the 'founding fathers' of sociology such as Durkheim and Weber.

We find evidence of the playful thesis and chapter titles and a range of options in chapter organization that we suggest disrupt or deconstruct, to a degree, the topic-based macrostructure. The first person is used widely to position the author within the research study and within the writing of the thesis. As the extracts discussed below from several of the theses show, reflexivity, often indexed by the use of 'reflexive I', appears commonly in the author's presentation of self.

The autobiographical self (Ivanič 1998) interleaves with a more sociologically oriented authoritative self in the creating of a discoursal self that, through the thesis Introduction in particular, presents an embodied author who has a story to tell and who shifts between a more personal, informal tenor and an academic tenor which locates them as 'at home' in a complex conceptual landscape.

Five of the ten have titles which echo the postmodern word play identified earlier, some more enigmatically than others; for example, 'Surprise and seduction: Theorising fashion via the sociology of wit'; 'Performance or presence? Examining the private parts of Australian medical education'; 'The blindness of the seeing eye: Testing anthropocentrism'. Other titles are more literal: 'The politeness ethic and the development of the public sphere in eighteenth century England'; 'Understanding alienation, subjectivity and relations among the beauty employees in the retail beauty industry'. As noted above, these latter titles nominalize key concepts and processes, eliding the presence of an agent, whereas the more playful titles again make use of the gerund to refer to research processes suggesting an active researcher subject (e.g. 'theorizing', 'testing'). As with the early corpus, in the majority of the theses (seven) the Introduction chapter sits outside the chapter numbering system as does the conclusion, again suggesting its metadiscursive and paratextual functions in overviewing/previewing the entire thesis and introducing the author to the reader.

Macrostructural disruptions and origin stories

All but one of the more recent sociology theses are primarily topic-based in their macrostructure. In the discussion that follows, we examine variations to the topic-based format as well as writers' presentations of their discoursal selves in their theses. Our focus is on the paratextual elements identified above through which the student authors narrate a story of the origin of their study and introduce themselves to their readers, although we do consider other components of the theses as relevant.

'CREATIVITY UNBOUND: An analysis of open collaboration between experience design and poietic practice' (Jansen 2015) is an outlier in that it conforms largely to the definition of a complex traditional thesis as it contains three separate studies (Chapters 3–5), each with an introduction and conclusion, a separate 'empirical investigation' section and a separate theoretical framework section. The title reproduced above is as it appears on the title page. The choice of all capitals for the first part of the title and the use of Tahoma as a font (not reproduced) make the thesis somewhat distinctive. Chapter 2 is titled 'methodology' and provides an overview of the study's ethnographic approach. The 'Introduction' (Chapter 1), however, demonstrates an affinity with the new humanities as it contains a reflexive personal narrative which provides an account of the origin of the study as arising from within the researcher's own experience and interests. As the extract below shows, the personal and the academic sphere are no longer separate:

> My interest in creativity stems from my own education within an environment that values strong work ethics and clear structures over imaginative and disorderly playfulness. Perceiving creativity and discipline on opposite ends of a spectrum, I was curious about those who express their creativity as a means to live. Initially, I chose to research creative practices in order to learn about seemingly less disciplined ways to productivity. But I learned that, instead, discipline lies at the heart of creativity, and that it was love, imagination, and cognitive framing that set creativity free. In addition, the relevance of collaboration became apparent to me when I played a competitive Alternate Reality Game. ...
>
> I wondered if our reaction to the game is similar to facing today's rapidly changing ways of organising life through new technologies. As a result of this experience, I paired my academic interest in creativity with collaboration in order to understand collaborative ways of production in contemporary global grassroots movements.
>
> (Jansen 2015: 14–15)

In the Introduction to her topic-based thesis, Oxley (2014) deliberately disrupts her readers' expectations, telling them what her thesis is *not doing* (our emphasis). Referring metadiscursively to the part genre she is writing (the Introduction), she paints a narrative picture of her initial intentions, only to undercut them to juxtapose the person she was when embarking on the thesis with the researcher she became, having completed the thesis journey. The thesis supervisor is represented as a character/catalyst in the genesis of the change in orientation that occurred to set the novice researcher on the right path in her quest for knowledge. This highly reflexive personal story is, at the same time, closely interwoven with more conventional academic and scientific discourse in a discussion of postnatal depression in fathers:

> While this introduction starts with a number of initial questions, and is held together by many others, my research began with just one straightforward query. This was a question that I could not hear when I first began articulating the methodology and intent of this inquiry. Linking back and extending my

> previous research on infanticide (2007) and couples' experiences of postnatal depression (2009), this study was always going to concern what it was like for fathers living through such a distressful and intimate experience. ... Stemming from my background in medical anthropology, it was going to utilise a phenomenological methodology, of which I was very familiar; to highlight provocative and insightful parts of first-person transcripts, to hear male voices (in their verbal form) telling of an experience largely considered female, and to critique and ponder current health policies and initiatives. While still opportune and innovative, it was to be a much more straightforward, less frustrating (but far less satisfying) thesis. Upon my writing of a behemoth literature review of healthcare practices in New South Wales in the lead up to my first annual progress review, without any clear philosophical insights, my supervisor, Vicki Kirby, looked at me and asked 'So what? This empirical detail gets us where?' At this stage in my candidature, I could not answer.
>
> (Oxley 2014: 3)

Oxley takes care to position her thesis's structure and content as consciously counter to the generic or expected, proposing an alternative: 'In this sense, the introductory chapter of this inquiry will not offer an in-depth literature review discussing the nature of postnatal depression. Instead, my argument leaves the crucial discourses and vital insights to transpire within the milieu of queries raised within each section of this thesis' (Oxley 2014: 2).

In her thesis on palliative care, 'Reading between the lives: The sociality of volunteering in palliative care', Holi Birman concludes her Introduction (which sits outside of the chapter structure) with the conventional outline of the thesis chapters and simultaneously comments on her intention to subvert rhetorical expectations:

> In what follows, I give an outline of the thesis chapters. Before doing so, however, I want to note that that there is increasing awareness of the value of facilitating a fluid and more generative conversation between past and present research (Olson 2010: 17) rather than a more positivistic and deductive approach, where results and discussions are presented in separate chapters. ... After outlining my methodology and methods of my research in Chapter 1, subsequent chapters go on to intersperse literature, theory, results and discussion, at times interchangeably.
>
> (Birman 2017: 21–2)

Holi explained in our interview that she changed supervisors at the end of her first year and began to rethink her project. 'It didn't seem to make sense at the time', she said, 'to … have just one methodology chapter, one literature review chapter, results, discussion, that was never really something that I considered. So it ended up that I would start writing sort of free form and then it would develop into a chapter' (Holi Birman, interview, 2021).

While Holi ultimately decided to make her methods and methodology chapter, Chapter 1, she emphasized the constant deconstructing via critique of received notions of methodology throughout her study: 'There was such a focus on bringing the methodology and critiquing the methodology and methods in each chapter, each chapter ended up … being kind of a discussion … it's the palliative context, what was happening in the interviews, how was I influencing what was happening, … a little bit of literature.' Her choices as to the form and shape of her thesis were also influenced by other sociology theses submitted in School of Social Sciences and supervised by her supervisor that she had read.

In chapter 1, in a subsection titled, 'Why palliative care?', she includes a confessional account of her childhood in India as she scrutinizes 'the different threads of a life' (p. 60) seeking to understand the sources of her concern with loss, grief and dying. Her narrative takes the reader back, not just to Holi's childhood in India, but to an assignment she wrote in primary school on her experience once back in Australia:

> One of my earliest memories of extended writing was a Year Five assessment which involved a biographic component. Perhaps for the 'shock' factor, I recall describing my title and role as 'Chief Body Spotter' in Varanasi, India, as an eight year old. I provided a detailed account of the bodies (more specifically parts of bodies) that floated into view each dawn and dusk as I travelled by canoe with my parents along the Ganges River and went on to provide an earnest account of how and why these bodies were so prevalent.
>
> (Birman 2017: 60)

She explained that writing in a personal voice had been an integral part of her studies as an undergraduate and Honours student at UNSW studying both sociology and anthropology as the writing of reflective journals had been encouraged and become something that 'happened, naturally … bringing in the personal, … it was a no brainer, because I didn't know anything different in a way'. She noted that she had tended to get a positive response from her supervisor and others to the more narrative components of the thesis.

Svelte (2019) also adopts a slightly subversive strategy when introducing her topic and herself, inserting a striking image just prior to the opening page of chapter 1 of her thesis. 'Surprise and seduction: Theorising fashion via the sociology of wit'. chapter 1 titled 'Introduction: A dress and an epigram' is preceded by a full-page photograph, labelled Figure 1.1, of a dress from an exhibition of the fashion of designer Jean-Paul Gaultier that took place in Melbourne in 2015 and that Svelte attended. The chapter begins with an account of what could be called an epiphany that she experienced that is presented as the origin story of the thesis. The narrative also takes the reader back in time to a moment before the thesis, 'I first saw an image of the dress …', which she then views in person in Melbourne in 2015 where she is 'seduced' by the dress:

> I will begin by reflecting on one of my inspirations for this thesis. This inspiration is a dress, but it is not just any dress. It is a Jean-Paul Gaultier creation from the 'Romantic India' haute couture collection of Spring/Summer 2000. This dress is a décolleté evening gown with chiffon bodice and a flowing tulle skirt, accentuated by elbow length gloves [Figure 1.1]. … I first saw an image of the dress in a magazine compendium of haute couture collections published after the collection's presentation in Paris, January 2000. … At the time, I was struck by the gown's whimsicality in mixing camouflage and couture in one exquisite creation. The contrast between the classically flowing line of a ballgown with the military motif of camouflage resonated with me as simultaneously shocking, memorable and above all witty. That is, in one singular garment, the apparition of Gaultier's couture presented a bold and amusing vision, encapsulated an astonishing idea of intellectual creativity, and demonstrated a wicked sense of fun. In synthesising camo and couture, this dress provided a compressed and compelling experience of surprise.
>
> While this particular dress has been frequently celebrated in print and in exhibitions, my first encounter with the dress in person was at *The Fashion World of Jean-Paul Gaultier: From the Sidewalk to the Catwalk* exhibition presented at the National Gallery of Victoria, Melbourne, in 2015. … Through its skilful construction, the dress produced in me a remarkable and striking effect of capture and immobilisation: I did not want to step away from it. … I could only surmise that this dress exerted on me an effect of irresistible seduction.
>
> (Svelte 2019: 13–16)

In this short extract, Svelte also introduces the two alliterative key words from her title, 'surprise' and 'seduction', and uses the experience of encountering the dress to raise several questions that will undergird the thesis as she moves into a more conventional academic mode to introduce the concept of a sociology of wit. Perhaps wishing to pre-empt any concern that fashion is not a suitable topic for a sociology thesis, she lets the reader know early on that 'Sociology is an appropriate discipline to consider the experience of wit in fashion as it mediates individual experience with collective phenomena' (p. 25) citing a number of academic texts to support her claim.

Similarly, in chapter 1 of Bok's (2017) thesis titled 'Understanding alienation, subjectivity and relations among the beauty employees in the retail beauty industry', under the chapter title, 'You've got to be a bitch', the author takes the reader back to the origin story of her thesis, sharing personal details of her life when she worked in the 'beauty industry'. Although there is no chapter called Introduction, chapter 1 effectively performs the paratextual functions noted earlier (see Figure 5.5 for Bok's Table of Contents). Towards the end of the two and a half page, highly personal, narrative introduction to the chapter, she introduces the sociological and philosophical concept of alienation and then concludes the section by linking directly to the topic of alienation, 'This thesis investigates this question':

> This thesis can be traced back to my time working in the retail beauty industry, between 2005 and 2008. I started out as a supervisor, switched to part-time roles when I pursued my masters degree, and was then promoted to a retail manager, all within the same company. …
>
> My fascination with the beauty industry started before I began working in the industry. When I was a teenager working in fashion retail, I always looked at the ladies from the cosmetic floor with awe. … To qualify for it, I supposed they needed to possess a certain look. … Did others in the industry feel the same ambivalence? My conversations with my colleagues soon revealed that I was not alone in being caught between contradicting feelings: that while we felt a sense of pride in our job, we couldn't help but feel alienated as well. …
>
> The alienation I experienced was more complex than the power struggle between the workers and employer. In fact, it felt oddly displaced to suggest that, as a beauty employee, or as a responsible person, I was not complicit in my situation. … Or to put the matter more directly, if I made the decision to stay, knowing the affect the job had on me, was it not likely that I was myself deeply divided about this industry that I loathed and desired? This line of reflection made me wonder if others in the industry experience similar ambivalence and internal division. This thesis investigates this question.
>
> (Bok 2017: 1–3)

Section 1.2 that follows directly is titled 'Alienation' and begins 'I will now turn to address the key term of the thesis, alienation. This is one of the most fundamental concepts in sociology' (p. 3) and adopts a much more traditional analytic voice to discuss the concept of alienation as understood in the field

Understanding Alienation, Subjectivity and Relations among the Beauty Employees in the Retail Beauty Industry

Chapter 1: You've Got to be a Bitch
1.1 Introduction
1.2 Alienation
1.3 Service Work
1.4 Literature Reviews
1.5 The Gaps
1.6 Research Questions
1.7 Research Approach
1.8 Thesis Chapter Outline
1.9 Concluding Remarks

Chapter 2: Behind the Counter
2.1 Introduction
2.2 Producing and Selling Meaningful Appearance
2.3 Retail Beauty Industry
2.4 The Store
2.5 The Beauty Companies
2.6 Beauty Retail Employees
2.7 The Work of Beauty Retail Employees
2.8 Concluding Remarks

Chapter 3: Emotional Labour
3.1 The Managed Heart
3.2 Emotional Labour and Work Alienation
3.3 Exploring the Managed Heart
3.4 Management of Feeling
3.5 Feeling Rules
3.6 Concluding Remarks

Chapter 4: Emotional Labour and Beauty Retail Employees
4.1 Introduction
4.2 The Making of Beauty Retail Employees
4.3 Customers
4.4 Management
4.5 Concluding Remarks

Chapter 6: Beauty Identity and Beauty Consumption
6.1 Introduction
6.2 The Ideal Beauty
6.3 Consumption at Work
6.4 Cracks in the Mirror
6.5 Concluding Remarks

Chapter 7: Beauty Retail Employees and their Relations
7.1 Introduction
7.2 Customers
7.3 Colleagues
7.4 Management
7.5 Neighbours/Competitors
7.6 Concluding Remarks

Chapter 8: Closed Exchange and Genuine Meeting
8.1 Introduction
8.2 Meeting at the Counter
8.3 Closed Exchanged and Open Dialogue
8.4 *I-It, I-Thou* and Genuine Dialogue
8.5 *I-It*
8.6 *I-It*: Hochschild, Lacan and Hegel
8.7 *I-Thou*
8.8 Genuine Dialogue
8.9 Concluding Remarks

Chapter 9: Beauty and Genuine Meeting
9.1 Introduction
9.2 Norah and Charlie
9.3 A Closed Exchanged
9.4 Genuine Meeting
9.5 Jane and the Bride
9.6 Angie and Friends
9.7 Beauty in the Industry
9.8 Concluding Remarks

Chapter 5: Mirror Stage, Subjectivity and Desire
5.1   Introduction
5.2   About Jenny
5.3   Jenny's Private Emotions
5.4   Jacques Lacan as Cultural Analyst
5.5   Mirror Stage
5.6   Desire
5.7   Jenny, Ideal-I and Alienation
5.8   Concluding Remarks

Chapter 10: Conclusion
10.1   An Overview
10.2   Emotional Labour and Alienation
10.3   Subjectivity and Alienation
10.4   Un-alienated Possibilities
10.5   Reflections

Figure 5.5 Table of Contents (Bok 2017).

of sociology. The remaining subsections that follow are the more conventional generic headings, Literature Reviews, The Gaps, Research Questions, Research Approaches, Thesis Chapter Outline and Concluding Remarks (see Figure 5.5 for detailed Table of Contents); however, within these, the personal voice of the author is present and could be said to be 'braided' within the theoretical sections that review the key theorists whose work she will draw on, Hochschild, Lacan and Buber. This braided/hybrid style continues through the other chapters where theoretical and empirical chapters tend to blend. Bok makes this clear in Chapter 1 where she writes 'my aim … is to set up dialogues between these theoretical writings and the data collected during my study. … Chapters 5 and 8, where I undertake this task, should be considered as theoretical chapters as much as empirical ones' (Bok 2017: 43). Through her adoption of this dialogic format, Bok thus disrupts conventional expectations of the thesis' structure.

Emilie Auton (2018) waits until Chapter 5 of her thesis titled 'Performance or Presence? Examining the Private Parts of Australian Medical Education' to present her authorial self to the reader. Like Birman, Auton chooses the methods chapter 'An Education in Methods, Ethics and Medicine' to do so. She begins the chapter by aligning herself with sociologists of medicine and their origin stories, depicting these as a familiar trope, but then takes this further into the private parts of her own life, inserting her autobiographical self directly into her sociological text, thus mixing her intimate and academic worlds. As with the other reflexive extracts discussed above, this intermingling of the private self with a more academic self can be understood as enhancing the author's claims to validity (see Schwandt 2015, as cited above).

> A striking number of sociologists disclose how their own work into medical education began. The stories usually begin with the observation of a medical student or practitioner they know or through their own experiences of medical education (see Conrad 1988; Hafferty 1991; Sinclair 1997; Kapsalis 2001; Lempp 2003; Luke 2003). My path to this topic was remarkably similar. However, it was not simply questions that came from the medical world that piqued my interest; the daily reminder of what medical life really entails has acted as an anchoring point for me too.

> I live with a person who works in the medical field and often discuss the realities of his day – the struggles, the absurdity, the horror, the thrills, the messiness of human life and human bodies as well as the indifference of medical work. Moving between these accounts and my own days writing about the sociology of medicine meant that I was constantly moving between the two worlds. As a result, I have rarely been tempted to forget that medical professionals are real people who embark on difficult and disturbing work. This has undoubtedly affected the way I have researched this topic and the arguments I make in this thesis. More broadly, researchers that bridge the medical profession with the sociological profession have the potential to uncover important findings not apparent in isolated research.
>
> (Auton 2018: 97)

Her hyper-awareness of the constructed, written nature of her text is signalled from the opening page of her introduction when she writes, 'I wish that I could provide a single anecdote about intimate examinations that acts as a microcosm for the whole thesis, but things aren't that simple. Everyone will have heard innumerable horror stories about intimate examinations' (p. 1). Whereas others might use the anecdote as a way in, she deliberately undercuts the trope; the remainder of the introduction adopts a fairly conventional academic voice. Her thesis adopted a two-part structure; chapter 5, 'An education in methods, ethics and medicine', was the final chapter of Part 1. In a slightly disruptive move, one of her empirical chapters preceded the methodology chapter.

Several of the student authors we interviewed for this study indicated that the supervisor had played a key role in shaping the organization of their thesis as well as influencing their writing which is perhaps not very remarkable given the significant role of the supervisor in a student's PhD. After all, as Kamler and Thomson (2014) have pointed out, the supervisor can, in some sense, be seen to be standing in for the examiner(s) or for peer reviewers. What is worth noting, however, is the extent to which a supervisor over a number of years in a particular school may influence both the forms disciplinary knowledge takes within a specific field and its presentation in a doctoral thesis.

Our examination of the Tables of Contents reveals a surprising degree of diversity within the topic-based macrostructure of the sociology theses. While five of the theses are based on empirical studies in the more traditional sense of the term, that is, involving methods such as interviews and participant observation, several others adopt deconstructionist methods which involve close reading of 'texts' which can be the human body, a movie or other texts. Four of the Tables of Contents show a chapter or subsection with the title 'methods' or 'methodology'. In her introduction, Carlin (2016) sets out the textual method and her Table of Contents provides an outline of her approach (see Figure 5.6 for the first page):

> The conflicting views pro – and anti-circumcision groups have on circumcision puts them at an impasse. My method for challenging this impasse is to treat perspectives on circumcision as texts. In other words, they can be analysed and read as texts. To this end, my dissertation utilises for its analysis a textual method.
>
> (p. 13)

The two theses that employ deconstructionism as a methodology do not include the personal narratives noted so far. Dalziell puts forward a claim to reflexivity which is couched in the highly conceptual language of deconstructionism:

> I proceed from the exploratory space made available if we relinquish the desire to find absolutes, final truths, or singular readings. Instead of positioning myself outside of this problematic (and thereby beyond the self-deconstructing impulse or configuration of any text), my imbrication within this question ensures that my analyses do not claim to be exempt from the reiterations of the anthropocentrism that I reveal in other thinkers' works.
>
> (Dalziell 2018: 12)

Although the first person is used throughout the introduction to Tan's (2015) thesis, 'The Politeness Ethic and the Development of the Public Sphere in Eighteenth-Century England', it is probably the least reflexive of the corpus; 'I' is used primarily to organize the discourse. The introduction begins with the subheading 'A Singaporean perspective' and the opening paragraph introduces the thesis to the readers as 'a personal attempt'. She identifies herself as

Written through Blood: The Moral Complexities of Jewish Ritual Circumcision

Acknowledgements	Girard
Introduction	Desire and Violence
Circumcision as text: Judaism	Sacrifice and Victim
Circumcision as text: Circumcision activists	Derrida's Response
	Derrida's Ontology
Circumcision as text: Intactivists	Biblical Sacrifice
Theory as text: Violence	Manichaean Violence Reconsidered
Theory as text: Jacques Derrida	Chapter 2. Conceptualising Circumcision Introduction
Derrida and text	
Derrida and circumcision	What is circumcision?
Theory as text: Judaic Scholarship	Image 1. Uncircumcised and circumcised penis
The body as text	
Thesis argument	Image 1. Surgical circumcision devices
Chapter 1. Morality and the Primordial Moment of Violence	Image 3. Jewish ritual circumcision instruments
Introduction	The landscape of a predicament
What is Violence?	Terms of the contemporary circumcision debate
Freud	
Totem and Taboo	Circumcision, health, autonomy:
Unity through Flesh	Activists and Intactivists

Figure 5.6 First page of Table of Contents (Carlin 2016: 4).

'Singaporean', in opposition to 'the English', and uses this distinction to launch the motivation for her study in the following paragraph:

> This thesis began as a personal attempt to understand why neo-classicism still resonates today, as seen in the antique collections and interior decorations of some English and Australian homes. The desire of the English to connect with the past stands in contrast to the value-orientation of postmodern Singaporeans, whose general appreciation of the new, involves a rejection of all things old. …
>
> Not only did I notice that the English seem to venerate the past, I also noticed that neo-classical reproductions of the Georgian period are particularly

associated with the notion of good taste. ... I have learnt that this notion of good taste in the neo-classical tradition is related to the attributes of symmetry and proportion, as well as a disdain for ostentation, but I wanted to understand what else was involved. How far did this aesthetic reach in people's lives in the past?

(Tan 2015: 1)

The introductions to the theses in the 2020 sociology corpus demonstrate in the main the persistence of the distinguishing characteristics of the new humanities PhD as noted in Starfield and Ravelli's (2006) study. While there is evidence of conscious disruption of the topic-based macrostructure, they continue to adhere to the prototype of the thesis introduction. All have a section, typically towards the end of the chapter, in which they outline and overview the thesis structure, sometimes by means of a sub-heading. The majority identify a gap or a niche in previous research in order to build an argument for the justification of the study. Almost all have clearly identifiable research questions in the Introduction and again the vast majority clearly signal the study's contribution, often in the chapter overview section. Reflexive and narrative elements that clearly locate the writer as an embodied participant in the study are evident. As Schwandt (2015) and Hood (2010) have both pointed out, reflexivity and narrative elements can work to warrant the researcher's claims as to the study's validity; it may be that this is one of the functions of the increased evidence of reflexive and personal narratives in the thesis introductions of the sociology corpus.

History theses: Monographs rule

As discussed earlier, Starfield and Ravelli's (2006) paper situated two of the theses in their history corpus as demonstrating characteristics of the new humanities. In the 2020 corpus, two of the history theses can be said to exhibit the reflexive elements identified above as pertaining to the new humanities; as discussed below, these two theses align with a particular branch of history, namely oral history. The remaining eight theses in the new corpus, however, in their macrostructures and introductions, are more similar to each other than to the new humanities theses identified in the 2006 and 2020 sociology corpora. All the theses adopt a topic-based macrostructure and have, to a greater or lesser extent, a chronological organization. Only one of the ten theses has an Introduction chapter that is Chapter 1; all others sit outside of the chapter numbering system.

All but two of the theses deal with topics from eras that pre-date the early twentieth century. These are the two theses identified as more reflexive and they are somewhat different in methodology as one defines itself as participatory history and the other as oral history with both drawing extensively on interviews and including autobiographical elements. The introductions to these latter two theses also distinguish themselves through their use of the first person in more reflexive ways rather than simply as a means of organizing and signposting the discourse. They will be discussed further below.

The introductions to all ten history theses contain a component in which the subsequent chapters are previewed; in several of the theses this is signalled via a subheading such as 'chapter outline'. There is a degree of variation in the internal organizations of the chapters with five theses in the corpus including subsection headings in the Table of Contents; in two of the theses the subsections are numbered. The Table of Contents of Zubrzycki's (2018) history PhD (see Figure 5.7) displays a number of subsections for each chapter clearly revealing the thematic and narrative organization of the text, whereas Egan's (2019) Table of Contents (Figure 5.8) displays chapter headings only without subsections, emphasizing the chronological ordering of the macrostructure with the inclusion of several dates and time periods. Zubrzycki's extended use of subheadings allows him to use literary devices such as alliteration and metaphor to evoke the exoticism of the East, and the repeated use of the words 'magic/magical/magician' reinforces the sense of mystery he seeks to evoke. Egan's more terse Table of Contents on the other hand does not give the reader as much of a foretaste of what is to come. That said, as discussed further below, both are clearly history PhDs.

Above all, all ten history theses in their Introductions demonstrate a strong disciplinary alignment. Each has a component in which they discuss the historiography of their chosen topic and explicitly use the term 'historiography'. This section functions as a literature review cum methodology and also serves to scope out the research space for the proposed study, for example, 'In order to achieve its aims, this cultural history uncovers and examines a range of mnemonic products and practices related to the Messines and third Ypres campaigns that have received little attention in Australian historiography to date' (Haultain Gall 2017: 23). Similarly, all but one of the theses clearly signify their belonging to the field of history in their title choices. Each title contains a reference to a specific historical period, mostly via dates delineating a time period, for example, 'Power and dysfunction: the New South Wales Board for the Protection of Aborigines 1883–1940' (Egan 2019); 'Transnational exchanges in magical knowledge and methodologies between India and the West, 1813–1940', while others reference

Transnational Exchanges in Magical Knowledge and Methodologies between India and the West, 1813–1940

Acknowledgements
Abbreviations
List of figures
Introduction
Defining performance magic in a transnational context
The universality of the magician's craft
Transnational exchange and making of world magic
Time frames and structural parameters
Chapter outline

Chapter One
Magic and Transnationalism: Indian Jugglers in the West
Magical India and the accumulation of mimetic capital
Early European and Mughal accounts of Indian magic
The arrival of the first Indian magicians in Europe
From marginalised figures to performers in their own right
The beginnings of 'world magic'
Indian jugglers and their influence on the political and literary lexicon
Conclusion

Chapter Two
The Magician's Gaze
Indian magic and the Imperial project
Manning the barricades: Indian magic as a theme in imperial literature
Robert-Houdin and the 'dramas of proof'
The role of the magician's memoir in cultural imperialism
Magical imaginations: The early writings of magicians on India
Contestation and the hierarchy of power
Conclusion

Chapter Three
Contrasting Magical Narratives:
The Indian Basket Trick and Aerial Suspension
Appropriating Indian magic
Don't be Fooled by the 'Mild Hindoo'
Forms of appropriation
The 'great', 'original', 'real', 'first' and 'most authentic' Indian Basket Trick
Taking on the Spiritualists
Originality, respectability and the rebranding of Aerial Suspension
The return of Orientalism in magic
Conclusion

Chapter Four
Magic, Emigration and Labour
Magic for the masses: Choreographing India at international fairs
Networks of recruitment
Apathy and abuse: The case of the Oriental Troupe
'India comes to London': The implosion of the periphery on English popular culture
Reforming the Emigration Act
Conclusion

Chapter Five
Farewell to the Fakirs: Creating a New Performance Paradigm
Magic for the masses
The role of magic societies
Contestation and collaboration
Magic journals and the Westernisation of Indian conjuring
Learning from the masters
The slow evolution of Indian street magic
Conclusion

Figure 5.7 Table of Contents history thesis (Zubrzycki 2018; first 5 chapters).

Power and Dysfunction: the New South Wales Board for the Protection of Aborigines 1883–1940

Abstract	Chapter 3: The zealot from Parramatta
Table of Contents	Chapter 4: The 'almost white' children, 1904–1910
List of Figures	
List of Tables	Chapter 5: Enter the bureaucrats, 1916
Terminology	Chapter 6: The girls return
List of Abbreviations	Chapter 7: If the 'white parents object'
Acknowledgements	Chapter 8: Winds of change
Introduction	Conclusion
Chapter 1: A faltering start to 'protection', 1883	Bibliography
	Appendices
Chapter 2: Policy drift, 1883–1897	

Figure 5.8 Table of Contents from a history thesis (Egan 2019).

a specific period such as 'the long nineteenth century' or the 'gilded age'. In contrast, the sole sociology thesis in the 2020 corpus with a historical period in its title is 'The Politeness Ethic and the Development of the Public Sphere in Eighteenth-Century England' (Tan 2015).

The history theses for the most part follow a book-like organization (see, for example, Figures 5.7 and 5.8). They are conceived, from the outset, as research monographs and do not display the generic headings (apart from the occasional 'chapter outline' subheading see Figure 5.7) that clearly signal that the work is a thesis that we saw in the sociology corpus. It is striking that five of the ten theses have been 'turned into' books published by either university presses or by more generalist publishers. Two of the PhD graduates whom we interviewed in fact told us that they had a book in mind while writing their thesis.

Mark Dunn explained that from the outset he conceived of his thesis, 'A valley in a valley: Colonial struggles over land and resources in the Hunter Valley, NSW 1820–1850' as the book it would become: 'I think it's just in the nature of being a historian that we probably are thinking that at one point, some point, we would like to have a book.' In this he was encouraged by his supervisor who had had several students write PhD theses that became books. Mark referred to her influence in our interview, 'one of the directions she did give me, which was excellent, was to write the thesis with the idea that we would publish it … so essentially, present it as an academic piece, but, you know, sort of narrative style that could be easily transformed if we ever went ahead to publishing it'. He also said that he had modelled his structure very much on the organizational style of his supervisor in her books. As with the sociology theses discussed earlier in this chapter, the advice of an experienced supervisor in shaping the form the thesis takes is crucial.

Mark's thesis macrostructure has a clear chronological organization that takes the reader from the geological pre-history of the Hunter Valley, describing its Aboriginal inhabitants and their dispossession, the convicts who settled there and the varied attempts to establish white settlements in the period under investigation. Mark had completed his undergraduate studies in the UNSW history department some years before starting his PhD and attributed his choice of approach to his thesis as being very much influenced by his prior education telling us, 'I'm probably a product of UNSW 1989 to 94 so … I like that sort of chronological approach. … I thought, I'm telling a story here. I'm not trying to write a historiography or anything of that nature but also to put in the themes that sort of ran through … as well.'

For Matthew Haultain-Gall, turning his thesis into a book was also very significant. He explained to us that as he had, for a variety of reasons, decided not to pursue an academic career, publishing the book had become 'the end goal for me'. In his view, an academic book alone would not automatically lead to an academic position, 'it's the seed now … then you need, you know, all the other publications to go along with it'. Matthew credited a course on writing a thesis proposal with helping him conceptualize the organization of his thesis introduction but also noted the influence of other theses he had looked at:

> It [the course] got me thinking about more of the wider structure of the thesis as well, because the thesis proposal really laid down the introduction and the roadmap … got me thinking more about the overall structure. … What am I doing in the introduction? I have to introduce very quickly. I have to introduce the background, the context, and I have to introduce the literature, the theory that's going behind it. At least in the history theses that I'd read, the literature all seemed to come early. I read a few sociology ones as well and they all seemed to come very early on.
>
> (Matthew Haultain-Gall, interview, 2021)

The organization of Matthew's chapters is chronological, beginning with accounts written during and directly after the First World War, through the 1920 and 1930s, the Second World War and into the twenty-first century. Matthew referred to his thesis as a 'cultural history' and stressed, both in the thesis itself and in the interview, that his interest was not the First World War battles themselves but in how, over time, Australians have remembered and represented the 1917 Belgium campaigns in which Australia suffered great losses: 'It was a history of the memory of a battle and not the history of a battle itself.' Nevertheless, deciding whether to write about the battle presented him with a challenge: 'Only issue that I had was where are we going to talk about the actual battle and I actually don't do that in the thesis or I managed to sort of shoehorn it into the first chapter [chapter 1], whereas, in the book it ended up being a separate sort of section that ended the introduction.' He reported discussing options with his supervisors and ultimately deciding to introduce an account of the battles through the writing of one of the war correspondents whose work he analyses in chapter 1 which he felt would give readers a sense of the battles while not losing the focus on memory. He differentiated a cultural history from what he saw as the more formulaic approach of a military history:

> Military histories and cultural histories are very different approaches. Military history is very staid and a military history would have had a very clear structure. It would have would have been easy to introduce the objectives of the campaign, that particular unit that I was focusing on or whatever I chose to focus on. There would have been clear signposts of what to do, based on past studies, but in in my case there've been cultural histories of the First World War, but less so on battles and only a couple have come out during the same time that I that I wrote my thesis so I didn't have a set sort of model to go on. I sort of had to find my way a little bit based on what was already out there and based on how I imagined it, which was, early on, breaking it down into the different points as well, saying, okay, each chapter is a major idea leading me to a certain point but always being flexible, based on the research.
>
> (Matthew Haultain-Gall, interview, 2021)

Matthew's thesis was notable for the absence of the first person from all sections other than the acknowledgements. He commented in our interview that he had made a deliberate choice to 'steer away from I' and use 'the author' on a few occasions instead of the first person singular pronoun and that this seemed 'more appropriate from the examples that I'd read, certainly'. In the book, however, he did use 'I', 'for that personal feel at those particular moments … in fact, the book is prefaced by how I came to my thesis or at least a story of how I came to my thesis but I didn't think that that would have suited the thesis genre'. He justified his choices saying 'in the thesis, simply because I knew that the audience is limited to two or three readers because they're not so interested in my story, or at least that was my understanding, it was more, you know, the content of the active, academic reflection'. Being aimed at a wider readership, the book could, he felt, adopt a more personal tenor.

Both Mark and Matthew had completed their undergraduate studies at UNSW and can be seen as having been socialized into the discourse community of the history department and the wider field. Matthew articulated the tacit knowledge at play in thesis writing when reflecting on his choice in regard to the first person: 'My academic godparents or grandparents or whatever they're called. I didn't notice stylistically that they used the first person in much of their writing, unless it was in say a preface or something like that.'

Participatory and oral histories

Two theses in the 2020 history corpus define themselves as either participatory or oral histories and differentiate themselves from the other theses in the corpus in that the authors position themselves as actively engaged in the events and topics under investigation. Both theses contain some of the reflexive characteristics of the new humanities and it is worth noting that in her comparison of traditional and postmodern features of a corpus of history PhD theses introductions, Sawaki (2014) identified what she called 'participant history' as containing postmodern elements characterized by autobiographical narratives. One of these two theses is the sole history thesis that does not indicate a specific time period in its title – 'The proliferation of medical specialisation: A participatory account' (Kern 2017) – and the other is Robinson's (2018) oral history which will be discussed below. Both authors' use of qualitative methodologies such as interviews also distinguish their theses from the rest of the corpus.

In the opening paragraph of Kern's introduction, the author, a retired medical specialist, recounts the origin of his thesis which unfolds following the narrative quest pattern noted in the sociology corpora:

> Three events precipitated my interest in the proliferation of medical specialisation. When I was a senior resident at the Prince of Wales Hospital (POW), I wrote a paper on the complications of fractures of the femur in the elderly (Kern 1962: 554–557). To my surprise, I found that the major problems were not surgical (that is, wound infections or operative failure), but medical (that is, pneumonia, heart failure, urinary tract infections and bedsores). My paper on the subject

concluded that these fractures should be treated as medical emergencies rather than surgical ones. I also realized that the exclusive management of these cases by orthopaedic surgeons could be harmful.

Many years later, after I had retired, I attended a meeting of the Historical Section of the Royal Australasian College of Surgeons (RACS) in Adelaide. One of the presentations was by a retired orthopaedic surgeon from New Zealand who traced the history of the increasing specialisation within the specialty of orthopaedics, beginning from the 1960s. I realised that this process had occurred in my own specialty of paediatric surgery and in which I had participated. On the way home to Sydney on the aeroplane I met and spoke with Dr David Littlejohn (see Chapter 5), who had been one of my trainees at POW. He now practised in Wagga Wagga, where I had spent a term in 1961. It struck me that a comparison between the specialist populations then and now might shed some light on the process of proliferation in medical specialisation as a whole. To that end, it seemed worth talking to more people.

(Kern 2017: 1)

The author offers justification for the approach, in which he carried out over a hundred interviews, many with former colleagues, contrasting it with more traditional quantitative methods:

The personal stories of the interviewees, and their participation in the developments discussed in this thesis, while not carrying the epistemic authority of large scale survey projects, were an invaluable aid to this author/participant in the reflexive process, and helped to produce a more balanced and nuanced view of the proliferation of medical specialisation.

(Kern 2017: 2)

The first person is used widely through Kern's introduction with the chapter concluding with a summary of the author's career trajectory which functions again to justify his epistemic authority to investigate the topic, 'I am therefore reasonably well-placed to discuss specialisation in medicine from a participatory point of view, as I have experienced practically all the modalities of a medical practitioner' (p. 11). At the same time, the introduction chapter contains a review of relevant literature on the history of medical specialization which resembles the historiographical sections of other history theses in the corpus. It also has a chapter overview section previewing each of the following seven chapters. It is topic-based, with an Introduction and a Conclusion sitting outside of the chapter structure and in this is similar to all but one thesis in the corpus which, although topic based, has the Introduction as Chapter 1 (de Cambiaire 2016).

The other thesis in the history corpus that shares some characteristics of new humanities theses is 'The lesbian presence in feminist, gay and queer social movements in Australia, 1970s–1990s' (Robinson 2018) which defines itself as an oral history: 'The definitive approach or method of this research project has indeed been its oral history component: interviewing and recording the experiences of women who lived through and defined a significant shift in the cultural and political visibility of lesbianism' (p. 37). Like Ian Kern, Sophie Robinson, the author, also positions herself as a participant: 'The connections I have with my archives have been two-fold, as researcher, and as a participant in the various lesbian and feminist communities I am tracing' (p. 36). She carried out thirty interviews for her study and was given access to some of the personal archives of participants in the social movements she studied. In her Introduction, she positions herself clearly as having the legitimacy to carry out her study: 'As a self-identifying lesbian who has gained some degree of local community standing as a representative of LGBTQ+ history group "Pride History Group" my disclosure as a lesbian was not always needed or questioned' (p. 37). Through her choice of oral history and a feminist standpoint, she also announces a challenge to traditional history:

> I have considered – as I expand below – how my archival choices are informed by my own feminist politics and participation in contemporary feminist politics, including within lesbian communities.
>
> My commitment to oral history, which can be overlooked as overly subjective, memory-based and therefore less amenable to rigorous scholarly enquiry, is one key way I challenge traditional history and archival practices.
>
> (Robinson 2018: 34)

At the same time, her thesis macrostructure adopts the explicit chronological and topic-based organization of the other history theses in the 2020 corpus, apart from Kern's. In our interview, she commented: 'I've always been good at doing conventional history as well and conventional history writing … In honours I did a similar thing. I was writing unconventional history, but … within the kind of conventional format.' Sophie stressed the paratextual nature of both introduction and conclusion in that 'how the intro and the conclusion would look and read and feel' was the focus of a good deal of discussion with her supervisors in terms of 'just challenging the traditional format':

> My introduction, is obviously a literature review blended into this kind of introductory statement and positioning and the conclusion is like a postscript, also a positioning piece, kind of taking stock of where the movement is now and

where I am now and how this is all related to this kind of bigger personal history. So conventionally, it's got that structure but we really did try to think about how the intro and the conclusion could do something quite different.

(Sophie Robinson, interview, 2021)

Her introduction resembles those of many of the sociology theses in that it embeds a personal account of the thesis's origin in a short paragraph which locates her own consciousness raising in encounters with key feminist writings in the course of her studies:

> My desire to explore Australian lesbian feminism developed via a 'long cumulative labour of transformation', to use Meaghan Morris's phrase in relation to her own development as a feminist activist and researcher. As an undergraduate Women's and Gender Studies student I became increasingly fascinated with the sexual liberation movements that shifted the social and cultural landscape of Western societies during the 1970s, especially the Women's Liberation movement. While I had read Germaine Greer's *The Female Eunuch* (1970) before I started university, by second year I was exposed to the more expansive writing of second wave feminism such as Anne Koedt's 'Myth of the Vaginal Orgasm' and the Radicalesbians' 'Woman-Identified Woman.' I recall being struck in an undergraduate History of Sexuality course by the significant conflation of lesbianism and feminism during the 1970s.
>
> (Robinson 2018: 17)

Sophie also emphasized the extent to which the intersection of history and gender studies at UNSW as well as her own trajectory from undergraduate to PhD student in history and gender studies at UNSW shaped her research choices. Her comments highlight again the significant influence of the culture of the discipline as conveyed by the supervisors to the student and the processes through which a student becomes enculturated:

> I've always been working within the discipline of women's and gender studies and history at UNSW. They're deeply intersected obviously at our university and I guess the way I've learned how to be a historian, how to write history and what historiography is, very much informed by a feminist history and a gender history approach, which is at all times, trying to challenge the traditional ways of writing and analysing the archives of history. … My thesis writing is definitely informed by those interventions into the historical canon and the shift in historical research.
>
> (Sophie Robinson, interview, 2021)

Blurred genres?

To what extent do we see signs of genre blurring in our 2020 history corpus other than in some aspects of the two participatory history theses discussed above? Overall, it seems that the history PhD theses most closely resemble the research monograph prototype. The chronological, topic-based macrostructure evident in the 2006 history theses is in use in the 2020 corpus and, this has been the case, as we point out in Chapter 4, since the earliest examples in our study. The use of personal narratives in the two oral histories distinguishes them from the other eight, but they nevertheless clearly identify as history theses. There is no evidence of the layout and font playfulness found in Wessell's (1999) thesis discussed earlier. There is indeed little evidence of genre blurring, with all of the ten theses submitted between 2015 and 2019 aligning strongly with the discipline of history and having an introduction that does not evidence much author reflexivity other than in the two theses specifically discussed above.

When compared to the 2006 corpus, the use of the first person in the history corpus Introductions is more prevalent. 'I' is, however, mainly used to organize and signpost the introduction for the reader or outline an argument, as for example, 'However, as I argue in this thesis' (Egan 2019: 2); 'as I demonstrate' (Keating 2017: 7); 'the other major theme I will explore' (Zubrzycki 2018: 12).

Most of the theses in the corpus identify a research gap through the historiographical section of the introduction, for example, 'Yet, they have been viewed in isolation from each other and overlooked in the push to globalise Australasian histories. Why has this occurred?' (Keating 2017: 26) or 'Less attention has been paid to the Board itself, and to the political and social trends that shaped the Board's policy direction. This thesis endeavours to fill this gap' (Egan 2019: 2).

While the reflexive personal narratives common to the sociology corpus are absent, apart from in the two theses already referred to, the history theses may, however, open with a brief 'scene setter' or anecdote that conjures up a moment in time before proceeding with the topic. Usually not longer than a paragraph, often specifying a date and introducing a specific historical personage or grouping, these paratextual elements seek to introduce the reader to the topic and 'transport' them to the period under investigation:

> On 10 October 1902, the Melbourne feminist newspaper Australian Woman's Sphere featured 'An Open Letter to the Women of the United States'.[1] It was written by Vida Goldstein, the newly elected secretary of the International Woman Suffrage Committee, on her return from six months touring America.
>
> (Keating 2017: 1, opening paragraph)

William Ferguson and Jack Patten, two Aboriginal men from southern central New South Wales who had become seasoned campaigners for Aboriginal rights, were in no doubt about the intentions of Aboriginal 'protection' in Australia when they published their 1938 pamphlet, *Aborigines Claim Citizens Rights!*

(Egan 2019: 1, opening paragraph)

In 1933, Sir Denison Ross, the vice-president of the Magician's Club of London, declared that aside from the manipulation of cards, all the best European conjuring tricks were derived from the East.

(Zubrzycki 2018: 1, opening paragraph)

At the turn of the twentieth century, The Young People's Society of Christian Endeavor (CE), or the 'Endeavor Movement', was the largest Protestant youth group in the world.

(Caroll-Dwyer 2015: 1, opening paragraph)

Conclusion

The time period that has elapsed since the collection of the initial corpus of twenty theses from each of sociology and history at the University of New South Wales is probably too short to gain a clear sense of the extent to which any patterns observed may indicate genre change or longer-term stability. While a fairly superficial view may assign the majority of the sociology and history theses that constitute our recent corpus to the topic-based category, closer examination suggests that forces of disruption may be at work, particularly in the case of the internal organization of the sociology theses. Thompson (2013: 286) has commented that the 'topic-based' macrostructure 'tends to be a catch-all for a wide range of frameworks that do not fit into the traditional IMRD patterns' and it may well be that further research on a larger corpus, from a wider range of institutions, could shed more light on its usefulness as an analytic category.

Certainly, within the recent sociology corpus, the influence of concerns in the field itself as to writer representation, researcher positionality and the act of writing that were identified in the earlier study is clearly evident and appears to be of concern to the student writers. The use of personal narrative is evident and would appear acceptable to examiners of these theses. While the theses would seem to align with the new humanities as delineated by Hodge (1995), at the same time they locate themselves clearly within sociology as a field of study.

Similarly, the history theses are positioned clearly within the discipline of history, adopting chronological and thematic macrostructures, and, apart from the oral history and the participant history theses, show no evidence of writer reflexivity as observed in the sociology corpus. There is stability here too. Wessell's thesis from the 2006 corpus appears to be somewhat of an outlier but then it is important to remind ourselves of its explicit location within cultural studies (see above). As discussed in Chapter 2 (see also Chapter 10), the notion of family resemblances and prototype allow us to see PhD theses as being more or less typical of a particular category but still be members of that category, namely history theses in this instance.

The theses in each corpus are clearly doctoral theses. The components studied in this chapter function paratextually to indicate to the reader that the text they will encounter is indeed a doctoral thesis. They have title pages which state this and administrative texts which must precede the table of contents indicating they have met various institutional requirements. The Introductions, in the main, function to both introduce the student writer/researcher and align them with a particular approach to their chosen field. All contain an outline of the thesis and the chapters to follow. They signal research gaps through reviewing previous studies, announce the study's purpose and preview the thesis's contribution to the field. In this there is continuity.

A key force for stability in each of the fields under investigation that emerged more clearly through the interviews would appear to be the supervisor who guides the student either explicitly or more implicitly into an understanding of the generic expectations of a PhD in their specific area. The supervisor then embodies and conveys the wider disciplinary expectations. Fellow students may also play a similar role as our interviewees identified their reading of other theses and talking with peers on a regular basis as sources of influence.

We are left to ponder Hodge's prescient comment: 'It is not clear how long the "New Humanities" will be able to retain its sense of being subversive or revolutionary, its openness to change, its commitment to openness, or how many times the activity of deconstructing the genre of the PhD will be challenging and productive' (Hodge 1995: 39).

6

Professional doctorates

Professional doctorates are a significant diversion from the conventional doctoral thesis/dissertation. This chapter discusses the development of professional doctorates and, in particular, the Doctor of Education (the EdD), a research degree that is often offered to education practitioners as an alternative to the PhD. The chapter focuses on EdD degrees offered in four different countries: the United States, the UK, Canada and Australia. Similarities and differences between the theses that students write in each of these countries are examined. We also consider EdD theses in relation to features of new humanities theses as discussed in the previous chapter.

Professional doctorates

The term 'professional doctorate' emerged in the United States where, in 1920, Harvard University introduced the Doctor of Education degree (Burnard 2016). This was followed by the establishment of an EdD at Columbia Teachers College in 1934. Institutions such as the University of California Berkeley, Stanford University and the University of Michigan followed thereafter (Perry 2014). The EdD has been offered in the UK since the 1990s, first at the University of Bristol (Poole 2012). It is now available in Canada and Australia, among other countries (Ellis and Anderson 2009; Scott et al. 2008; Smith 2008). There are, of course, other professional doctorates in the humanities and social sciences such as the Doctor of Social Work, the Doctor of Psychology, the Doctor of Nursing, Doctor of Health Science and the Doctor of Theology. In addition, a number of universities offer a Doctor of Professional Practice which is aimed at a specific professional group, such as health practitioners. The Doctor of Professional Practice may also have a broader focus and be aimed at practitioners in a range of occupational areas and have a transdisciplinary rather than specific disciplinary focus. It is the Doctor of Education, however, which will be the focus of this chapter as it is a professional doctorate that is widely offered and the professional doctorate that has been most discussed in the literature on doctoral education (Hawkes and Yerrabati 2018).

The Doctor of Education

A key feature of the EdD, as with all professional doctorates, is its connections with professional practice (QAA 2020) and its aim to prepare researching professionals, as opposed to professional researchers as is the case with the PhD (Lunt 2018). That is, the EdD is aimed at

> experienced professionals who wish to develop and reflect on their own practice, to deepen their understanding, enhance their critical and analytical abilities, and to turn a research lens to their professional context in order to enhance it.
>
> (Lunt 2018: 4)

The EdD thesis, further, involves the generation of new knowledge and expertise that will inform and underpin professional practice (Smith 2008). Thus, while, in her words, 'the process and focus of study may differ from the PhD … the outcomes are considered the same in terms of the level of knowledge and expertise developed and their intellectual rigour' (Smith 2008: 10).

The EdD has a coursework as well as a thesis component, although the thesis is sometimes shorter than that of the PhD. An EdD thesis is typically about 50,000 words in the UK (Scott et al. 2008) and 200 or so pages in the United States (Storey et al. 2015). The EdD is often compared with the PhD in terms of its value and prestige (Storey and Hesbol 2014). In fact, Harvard decided to discontinue its EdD in 2012 and replace it with a PhD with some (although not Harvard) pointing out that the EdD has been seen as a lesser alternative to the PhD (Inside Higher Ed 2012; Perry 2014; Poole 2012). The difference between the EdD and the PhD further, for some, is rather blurred (Levine 2007). The EdD, however, is still widely offered in the United States (Storey et al. 2015) and several other countries and it is the purpose of this chapter to examine the theses and dissertations that are written for these degrees in different countries and universities, specifically in the United States, the UK, Canada and Australia, to see to what extent there are similarities in what students write across institutions and in different geographic locations and in what ways they might be different. A study into the EdD carried out for the Carnegie Project on the Education Doctorate in the United States (Perry 2017) found that students were typically writing traditional five-chapter dissertations for their degrees (Storey et al. 2015; Storey and Hesbol 2014); that is, simple traditional theses of the kind described in Chapter 4 of this book. Anderson and Okuda's (2021) study of doctoral theses at the University of British Columbia in Canada examines Education PhDs theses over a fifty-two-year period, which showed a change in preference from simple traditional to other thesis types over the years (see below for further discussion of this study).

Data and analysis

Forty EdD theses were collected for this chapter, ten each from universities in the United States, the UK, Canada and Australia. The US theses were from Columbia University and Arizona State University, and the UK theses from University College London and the University of Bath. The Canadian theses were from the University of British Columbia and the University of Alberta. The Australian theses were from the Queensland University of Technology and Western Sydney University. Five theses from each of these universities were included in the data set, although, in some cases, more were obtained in case they were needed to further explore observations made in the analysis of the smaller sets of theses. The US and Canadian dissertations were obtained through a search of the ProQuest database and the UK theses by searching the British Library EThOS database. The EdD dissertations were not always easy to locate however as, at times, they were listed as a PhD on the front page of the database whereas in reality they were an EdD. The Australian theses were also difficult to find and, in most cases, required an intensive search of individual libraries' online catalogues where an EdD is on offer.

The starting point for the analysis was the thesis types that have been found in previous research into doctoral writing such as those outlined in Chapter 4. Other data sources however were also drawn on such as university handbooks and guidelines for EdD studies as well as published accounts of students' experiences of having undertaken an EdD. Reviews of the EdD such as the Carnegie Project on the Education Doctorate (Perry 2017; Storey et al. 2015) and the UK Quality Assurance Agency for Higher Education's reports on doctoral degrees (QAA 2020) were also examined. In addition, students and supervisors were interviewed to further explore matters that arose in the analysis.

Findings

The United States

The choice of universities to examine in the United States was informed by a publication titled *21 Best Doctor of Education (EdD) Programs* (https://www.eddprograms.org/schools/best-doctor-of-education-programs/) which provides advice to prospective students on choices of universities for undertaking an EdD degree. The publisher of this website uses *US News and World Report* and *Times Higher Education* rankings and published completion rates, as well as other sources, to make their recommendations. The top EdD in its ranking is the degree offered by Columbia University's Teachers College and so it was chosen as one of the universities from which to obtain sample dissertations. The other university chosen, Arizona State University, was lower-ranked but still highly recommended institution in their ranking.

The EdD at Columbia Teachers College is offered across a number of areas of concentration: namely curriculum studies, early childhood education, early childhood policy, educational leadership and school change, gifted education, and literacy education. These areas are further divided into areas such as applied linguistics, education leadership, art and art education, and music and music education. In all, Columbia Teachers College runs more than seventy EdD programmes, by far the largest set of EdD offerings in the United States. As with all US doctorates, EdD students at Columbia undertake a substantial amount of coursework before they reach the dissertation phase of their degree. They also have to submit a programme plan, pass a certification examination and write a qualifying paper in order to proceed to the dissertation.

Five EdD dissertations from Columbia Teachers College were examined for the chapter. They were in the areas of art education (3), music education (1) and education leadership (1). The dissertations were, on average, 240 pages long although one was longer at 300 pages. All of the Columbia dissertations had a simple-traditional format in that they broadly followed an Introduction, Literature Review, Methodology, Findings, Discussion and Conclusion pattern of organization. An example of one of the Columbia EdD dissertations is shown in Figure 6.1. These traditional chapter headings can be seen in the Table of Contents of her thesis. The subheadings within Chapter 1, similarly, reflect the areas that would be expected to be covered in a thesis introduction, as do the subheadings within the methodology, findings and discussion, and conclusions chapters.

Going home: Professional Integration of Chinese Graduate Degree Holders from United States Colleges and Universities in Art Education

Chapter I – Introduction
Background of the Problem
Problem Statement
Research Questions
Limits of Study
Assumptions
Personal Suitability
Educational Aims and Benefits
Organization of the Dissertation

Chapter II – Literature Review
Introduction
Theoretical Approaches to Reentry Adaptation
A Historical perspective on Returned Chinese Students in Art Education
Contemporary Studies on Returned Chinese Students and Professionals
Chapter Summary

Chapter III – Methodology
Introduction
Type of Study
Instruments
Data Collection Process
Methods of Data Organization
Limits of Study
Revision of the Proposed Timeline
Chapter Summary

Chapter IV – Findings
Introduction
Case Study 1: Yingshi Yang
Case Study 2: Julia Li
Case Study 3: Mido Cao
Case Study 4: Mingyang Sun
Case Study 5: June Han
Case Study 6: Shu Cao Mo
Chapter Summary

Chapter V – Discussion
Introduction
Theme 1: Challenges
Theme 2: Change
Theme 3: Competence
Chapter Summary

Chapter VI – Educational Implications
Introduction
Implications for Reentry Adaptation
Implications for Arts Education Programs in China
Chapter Summary

Chapter VII – Conclusions
My Reflections on the Research
Revisiting the Research Questions
Implications for Future Studies

Figure 6.1 An example of a Columbia Teachers College simple-traditional EdD dissertation (Liu 2021).

Arizona State University describes its EdD as a programme that is

> designed for practicing educator-leaders working in a range of settings who want to transform and improve their practice and create better learning opportunities for students of all ages. Students in the program begin as accomplished teachers, teacher leaders, principals, superintendents, higher education professionals, or leaders in other educational contexts working to implement change in their local place of practice.
>
> (ASU Mary Lou Fulton Teachers College 2021: 3)

The Arizona State EdD is offered in both on campus and online modes. The programme is designed for educational leaders who wish to improve their current place of practice or to advance in their professional careers rather than for people who are aiming for an academic tenure-track career. EdD students at Arizona State also complete coursework with both professional and research orientations and a number of hours of advanced studies which focus on disseminating research and guidance in developing research skills.

The EdD dissertations at Arizona State University were all in the area of educational leadership and innovation, the prime focus of the programme. Five dissertations from this programme were examined for the chapter. They were shorter than the Columbia Teachers College dissertations, on average 130 pages. They were all, however, as with the Columbia Teachers College dissertations, simple-traditional in their pattern of organization except that, in most cases, 'Theoretical Perspectives and Research' was used as a chapter heading instead of 'Literature Review'. An example of this can be seen in the Arizona State simple-traditional EdD dissertation shown in Figure 6.2. The other chapters have conventional thesis titles, Introduction and Purpose of the Study, Method, Data Analysis and Results, and Discussion.

In sum, then, the analysis of the two sets of US EdD dissertations confirmed the findings of the Carnegie Project that students, at least in the institutions examined here, wrote standard simple-traditional EdD dissertations. The length of the dissertations was in the same range in terms of page numbers as in the Carnegie Project's findings, although the Arizona State dissertations, at an average of 130 pages, were somewhat shorter than the Columbia dissertations which had an average length of 240 pages. As was also found in the Carnegie Project study, the dissertations addressed immediate needs in professional practice. In each of the dissertations, the 'problem of practice' being addressed derived from either a 'felt difficulty' that the student was facing in their

Preparing Teachers for Diverse Classrooms: Developing Intercultural Competence

1 **Introduction and Purpose of Study**
National Context
Local Context
Purpose of the Study
Research Questions

2 **Theoretical Perspectives and Research**
Intercultural Development Continuum
Related Studies
Transformative Learning Theory
Related Studies
Discussion

3 **Method**
Setting
Participants
Role of Researcher
Innovation Overview
Innovation Outline
Methodology
Instruments

Data Sources
Trustworthiness

4 **Data analysis and results**
Data Analysis
Quantitative Analysis
Qualitative Analysis
Procedure
Data Collection Timeline
Results from Quantitative Data
Results from Qualitative Data
Summary of Results

5 **Discussion**
Integration of Quantitative and Qualitative Data
Explanation of Results
Outcomes Related to Previous Research and Theory
Personal Lessons Learned
Limitations
Implications for Practice
Implications for Research
Conclusion

Figure 6.2 An example of an Arizona State University simple-traditional EdD dissertation (Brady 2020).

workplace or a 'real-world dilemma' that was 'situated in larger educational policy and procedures that created dilemmas for educators in their daily work' (Ma et al. 2018: 17).

The UK

The EdD in the UK tends to be offered on a cohort basis and is more applied in nature than the PhD. This cohort basis lends itself more to the sharing of experiences among students than is the case with the PhD. Completion times and rates also seem to differ from the PhD with fewer EdD students seeing the degree through to completion compared to the PhD (Poole 2012; Taylor 2008). There has also been debate about the place of the EdD in UK universities versus the PhD, with some universities having been reluctant to offer an EdD (Park 2005, 2007).

A review of the EdD in Britain carried out by Poole (2012) obtained data from sixteen English universities by means of a survey and follow-up interviews. He focused on three specific topics in his research: the specifics of an EdD compared to a PhD in Education in terms of learning experiences, programme aims and modes of assessment; the EdD *viva voce* in terms of its strengths, weaknesses and purposes; and 'originality' in the EdD, including how supervisors and examiners decide whether an EdD displays 'doctorateness' (Poole 2015). Poole (2012) found that the EdD was more supportive for students than the 'lonely' PhD. He also found that the EdD takes students to the same, or similar, end point as the PhD in terms of skills and knowledge. His respondents also said that they didn't expect less originality in the EdD than the PhD. There was also strong support for the viva voce as a compulsory part of the assessment and guarantor of academic standards for the EdD.

In the UK, the EdD has a coursework component in contrast with the UK PhD which typically does not. The aim of the coursework component is to scaffold students' learning as well as to provide structure to the EdD. This is especially important for students in helping them to engage with their supervisors as well as to interact with other research students so as to avoid the feelings of isolation that are typical of part-time study of this kind. The structure and support offered in the UK EdD, thus, appeal to busy professionals who are very often working at the same time as they are studying (Burgess et al. 2006). The cohort feature of the UK EdD, further, strengthens students' learning, much of which comes from the sharing of experiences between the students (Hawkes and Taylor 2016). Students undertaking the EdD, further, are often experienced professionals returning to study after a break away rather than undertaking a doctoral degree immediately after a first degree as is often the case with the PhD (Smith 2008). The extra support provided in the EdD, thus, is extremely important for these students.

Savva and Nygaard's (2021a) *Becoming a Scholar: Cross-cultural Reflections on Identity and Agency in an Education Doctorate* looks at students' experiences of undertaking an EdD at the University College London (UCL) Institute of Education. The book is based on accounts of a cohort of students, none of whom lived in the UK, but came together to do the degree on a part-time basis while continuing to live and work in their home countries. They are described by Savva and Nygaard (2021b) as 'peripheral students' in the academy, partly due to them being distance students, but also due to them being international students, mature and returning students, and part-time students. For many of these students it was a challenge to balance full-time employment with part-time academic studies and family responsibilities. The students chose research topics related to their work environments in line with the goal of the EdD to develop 'reflective practitioners' (Burgess et al. 2006). The students found that they needed a strong sense of agency, willingness to adapt to changing circumstances, and resilience in order to navigate the challenges they faced. They also found they were challenged by their change in status when doing the degree, from the expert status they held in their professional lives to the novice status they encountered when starting out as doctoral students. As Savva and Nygaard point out, 'We struggled to align who we were on the inside with who we could be on the outside – all the while adapting and negotiating the identities nested within us' (p. 169). It is the EdD theses from this cohort of students that are examined in the next section of the chapter.

University College London launched its EdD in 1996 (Lunt 2018). It is available in the following areas:

- Culture, communication and media
- Curriculum, pedagogy and assessment
- Education, practice and policy
- Learning and leadership
- Psychology and human development

There are three taught courses in the UCL EdD. These courses focus on professionalism in education and methods of enquiry. At the end of the taught phase, students submit a portfolio of work which needs to be approved by their supervisor and a 2,000-word reflective statement. In addition, students undertake two non-assessed courses from UCL's training programmes for doctoral students. There are also workshops students attend for an Institution Focused Study (an IFS) which provides a bridge between the taught modules and the thesis they need to write at the end of the degree. The purpose of the Institution Focused Study is to enable students to carry out a small-scale study based on their own institution. Students submit a 20,000-word research project for this component of their studies (Hawkes and Taylor 2016).

The thesis which students complete at the end of the degree has an upper word limit of 45,000 words and is required to

> make a distinct contribution to the knowledge in the field of study and afford evidence of originality and a capacity for autonomous research. The thesis usually relates to the IFS and the work carried out in the taught part of the programme.
> (UCL 2021 online)

Students undertaking the UCL EdD, thus, do a substantial amount of writing in their degree apart from the actual thesis.

The theses in the UCL sample were all simple traditional in their patterns of organization, although some of the results chapters had topic-based headings as in Nygaard's (2019) results chapters 'What does it mean to be a woman at PRIO? Situating gender and professorship' and 'Sites of negotiation and agency in everyday writing practices at PRIO'. Three of the theses, further, contained an impact statement in which the students elaborated on the contribution their research makes to the field as well as their particular workplace. The impact statements were several pages long and talked about the student's research trajectory as well as the impact they hope their work will make.

Poli's (2017) thesis 'Professional women in higher education management – Practices, career strategies and approaches to leadership' contained a section titled 'The EdD as a reflective and intimate journey' in which she talked about her reasons for doing the EdD, how she struggled with some of the earlier modules she undertook, and how she fought to make her voice heard as a woman and to establish herself in the male dominated field of higher education. She relates, however, how she became more confident in expressing herself as she progressed through the degree 'module after module, I saw myself become more capable to hear my voice first, then speak out my thoughts as never before' (Poli 2017: 12).

Poli also talks about becoming a 'blended professional' (Whitchurch 2009) during her studies where, instead of compartmentalising herself as either a professional or an academic, she established an identity which drew from both her professional and academic domains. This hybrid identity, she says, allowed her to develop her expertise as an academic by building on her professional expertise. It affirmed her pride in belonging to her professional community at the same time as complemented the academic person she was becoming. The practice of shifting from one to the other domain, the academic and the professional, became common for her during her studies (Necas and Poli 2021).

O'Keeffe (2016) also includes a reflective section in the opening pages of her thesis. She described her thesis writing journey thus:

> Initially the research process was messy, I felt confused and while reading broadly about *learning* I did not identify a specific conceptual framework to hinge my research upon. Nonetheless, during this time I realised that writing and rewriting were crucial to the process of analysis, interpretation and generating findings ... I began to trust the ambiguous process of qualitative and interpretive research. As one of my peers asserted, 'research is not plug and play'. Rather

the research process is about moving continuously forward with a question, to which there is no right answer and that continual engagement will help with making sense of the findings.

(O'Keeffe 2016: xvii)

She adds:

The EdD has been an identity journey allowing me to better understand myself and to become critically aware of my position within societal, cultural and political legacies ... While the research process began with vagueness ..., having completed my thesis, I am now in a position to better understand and influence activities in higher education and in the field of academic development.

These extracts, thus, show how the experience of doing the EdD is just as important as its final product, the thesis.

The EdD at the University of Bath was introduced as part of a broader development of professional doctorates at that university which also includes a Doctor of Business Administration in higher education management, modelled on the structure of the EdD, four taught courses plus a thesis (Jamieson and Naidoo 2007). The Bath EdD has students enrolled in the degree from across the world. It is taught through a mix of summer and winter school intensive on-campus units, off-campus study and directed learning units. The taught courses involve the writing of four 8,000-word assignments that are assessed by two markers (Poole 2012). The thesis for the EdD at Bath has a limit of 45,000 words, the same as the EdD at University College London. The research focus of the thesis draws from the taught component of the degree as well as the students' existing work and interests. Bath describes its EdD, thus, as a degree which is

aimed at experienced educational professionals and sets out to place you at the leading edge of your professional field in terms of knowledge, awareness and understanding ... The degree is designed to engage current practitioners with knowledge, awareness and understanding of the philosophical, organisational, political, social, managerial, interpersonal, and technical dimensions of schools and other educational institutions.

All of the EdD theses from the University of Bath, as with UCL theses, were simple traditional in their organization. The University of Bath EdD theses did not, however, contain an impact statement or a reflective component as was the case with the UCL EdDs. The main section titles from the table of contents of Poole's (2012) simple traditional thesis are shown in Figure 6.3. As can be seen, it is very traditional in the areas it covers in its five chapters: an introductory

Perspectives on the EdD from Academics at English Universities

Introduction	**Chapter 4 Questionnaire and Interview** Data Analysis
Chapter 1 Literature Review	4.1 The questionnaire
1.1 Recent Developments in Doctoral Education	4.2 Interview data and discussion
	Chapter 5 Limitations, Conclusions and Implications
Chapter 2 Research Design	
2.1 Introduction	5 Introduction
2.2 Research questions	5.1 Limitations of the present study
2.3 Research methodology	5.2 Conclusions
	5.3 Implications for further research or debate
Chapter 3 Research Implementation	
3.1 Research methods	

Figure 6.3 Poole's (2012) simple traditional EdD thesis submitted at the University of Bath.

chapter which contains a literature review, research methods chapters, a data collection and analysis chapter, and a conclusions and limitations chapter. His data collection and analysis chapter also contain a discussion of his findings in relation to previous research, rather than being a stand-alone discussion chapter.

Both the UCL and the University of Bath EdDs, thus, fit with the UK Quality Assurance Agency for Higher Education statement on the characteristics of professional doctorates. That is, they contain research projects which are located within the candidate's professional practice and are assessed through submission and examination of a thesis and an oral examination (QAA 2020).

Canada

There seems to have been less expansion of professional doctorates in Canada compared to the United States and the UK. Professional doctorates are not, however, new in Canada with the first Doctor of Pedagogy degree (now an EdD) being awarded by the University of Toronto in 1898 (Kot and Hendel 2011), a degree it still offers. One of the reasons Kot and Hendel (2011) give for this lack of development is the increase in the offering of flexible PhD programmes for professionals in Canada as a result of a trend to reinvent the traditional PhD rather than to develop professional doctorates (Allen, Smyth and Wahlstrom 2002). There has also been a resistance on the part of state governments to fund and thereby support professional doctorates (Kot and Hendel 2011). Notwithstanding, a number of Canadian universities do offer professional doctorates, including the EdD, which is the focus of this section of the chapter.

In Canada, as in the United States and the UK, the EdD contains coursework and a thesis which reports on original research, the examination of which includes an oral examination. Information on the University of Alberta's webpage for the EdD states that the EdD is equivalent to the PhD, except that the thesis in the EdD degree may be more practically oriented than the PhD. At the University of Alberta EdD students undertake two years of coursework, including a wide range of research methods options, before starting on the thesis component of their degree. In order to proceed to the thesis stage of the degree, students must prepare and orally defend a written candidacy paper which outlines their proposed study and reviews relevant theory and research.

Students can undertake the EdD at the University of Alberta in a wide range of areas, including Aboriginal Education, Art and Media Education, Arts-Based Research and Participatory Research, Career and Technology Studies, Curriculum Studies, Drama Education, English Language Arts Education, Mathematics Education, Music Education, Physical Education, Religious and Moral Education, Science Education Second Language Education, Social Studies Education, Teacher Education and Technology in Education (University of Alberta 2021). There is no specified upper word limit for the EdD thesis on the University's website, but the EdD theses collected for this chapter were in the range of 157–219 pages, a similar length to PhD theses in Education at that university.

All of the University of Alberta EdD theses collected for the chapter were simple traditional in their patterns of organization, although one of the theses (Nixon 2007) took a theme, 'tapestry', which was developed in combination with more conventional chapter headings as the thesis progressed (see Figure 6.4).

On the opening page of her thesis, Nixon explains her choice of tapestry as a theme for her study:

> As I began this journey, the image of the creation of a tapestry came to mind. Rich and vibrant colors blended with different textures and patterns, and all combined to create something new, something unexpected. This process, this act of creation, takes into account the varied experiences that I acquired while working with students in a number of roles. My professional reading adds to the tapestry, and the teacher and the students are the main threads – colorful, quirky, unique. The final product, the summary, is a composite of all the pieces,

---

A Study of the Reading Experiences of 'At Risk' Grade 10 Students

Chapter 1: Introduction: The Start of the Tapestry

Chapter 2: Review of the Literature: Assembling the Threads

Chapter 3: Research Methodology and Design: Making a Plan

Chapter 4: Analysis of the Data: Taking the Threads Apart

Chapter 5: Data Collection and Analysis: Filling in the Gaps

Chapter 6: Pulling the Threads Together

Figure 6.4 Chapter titles in Nixon's (2007) University of Alberta EdD thesis.

complex, yet simple; well worth, I believe, sharing. As with many creations, the final product is often not what one expected.

(Nixon 2007: 1)

The theses submitted for the EdD at the University of British Columbia (UBC) showed much more variation than the University of Alberta EdD theses as well as the US and UK theses reviewed earlier in this chapter. One of the UBC theses was simple traditional, three were topic-based and one was a doctorate by publication. One of the UBC topic-based theses was an account of a three-act ethnodrama (sometimes called performance ethnography) which examined school principals' understanding and response to homophobia in a school district in British Columbia (Perkins 2012). The student's thesis describes the ethnodrama which was titled 'Do we really need to discuss this?' Perkins both wrote and directed the ethnodrama. The chapter headings from Perkins' (2012) thesis are shown in Figure 6.5. Chapters 1 and 2 of the thesis provide background to the topic of homophobia. Chapter 3 outlines what ethnodrama is and Perkins' experience with ethnodrama. She also includes her own experience of having handled homophobia as a school principal, part of which she presents as a 'remembered' ethnodrama, presented in the text in scripted form. She then explains the characters in the ethnodrama, where and when it is located, why it was produced and the read-throughs and rehearsals that took place before the actual performance of the ethnodrama through which she presents her research findings. Chapters 5 and 6 present the three acts of the ethnodrama as in the script for a play. Perkins adds director's notes to the chapters which include her reflections on the performances as well as discusses the ethnodrama in relation

How School Principals Understand and Respond to Homophobia: A Study of One B.C. School District Using Ethnodrama

Chapter One:	Prologue
Chapter Two:	Behind the Scenes – History and Context
Chapter Three:	Setting the Stage
Chapter Four:	An Ethnodrama – Act 1
Chapter Five:	Act Two
Chapter Six:	Act Three
Chapter Seven:	Conclusion

Figure 6.5 Chapter headings in Perkin's (2012) University of British Columbia EdD thesis.

to broader discussions of homophobia in the published literature. Chapter 7 presents conclusions, a summary of the study's findings, limitations of the study and implications for policy and practice. The chapter headings of her thesis reflect each of these components in overall terms.

Perkins starts each chapter with a vignette. Sometimes this is from her own experience as in the opening to Chapter 1:

> On Monday morning as I completed my routine check of the girls' bathroom, I heard someone throwing up. Destiny opens the door and bursts into tears. Her best friend had just spilled her biggest secret. Her mother was living with another woman. Destiny was in pain.
>
> (Perkins 2012: 1–2)

Other times the vignette is from the published literature, as in the opening to Chapter 2:

> Although the rule is seldom explicitly stated, the closet seems to be the only option for those who want to become administrators.
>
> (Lipkin 1999: 206)

The range of thesis types shown in the UBC EdD theses is reflective of the range of thesis types found in the work of Anderson et al. (2020, 2021) who examined the macrostructures of Education doctoral theses in Canada more broadly. In a subsequent study which looked at the development of Education PhD theses over a fifty-two-year period at the University of British Columbia

(Anderson and Okuda 2021), they found that while in the early days simple traditional thesis types were most common, in recent years other thesis types have become more popular for Education PhDs and there is now a move away at that university from the more traditional introduction, literature review, methods, results and discussion type thesis. This was also seen in the UBC EdD theses examined in this chapter.

Australia

Professional doctorates were introduced in Australian universities in 1990 (Ellis and Anderson 2019). Some of these early doctorates have continued to be offered while others have not (Malloch 2016). The Australian Qualifications Framework (2013: 63) describes professional doctorates as 'making a significant and original contribution to knowledge in the context of professional practice'. In comparing professional doctorates with the PhD, it continues, 'The emphasis in the learning outcomes and research may differ between the different forms of Doctoral Degree qualifications but all graduates will demonstrate knowledge, skills, and the application of knowledge and skills at AQF 10' [the top level of academic qualification in Australia].

Most professional doctorates in Australia contain coursework, although much less than in the degrees described earlier in this chapter. The EdD at Queensland University of Technology, for example, requires students to attend three intensive study schools and the Western Sydney University EdD requires participation in activities such as specified research training units, courses and workshops. These activities largely focus on preparing students for the research phase of their degree, however, rather than providing additional subject area knowledge.

As with the EdD in other parts of the world, the EdD in Australia attracts mid-career professionals in the areas of education and training most of whom do their studies part time. Some students will be seeking career advancement on the basis of the completion of the EdD while other will be wanting to work in universities. There are broadly two generations in the history of the EdD in Australia (Skamp 2019). The first was 'moderately conservative rather than innovative' (Malloch 2016: 72) in its attempt to measure itself against the PhD. The second aimed to move beyond this and aimed to 'produce useful or significant knowledge, where the usefulness of or significance of the knowledge is determined by its application, relevance and pertinence to a professional or workplace context, rather than to a body of knowledge within an academic discipline (as is the case of the PhD)' (Evans 1997: 178).

The current trend with the EdD in Australia, however, Malloch (2016) argues, has been to discontinue the EdD and to use its courses to support the studies of PhD students. The University of Sydney, for example, terminated its EdD several years ago and for a short time compulsory coursework into its PhD. Similarly, from 2020 all EdD students at the University of Technology, Sydney (UTS) have changed their enrolment to a PhD. The University of New South Wales however, which had previously discontinued its EdD, reintroduced it in 2019.

Maxwell (2016) has described the EdD in Australia as being 'at a crossroad' (p. 79) with the number of students graduating from the EdD being in decline. Strong EdD programmes do, however, still remain in Australia and it is two of these that are the focus of this section of the chapter, the EdD at the Queensland University of Technology and the EdD at Western Sydney University (formerly the University of Western Sydney).

Queensland University of Technology (QUT) has a strong reputation for professional doctorates having graduated 121 students from these degrees in the years 2010–2020. These are not all EdDs, however, but also include the degrees of Doctor of Creative Industries, Doctor of Health Science, Doctor of Juridical Science and Doctor of Business Administration. The QUT EdD has a focus on 'applied investigation and problem solving rather than on a contribution to pure research or to theoretical knowledge' (QUT 2021). It has a focus on enhancing students' professional practice and fostering the professional development of education practitioners. Students commence their studies with an interdisciplinary education studies unit which they complete in a one-week intensive study school. They then undertake further study schools during which they work on the methodology and design of their thesis. The thesis they write for the EdD is typically 80,000 words.

Students undertaking the EdD at QUT come from a range of backgrounds, including classroom teachers, gifted and talented teachers, school principals, school guidance and career officers as well as academic staff from other universities wanting to obtain a doctoral degree. Students choose the EdD because of its practical nature and see it as a way in which they can focus on their particular role in the education system. The topics they choose however 'seem to come in quite discernible waves' (QUT teacher and supervisor interview 2021). For example, at one point there were students focusing on ICT in education, then inclusive education, career advancement, sexualities in education and higher education. Students choose a range of project types and research approaches ranging from case studies to the analysis of statistical data by various education systems including those associated with Catholic, Independent and government schooling. The projects all, however, entail a single study rather than multiple studies and students have gone on to win prizes for their work.

A student we spoke to very much appreciated the scaffolded nature of the QUT EdD programme. She did, however, have problems with the genre of the doctoral thesis, even though she had been given very clear guidelines on how to organize it. An issue for her, in particular, was the academic language that it required. Even though she was an experienced writer of scientific reports, she said meeting the writing requirements of a doctoral thesis 'doesn't come easy' and were, for her, a struggle (QUT student interview 2022). This reflected a view put by a supervisor we interviewed who, equally, felt the genre requirements of a doctoral thesis were a challenge for their EdD students but, nonetheless, a necessary part of mastering the genre conventions of an Education research thesis (QUT supervisor interview 2021).

The QUT EdD theses collected for this chapter were all simple traditional and reported on a single study. Bui's (2015) thesis 'Using collaboration and technology to enhance Vietnamese students' English writing skills', however, adds a chapter titled 'Theoretical framework' after the literature review chapter which also occurred in a number of the other QUT EdD theses. She also gives topic-based titles to her findings chapters which is also a feature of a number of the other QUT EdD theses in the collection. Her thesis and the ones that are similar to hers, then, following the work of Anderson et al. (2020), could be considered a 'hybrid' simple traditional/topic-based thesis. The chapter titles for Bui's thesis are shown in Figure 6.6. Chapters 1–4 are conventional in their chapter titles, Introduction, Literature review, Theoretical framework and Research design, as is Chapter 8, Conclusion. Chapters 5, 6 and 7, however, have thematic titles related to the particular findings of the study.

Western Sydney University (WSU) is a relatively new university in Australia. It was formed in 1989 by bringing together a number of colleges and institutes of advanced education. Initially it was named the University of Western Sydney and in 2015 was re-named Western Sydney University. Apart from the EdD, UWS also offers professional doctorates such as a Doctor of Cultural Research, Doctor of Creative Arts and Doctor of Business Administration. WSU has a reputation for developing alternate models of education and their EdD is no exception to this.

Using Collaboration and Technology to Enhance Vietnamese Students' English Writing Skills

Chapter 1   Introduction
Chapter 2   Literature review
Chapter 3   Theoretical framework
Chapter 4   Research design
Chapter 5   Participants' experiences of L2 writing and perceptions of collaborative writing using wikis
Chapter 6   Participants' expectations of and strategies for collaborative writing
Chapter 7   Reflections and evaluation of the entire project and suggestions for future projects
Chapter 8   Conclusion

Figure 6.6 Chapter titles in Buis' (2015) EdD thesis from the Queensland University of Technology.

The WSU EdD is available in the following areas:

- Policy studies in education
- Curriculum studies
- Learning and teaching
- Socio-cultural studies
- Educational leadership and change

The EdD is described by WSU as a degree in practice-led research and research-led practice which should 'uncover new knowledge either by the discovery of new facts, the formulation of theories, the innovative re-interpretation of known data and established ideas, or the application of established knowledge in new contexts' (Western Sydney University 2017). A key focus of the WSU EdD degree is the relationship between research, scholarship and professional practice. Practice-informed research and research-informed practice, thus, are a critical part of the programme, with academic work and teaching practice being seen as 'mutually informed and mutually informing' (WSU supervisor interview 2022).

The WSU EdD requires students to produce an examinable portfolio of work which is normally text-based but may include other mediums of communication such as film, video or online resources. Clerk and Lee (2008: 17) ague that 'as a flexible form of doctoral production, the portfolio has the potential to evidence both textual products and graduate capabilities due to its capacity to accommodate a range of media forms and delivery contexts that address various scholarly and professional practice communities'.

The WSU portfolio commences with a narrative of personal, professional and scholarly development which is then followed by three scholar papers and examples of work-place-related research-based practices or products. The final submission is in the range of 60,000–90,000 words, which is similar in length to the PhD in most Australian universities.

All the WSU EdD submissions collected for the chapter were portfolios of scholarly papers and professional practice initiatives. The section headings in Leonarder's (2016) EdD portfolio 'Ethical decision making by school leaders in a period of neoliberal reform' are shown in Figure 6.7. The scholarly papers included in his portfolio, while following expectations for submissions to academic journals, do not however appear to have been submitted to academic journals at the point of submission of his doctorate.

The EdD at Western Sydney University, thus, could be considered a doctorate 'by portfolio' with an overall structure as summarized in Figure 6.8.

Ethical Decision Making by School Leaders in a Period of Neoliberal Reform

Overarching Narrative	
Scholarly Paper 1	Ethical decision making and its implications for schools and educational leadership
Professional Practice Initiative 1	The development of the ethical decision-making toolkit
Scholarly Paper 2	Scenario-based professional learning and its applicability for education leaders
Professional Practice Initiative 2	The ethical decision-making course for school leaders in the Macquarie region
Scholarly Paper 3	Educational leadership
Professional Practice Initiative 3	Practitioner study: Expectations, accountabilities and professional learning for educational leaders in an era of educational reform
Concluding remarks	

Figure 6.7 Section headings in Leonarder's (2016) EdD portfolio from Western Sydney University.

Narrative

Scholarly Paper 1

Professional Practice Initiative 1

Scholarly Paper 2

Professional Practice Initiative 2

Scholarly Paper 3

Professional Practice Initiative 3

Figure 6.8 Typical structure of the Western Sydney University EdD by portfolio.

An issue one of the WSU EdD supervisors raised in an interview was the challenge students faced with their writing. As mid- to senior-level practitioners they were used to writing reports and what could be broadly described as descriptive writing. Indeed, they generally thought of themselves as good writers. They struggled, however, with the requirements of academic writing and the overall genre expectations of doctoral writing. Indeed, he found he might say to a student 'It's beautifully written and it's quite interesting – but it's not research' (WSU supervisor interview 2022). A student we interviewed, indeed, said, 'No matter what you've written in the past ... there's nothing that prepares you for that style of academic writing' (WSU student interview 2022).

For these students, then, writing itself wasn't a huge challenge, but the requirements of doctoral writing were, or as one student put it, 'getting the mode of expression right' (WSU student interview 2022). Some students, further, a supervisor we spoke to said, had an impressive command of theory. Others, however, struggled with the theoretical component of their studies.

The EdD and new humanities theses

In the previous chapter we discussed features of new humanities theses such as reflexivity, the use of personal narratives, playfulness in thesis and chapter titles, use of alternate layout, font, patterns of organization, and reference to postmodern and poststructural theorists in the discussion of the thesis topic and analysis of the data. They were, in many ways, similar to the origin stories in new humanities theses that we discussed in Chapter 5. Reflexivity and personal narratives were features of many of the EdD theses we examined for this chapter. For example, Capezzuto (2021: 30), in his thesis 'The hands of Johannes Whisler: A historical study of handwriting and drawing' from Columbia Teachers College, provides a reflective description of his role of a researcher in which he acknowledges his theoretical disposition and biases:

> My role is informed primarily by a constructivist worldview, by which – according to John Creswell (2014) – meaning is inductively derived from the researcher's direct experience of a context and interaction with sources of data. I gathered data through a formal analysis of Whisler's cyphering book, and primary and secondary historical research. As a historical researcher working in a constructivist paradigm, I interpret a past reality for a present understanding of that reality.

Capezzuto uses 'I' to position himself within his study and the writing of his thesis, an example of what Macbeth (20021) terms textual reflexivity. In doing this he foregrounds rather than elides his role in the process of carrying out the research. His personal voice returns in his concluding chapter when he reflects on what he has done in saying:

> I have presented this dissertation against a cultural backdrop in which literacy in various lexicons of signs is promoted as the driving force of meaning making and communication.
>
> (Capezzuto 2021: 195)

and

> I end with the consideration of handwriting as a life process or, more specifically, one mode of a life process that includes other modes of symbol formation. Handwriting is an intrinsically social apparatus, but it is only by our individual explorations of it that it can work at all.
>
> (Capezzuto 2021: 196)

His thesis, however, is simple traditional in organization with distinct Introduction, Literature Review, Methodology, Results, Discussion and Conclusion chapters. It was also conventional in terms of the layout of the thesis and use of font. None of the poststructuralist theorists referred to in the previous chapter, further, were drawn on his research and analysis.

Levin (2021), in her Columbia Teachers College EdD thesis 'Holding on to millennial teachers: Learning from aspiring leaders' experiences about why they stay', provides a reflective account of her teaching experience as a way of positioning herself within her research:

> I began my teaching career in 2001, in New York City. The students I taught were all Millennials (born between 1980 and 2000). These particular students were additionally labelled "at risk" and "second chance." The school I taught at was labelled "alternative" and "transfer." These terms all allude to issues of retention, begging questions such as: How are these students effectively engaged in learning? How can the content and pedagogy be more relevant and authentic for them? How can we keep them in school?
>
> (p. 17)

Her thesis is also simple traditional and equally conventional in terms of layout and use of font (as were the other Columbia EdD theses) but ends with a section titled Researcher Reflections in which she says:

> The dissertation has been a challenging process that has required more intellectual grit and internal strength than I ever knew I had. Upon reflection, it seemed almost impossible at points that this project would ever be completed. It was not easy to accomplish while concurrently raising three children, working full-time, and relocating my family to a new part of the country (during a globalpandemic). However, once a pathway through the madness of this seemingly herculean task emerged, it suddenly became more manageable. With the help and support of my advisor, my husband, and my village, I have learned to accept my limitations (more effectively than before). After all, done is often better than perfect, as difficult as that is for a perfectionist to internalize.
>
> As a proud member of Generation X, studying these teacher leaders through a Millennial lens was very thought-provoking. Much of the literature sheds an unattractivelight upon the 20- to 40-year-olds who make up the largest cohort of workers in American history. But as my husband recently pointed out, maybe this generation is actually onto something. Maybe self-improvement is as important as societal improvement. Maybe voice, choice, and opportunity are less about feeling entitled and more about knowing what one needs to be successful in the work and satisfied as an individual. Perhaps prioritizing our own happiness to positively inform a whole set of outcomes for the greater good would help us all work smarter instead of harder. That is what I am walking away thinking about anyway.
>
> (p. 192)

Liu (2021), in 'Going home: Professional integration of Chinese graduate degree holders from United States colleges and universities in art education', provides an extended personal narrative in a section titled 'Personal Suitability' as a way of explaining her position in relation to her research. She talks about growing up in China, her time as an exchange student at the University of Bologna, moving to the United States to do her EdD and then her impending return to China as a degree holder from a US university to work in art education – the subject of her research. In the final chapter of her thesis in a section titled My Reflections on the Research, she says:

> The idea for this research stemmed from my own experience as a Chinese national who has spent years in the United States. Like many international students from China, I considered returning home to be a practical option for me because there were gaps between art education development in the United States and in China, and I wanted to make a change in my home country. However, sometimes I felt uncertain about the future because, although I learned about art education in the United States, I was not taught how to translate what I learned in the United States to a system of education in another country. Also, I have noticed that in today's world, this issue could be global because cross-border mobility continues to gain popularity worldwide. Therefore, I decided to research this issue with a focal point on Chinese returnees who studied art education in the United States.
>
> (p. 201)

Liu's thesis and the other two theses referred to above, while in other ways conventional in their layout, show there is clearly a place for these kinds of reflective accounts in Columbia Teachers College EdD theses, much as we saw in the discussion of sociology and history new humanities theses in the previous chapter.

A section titled Role of the Researcher also occurred in one the Arizona State University theses. In 'Preparing teachers for diverse classrooms: Developing intercultural competence', Brady (2020: 326) provides a reflective account which commences:

> As the daughter of two college professors from India who taught at various colleges and universities in Africa, I grew up attending international schools in Tanzania, Kenya, and Botswana. My academic and social experiences at these schools engaging with students and teachers from a plethora of different racial, religious, ethnic, and cultural backgrounds has had a significant lifelong impact on me. As a result, I have continued to be deeply interested in how people (both adults and children) interact with one another, especially with those who are

different from themselves, whether it be related to race, religion, ethnicity, culture, or sexual orientation.

None of the other Arizona State University theses contained this kind of account. Notwithstanding, all of the Arizona State theses ended with a section titled Lesson Learned in which the students reflected on what they had learnt from their research, although they were typically not written in a personally reflective way.

A number of the University College London EdD theses, while all conventional in their organization, also contained reflective accounts of the student's history and motivation for carrying out their research. Bukhatir (2018), for example, in 'Learning from experiences and investing in opportunities: A narrative inquiry about the career progress of public kindergarten principals in the United Arab Emirates', had an extended section titled Narrative Beginnings which included subsections titled Childhood, School and Education, Becoming a Teacher, Leaving Teaching to Start a Family, Becoming a Leader in a Private Bilingual School, Establishing an Early Years Setting and the Story of My Professional Doctorate, and Positioning Myself in the Study. Gishen (2020), in 'Evaluating a Curriculum Map for Undergraduate Medical Education: A Critical Analysis through Different Stakeholder Lenses', has a section titled Seeking Personal Utility Through This Research in which she outlines some of the personal influences which shaped her research. Other sections of University College London EdD theses which had this function were titled Positioning Myself in the Study (Hutchinson 2020), Personal Interest (Kinuthia 2021), The EdD as a Reflective and Intimate Journey (Poli 2107) and Reflective Statement (Nygaard 2019).

Reflective accounts were also a feature of the EdD theses from the University of Bath. For example, Poole (2012), in the opening lines of his Introduction, provides a personal account of his earlier attempt to obtain a PhD:

> In the mid-1990s I enrolled as a part-time MPhil/PhD student in applied linguistics at a British university. Despite successful transfer to PhD status, for various reasons (being required to take on extra responsibility at the – different – UK university where I worked; then getting divorced; then moving on 'unpaid leave' to a demanding overseas post; then my supervisor's unexpected early retirement), I did not complete my doctorate. Instead, in 2002, when I returned to my 'permanent' job, I tidied up the work already done and, guided by a senior colleague as supervisor, successfully submitted it for the award of MPhil.
>
> (p. 10)

A number of the University of Alberta and the University of British Columbia EdD theses wove narrative accounts into their text. Two of these were mentioned earlier in this chapter: Nixon's (2007) 'A study of the reading experiences of "at risk" grade 10 students' and Perkin's (2012) 'How school principals understand and respond to homophobia: A study of one B.C. school district using ethnodrama'. Beyond this, a section titled Role of the Researcher occurred in all but one of the University of Alberta EdD theses.

A University of British Columbia EdD thesis, similar to Poole's (2012) University of Bath EdD thesis, opened with a personal life story. It commenced thus:

> I grew up a pleaser, an accommodator, a good girl. But somehow it's never been enough. Now, I find myself a 50-something, divorced, professional woman, with two wonderful, accomplished, grown-up daughters and a few dear friends, wondering what it means to be successful, to have a successful life, to be a success.
>
> (Fraser 2007: 1)

Another University of British Columbia EdD (Johnson 2009) commences with a chapter titled 'The story begins' and includes a discussion chapter titled 'My story' in which the student reflects on her own professional history in relation to the findings of her study.

The Queensland University of Technology EdD theses were similarly conventional to the other EdDs we examined for this chapter in terms of their format and organization. A number of the QUT theses, however, contained personal accounts which explained the students' motivations for their study. One thesis that did this was Newton's (2009) 'Resisting education: A capital idea' which contained a section titled Role of the Researcher in which the student described his motivation and interest in the topic of his study. Orth (2015) also did this in his EdD thesis. Phan (2015) included a section titled From my Own Experience in which she explained her professional history in relation to the topic of her thesis.

The professional portfolios submitted at Western Sydney University, while very different from the other EdDs examined in this chapter, all contained a narrative section as it was a required component of the document the students had to submit for examination. Many of the Western Sydney University portfolios, further, drew on theorists such as Foucault (e.g. Leonarder 2016; Seto 2016) and Bourdieu (e.g. O'Brien 2016; Murphy 2016) for their thinking and analysis. These were all for portfolios submitted after 2016 which was the year before the university published their guidelines for their 'new look' EdD, suggesting these were theorists whose work had been given prominence in the coursework that the students did in the re-structured degree.

What we saw, then, was that while many of the EdD submissions we examined contained features of new humanities theses such as reflexivity and personal narratives, there was much less playing with thesis or chapter titles, layout, font and patterns of organization when compared to the new humanities theses described in the previous chapter. There was, however, playfulness and the use of the gerund in the title for Nygaard's (2019) thesis, 'Ready or not: Negotiating gender and institutional environment on the path to professorship', the gerund suggesting something that was still in progress rather than a finished state. Johnson (2009) in her EdD thesis from the University of British Columbia, 'Preparing to appear: A case study of student activism', uses the gerund for a similar effect as did Newton (2009) in his thesis from Queensland University of Technology, 'Resisting education: A capital idea', also showing playfulness with 'A capital idea' in his thesis subtitle. Nygaard's (2019) UCL thesis, however, was the only thesis in the data set that used alterative font on its title page. Nygaard also used the work of theorists such as Butler and Bourdieu in her thesis as did Poli (2017). At one of the other universities, Western Sydney University, students also drew on the work of theorists which were features of the new humanities theses we examined in the previous chapter. So what we see then is the inheritance (see Chapter 2) of parts but not all of new humanities theses into EdD theses and genre change where reflexive features, personal accounts, the use of the gerund in thesis titles, and the work of postmodern and poststructural theorists (Phillips 2016) are now accepted in EdD theses but do not necessarily occur in every instance of them.

Conclusion

Most of the EdDs theses examined in this chapter were simple traditional, although there were other aspects of new humanities theses in the submissions as we have just discussed. The continuity of simple traditional thesis types is in contrast to PhD theses where there is typically much more variety in terms of thesis types (see Anderson et al. 2021; Paltridge and Starfield 2020b). This dominance of simple traditional EdD theses is, in part perhaps, because of the centripetal pull (see Chapter 4) of more traditional PhD dissertations and discussions (and debates) about similarities between the EdD and the PhD. The findings of the chapter, thus, largely fit with Carnegie Project discussions of EdD theses and the prominence of traditional five-chapter dissertations in these degrees (Perry 2017). Exceptions to this, however, were found in the University of British Columbia EdD theses examined in this chapter where the range of thesis types was similar to Education PhD theses currently being submitted at that institution. This is perhaps not surprising given that the University of British Columbia has been at the centre of discussions about the future of the doctoral thesis in Canada (see e.g. Paré 2019; Porter et al. 2018). The EdD at Western Sydney University was also (markedly) different from the other EdDs examined in this chapter. Indeed, it was the only university in the group of theses that was studied where there was a clear case of genre change in terms of what an EdD submission should contain in terms of the text students submit for examination and how it should be written.

Change in EdD submissions, however, is not just occurring in Canada and Australia. Storey and Hesbol (2014) discuss examples of EdDs in the United States that are somewhat different from those that have been discussed in this chapter. At the University of Southern California, for example, most EdD students work in small groups to produce dissertations around a common theme, working with one or two advisors as well as with other students in their group. The student outputs are the same – a stand-alone dissertation – but the way they get there is somewhat different. Marsh and Dembo (2009: 8) describe the research process thus:

> Students participating in thematic dissertations meet both formally and informally in all stages of their projects. This model of collaboration is apparent throughout the dissertation process. Students can assist each other in every aspect of the task and can critique and learn from each other's efforts. As a result, the thematic dissertation group increases individual productivity and accountability and can produce robust studies that may make a significant contribution.

EdD students at the University of Missouri-St Louis work in a dissertation team of two to three students to conduct research around a high impact 'problem of practice' (Storey and Hesbol 2014). At Vanderbilt University, EdD students produce a 'team-produced, client-consultant oriented' capstone project rather than a single-authored five-chapter dissertation (Smrekar and McGraner 2009: 46) which is both analytically rigorous yet reader friendly. As Pantelides (2013: 152) has noted, 'dissertations are not sole-authored works that offer new knowledge. Thus, collaborative inclusions and opportunities for co-authorship need to be acknowledged and valued as opposed to denied'. Dissertation change, Pantelides argues, is clearly happening, but 'for it to be authentic, all-encompassing change, it will and must happen slowly and naturally' (p. 149) which seems to be the case with the EdD.

There are, then, clear instances of genre evolution with the EdD, particularly at the University of British Columbia, Western Sydney University and at the US universities described above. While other EdD programmes discussed in this chapter held on to traditional thesis types, perhaps influenced by both the pull and prestige of the PhD, a number of universities have moved beyond this. The University of British Columbia drew on other thesis types beyond the simple traditional thesis and even allowed a student to make a performance piece the focus of her EdD thesis. Western Sydney University, while having used the portfolio idea in its EdD for some time, has more recently codified what students do by drawing up a set of regulations which give more structure and guidance to students for this type of submission. And at the University of Southern California, the University of Missouri-St Louis and Vanderbilt University, EdD students work collaboratively on their final research project in ways that are not typical of many other EdDs (or PhDs).

Beyond this, however, there is a uniqueness to the EdD in terms of its goal to train researching professionals as opposed to professional researchers (Burnard et al. 2018). Also, the experiences of EdD students seem to be very different from those of PhD students. Some students have described the EdD experience as 'inspirational and life-changing' (Burnard et al. 2018: 52). Indeed, Karen Ottewell (Ottewell and Lim 2016) describes how she did a PhD and then went on to do an EdD. While her PhD made the contribution to knowledge that was expected of it, she found that the EdD provided her with a critical reflexivity through which she could research her own and her community's professional practice with a view to being better at doing her job. The structured nature of the EdD is also appealing to students (Neumann 2005) as is the cohort nature of many EdDs through its ability to provide students with a network of critical friends who can both support and, at times, challenge them in their studies (Storey 2013). The cohort nature of the EdD also contributes to a sense of belonging for students as well as to their general well-being (Savva and Nygaard 2021c). Beyond this, the EdD has an explicit focus on research training and professional outcomes that are not features of all PhD in Education programmes (O'Mullane 2005).

7

Practice-based doctorates in the visual arts

This chapter examines practice-based doctorates, specifically in the area of the visual arts. As with other chapters in the book, doctorates are examined which were awarded in the United States, the UK, Canada and Australia. We examine theses and dissertations that have been submitted in each of these areas and compare them with previous research into thesis types, such as that discussed in Chapter 4, as well as our own earlier research on this topic. We also consider the extent to which practice-based doctoral theses in the visual arts share features of new humanities theses, as discussed in Chapter 5. We draw on interview data from four former PhD students and two supervisors to illuminate our discussion of the theses.

Practice-based doctorates in the visual arts are a relatively new arrival on the doctoral scene, primarily emerging in the UK and Australia from the late 1980s onwards and showing substantial growth through the 1990s and the first two decades of this century. These new kinds of doctorates differ from the more conventional doctorate in that they are comprised of a written and a creative component. Indeed, as Vaughan (2021: 333) points out:

> the doctoral contribution as thesis can no longer be automatically assumed to be contained solely in a written text. The doctoral thesis can be appropriately articulated and submitted for examination in diverse formats, including exhibitions, recordings, artefacts and artworks, as well as written text.

A number of changes in both British and Australian higher education led to the emergence of these doctorates. The merging of art colleges with polytechnics and then polytechnics with universities in the late 1980s was one of these changes (Bao, Kehm and Ma 2018; Borg 2007). Up until then, art schools had offered the Master of Fine Arts as their terminal degree (Buckley 2009; Gopalan 2018), essentially a creative work accompanied by a short, written commentary known as the exegesis (Paltridge 2004). Once art schools were incorporated into universities, they came under pressure to produce research that could be assessed in terms that were recognizable to and valued by other parts of the university, and, in particular, a research-based doctorate or PhD-level offering. This view is epitomized in a 1997 report by the UK Council of Graduate Education which states that 'creative works, no matter how highly esteemed, cannot in themselves be regarded as outputs of research. They can only become so in association with explanatory text' (UK Council for Graduate Education 1997: 17). Writing in 2000, however, Candlin claimed that in at least one university in the UK it was possible to submit a PhD that was entirely practice based, that is, with no accompanying text. This does not seem to have been the case, however, in most countries. Our study into PhDs in the visual arts in Australia (Paltridge et al. 2012a, 2012b, 2014), for example, found no evidence of this possibility, with all visual arts doctorates requiring a written component, although we found significant differences in the amount of written text that was required. MacLeod and Holdridge (2004: 157) noted, however, that 'some artists/researchers resist the provision of a written text' as they argue that 'their language is visual, and that to make work and submit a written thesis is equivalent to a double doctorate'. We made a similar observation in our research with some visual arts doctoral students asking why they had to write when they were already-established artists in their own right (Starfield, Paltridge and Ravelli 2012). Hamilton (2014: 370) refers to the practice-based thesis as a 'particularly demanding genre of writing. Unlike the traditional thesis, it requires the practitioner researcher to adopt a dual perspective – to look both out towards an established field of research, exemplars and theories, and inwards towards the experiential processes of the creative practice'.

Buckley (2009) commented that the role of the written text in visual arts PhDs still remained unresolved, despite there being 'widespread acceptance that the thesis may be constituted by multiple forms, ranging across painting, sound, performance, installation and text' (pp. 81–2). In our research, however, we found that the inclusion of a written thesis (or exegesis) was seen as being essential to ensuring the student's admission to the academy and an acknowledgement of what is valued by universities. Bao, Kehm and Ma (2018: 532) describe the relationship between the presentation of the student's creative work and the written text thus:

> The presentation … is accompanied by a text in which the candidate explains how he or she has arrived at the result or product by applying research methods. This is regarded as generating new knowledge through practice. Successful candidates are also expected to demonstrate how their work of art is related to other works of art in the same field (theoretical, historical, critical or visual context) and to evaluate possible effects.

In our data search for this book, we found few visual arts PhD programmes in the United States where, until recently, the Master of Fine Arts (MFA) was seen as the terminal degree in art schools, although this has now started to change (Jones 2009). Elkins (2014) identifies only six PhD level programmes in the United States. Our investigation found, for example, that the PhD at Ohio University was in the areas of dance, film, music and theatre training, not specifically fine arts. The School of Art and Design at Ohio University does have a fine arts graduate programme but only to the level of Master of Fine Arts. There is a visual component in the University of California San Diego PhD in art practice and a dissertation which is a quarter shorter than the normal length required for the PhD at that university (UC San Diego 2021a). The PhD in electronic arts at Rensselaer Polytechnic involves the creation of a practice-based presentation such as a gallery show or performance and the writing of a dissertation (Rensselaer Polytechnic Institute 2021a). The longest running of these programmes, however, is the PhD in fine arts at Texas Tech University that was first offered in 1974 (Texas Tech University 2020). The only PhD dissertations we were able to locate from Texas Tech, however, did not have a creative/practice-based component. Similarly, we were not able to obtain PhDs from the University of California San Diego which had a visual arts component even though information on the programme's website states that there is one. We were, however, able to obtain practice-based PhD dissertations from Rensselaer Polytechnic that included a creative component and which are discussed in this chapter.

Universities in Canada which currently have visual arts PhD programmes include York University, L'Université du Québec à Montréal, the University of Western Ontario and Ryerson University (Elkins 2014). A greater number of Universities in the UK, however, offer a PhD in the visual arts such as the University of Reading, the University of the Arts London (a consortium of art schools), the Glasgow School of Art, Oxford University's Ruskin School of Art and the Slade School of Fine Art which is part of University College London. In Australia, twenty-seven universities offer a visual arts doctorate, the first being offered at the Tasmanian School of Art and the University of Wollongong in the 1980s, in the latter case a Doctor of Creative Arts (Paltridge et al. 2011).

Data collected

A set of forty PhDs in fine/visual arts were collected for this chapter. The fine/visual arts PhD dissertations were from Rensselaer Polytechnic Institute in the United States, the Slade School of Fine Art in the UK, York University in Canada and the University of Sydney in Australia. The US and Canadian theses were obtained through the ProQuest database and the UK theses through the British Library EThOS database. The Australian theses were obtained through a search of the University of Sydney's online thesis repository. We were able to interview former PhD students from the Slade School of Fine Art, from the University of York and from the University of Sydney about their theses and explore reasons for the choices they made. We also interviewed a PhD supervisor from the University of Sydney and one from the Slade.

Findings

The United States

As mentioned above, the Master of Fine Arts (MFA) is still the most commonly offered graduate-level qualification in the United States and is the highest degree which most visual arts academics hold in US universities (Elkins 2014; Gopalan 2018). Rensselaer Polytechnic Institute, however, does have a visual arts PhD in Electronic Arts which was established in 2007. A set of ten Rensselaer Polytechnic dissertations were examined for this chapter. The PhDs we examined were in the areas of art, sonic image, video, wearable technology, film, performance and music. The Rensselaer PhD is described as a degree which is

> conferred for independent investigation representing an original contribution to knowledge, where knowledge is understood to incorporate an integrated combination of creative practice in the arts with theoretical and historical research.
>
> (Rensselaer Polytechnic Institute 2021b)

The core focus of the Rensselaer programme is the student's creative practice. This practice is informed by coursework taken both in the Arts Department and in other Rensselaer departments, in areas such as research methods, video, computer music, science and technology studies, architecture, animation, cultural studies, internet interventions, bio-technology, information technologies, genomic studies, musicology, cognitive science, mechanical engineering, acoustics, computer science, performance and communication studies. The dissertation phase of the PhD involves a public presentation of the student's artwork and a dissertation text.

All the Rensselaer dissertations we collected were topic-based dissertations with an Introduction, followed by topic-based chapters and a Conclusion. In some cases, the creative work was described within the body of the dissertation, and in others, it was listed in an Appendix. Not all the dissertations referred to any particular research methodology but if they did it was included in the Introduction and was not a stand-alone chapter. In every case it was clear what the creative work was and that the dissertation was a theoretical and reflective account of this work.

Figure 7.1 shows the Table of Contents of one of the Rensselaer dissertations. It is a practice-based dissertation titled 'Disruption, dis/orientation, and intra-action: Recipes for creating a queer utopia in audiovisual space' (Pirler 2019)

Disruption, Dis/orientation and Intra-action: Recipes for Creating a Queer Utopia in Audiovisual Space

1 INTRODUCTION
1.1 Statement of Purpose
1.2 Problem Statement
1.3 Overview of Methodology and Research Questions
1.4 Organisation of the Dissertation
1.5 Role of the Artist/Researcher
1.6 Artist/Researcher Assumptions
1.7 Disruption and dis/orientation in Avant Garde

2 LITERATURE REVIEW
2.1 The Lived Body: Space and Body
2.2 Towards a Multicultural Feminist Queer Utopia
2.3 Sensuous Space: Blending the Boundaries
2.4 Gender and Sexuality as Experimental Audiovisual Performance Literature

3 RELATED WORKS

4 PORTFOLIO
4.1 *Moved in Noir* (2016): Gender Performativity and Film-Noir
4.2 *Moved in Light* (2017): Queer Objects and Queer Utopia
4.3 *Surface Connections* (2018 – ongoing): Diffractive Improvisation

5 ADVICE FOR PRACTICE: RECIPES FOR QUEERING THE MULTISENSORY PERFORMATIVE SPACE
5.1 Disruption
5.2 Dis-orientation

6 Conclusions
6.1 What's next?
6.2 Conclusions

REFERENCES

APPENDICES
Full Credits of the Artistic Projects, Biographies of the Main Collaborators, and Supplemental Files
Appendix A: Full Credits of the Artistic Projects
Appendix B: Biographies of the Main Collaborators
Appendix C: Supplemental Files

Figure 7.1 Table of Contents of a Rensselaer PhD dissertation (Pirler 2019).

and is in the area of audiovisual performance. Pirler's written component is multimodal in that it contains forty-five figures, most of which are stills from the productions of her creative work and are located in the Portfolio chapter. The dissertation is unusual in that it contains a chapter titled Literature Review, the only dissertation in the data set to do this. The literature review, however, is a presentation of relevant work by some of the theorists influential in the new humanities and feminist thinking such as Ahmed, Barad, Butler, Foucault and others (see Chapter 5), rather than a review of previous research in relation to the topics of the student's creative projects. Chapter 3, Related Works, examines artistic works that embody the concepts presented in the literature review. The creative works which are presented in Chapter 4, Portfolio, are an audiovisual/movement performance project titled *Moved in Noir*, a performance/installation project, *Moved in Light* and a video project, *Surface Connection*. Supplemental files on the *Proquest* database provide access to these works.

In her dissertation, Pirler (2019) discusses how she developed her projects as well as positions her work in relation to the theories and concepts she presented in her literature review. Parts of her written text are reminiscent of other characteristics of new humanities theses, for example, in a section in her Introduction titled Role of the Artist/Researcher she makes a reflexive statement about where she is coming from as both an artist and a researcher:

> As a queer, feminist, and migrant sound artist who is deeply invested in audiovisual practice, I create performative spaces that hold complex intra-actions between disciplines, bodies, objects, and sensuous experiences. The constant tension of being "in-between" spaces – between being disoriented and oriented – has been a question for me. I am drawn to explore strategies to *re*-produce this conflict, opening bodies to be affected, and in turn, facilitating "a new way of thinking about the spatiality of sexuality, gender, and race." … As a product of the identities I hold, my practice highlights women's gaze on women as a function of queer desire and is intended as a critique of contemporary art sites that are male-dominated. This research and my artistic practice mainly feature women (or people who identify as women in a way that is significant to them) and/or queer artists who are informed by feminist and intersectional thoughts.
>
> (p. 10)

This section sets the tone for the rest of the dissertation in which she uses the first person 'I' to present her authorial self to the reader and to reflect on her research in a highly personal manner. Her text also functions as a paratext (Genette 1987; Pérez-Llantada 2021, see also Chapter 5) in that it sets up writer-reader relations for the rest of her dissertation. Pirler's topic-based chapter titles, however, are literal rather than metaphorical and there is no use of word play or playfulness in her thesis or chapter titles; they are all essentially descriptive.

The UK

The UK visual arts PhD theses were from the Slade School of Fine Art, which is part of University College London (UCL). Susan Collins, who had been director of the School from 2010 to 2018, told us that the doctoral programme at the Slade had begun in the 1990s. Initially there had been two routes, a practice-related one and a thesis-only one. The thesis-only route, like many other doctorates, required a text of between 80 and 100,000 words. The practice-related route did however have a practical component but the original contribution lay across both the practice and the theory, and it had a very substantial 60,000–80,000-word written component and was 'very theoretically driven'. Under Susan Collin's leadership and in conjunction with Professor Sharon Morris, then Head of the PhD programme, a practice-led PhD option was introduced which drew on the Slade's reputation for practice and would be equivalent to the other two options on offer. Susan Collins also drew our attention to what she felt to be a distinctive feature of the fine art PhD at the Slade: the availability of cross-disciplinary, secondary supervision from across UCL.

Students doing a PhD at the Slade now have these three options for their PhD. It can be practice-led or practice-related or they can submit just a written thesis. According to Susan Collins, the majority of the PhD students at the Slade are now enrolled in the practice-led stream which requires students to undertake studio practice that makes an original contribution to knowledge. Practice-led students are entitled to a studio space. In addition to the creative work, they also need to submit a written report of between 15,000–30,000 but no more than 40,000 words. Susan emphasized that

> the original contribution lies in the studio practice and there is a report that's pretty elastic, anything from 15 to 40,000 words as appropriate that is there to really explicate the practice. If people want to be hardcore theoretical in it, no one's stopping them but it's very clear that that route is for those [whose] original contribution lies in the practice itself.
>
> (Susan Collins, interview, 2022)

The practice-related option still requires a longer written component of 60,000–80,000 words which, together with the studio practice, makes an original contribution to knowledge and the thesis-only option requires a written submission of 80,000–100,000 words. The two practice-led theses discussed in some detail below offer a sense of the 'elasticity' Collins evokes.

Sarah Fortais, who graduated in 2018 from the Slade School with a practice-led PhD, confirmed that several years before she began her studies, the Slade divided the PhD into the three different streams: 'one was research led, one was practice led and one was practice related'. She explained that for practice-led research, 'they argued that the artwork is the thesis and that your writing component is really a report'. As Sarah noted in her report, her research involves 'building artworks to answer research questions' (p. 39). Another interviewee, Dawn Gaietto (also from the Slade), explained the distinction between practice led and practice related as follows:

> In practice led, the thesis is considered the visual work or the artistic work and then the written portion is referred to as a report so you're reporting on what you've done visually or through practice versus in the practice related, your text and your practical work are considered the thesis, so they are of equal import.
> (Dawn Gaietto, interview, 2022)

Sarah's account of how she decided on the practice-led route highlights a degree of contingency that shaped her choice of the practice-led PhD in that the provision of studio space throughout her project that was large enough to exhibit Russell, the giraffe in a spacesuit she was building, was important: 'There's only one space in the whole school [with] the ceiling high enough. I don't think I could have argued to have shown in that space if I wasn't there all the time.'

Her doctoral submission, 'Defining cool through a Bricoleur's studio practice' (Fortais 2018), aimed to define what it means to call a person or thing 'cool'; she adopted 'bricolage' as her methodology and identified fourteen 'sensibilities of cool' through her project inspired by moon landings and voyages in space. Her submission contained a written component titled 'Report' and a digital component on a USB stick where the artwork could be viewed. Her report was traditional complex in organization. It contained an Introduction, followed by a chapter which reviewed literature relevant to her methodology and conceptual framing of her study and another chapter which discussed the NASA Apollo missions and their significance for her creative project. Three chapters then present her artworks which were separate but linked studies and they are followed by a Conclusion chapter. The sections of her Table of Contents are shown in Figure 7.2. The acknowledgements section for her thesis (see Figure 7.3) was presented in graphic form as a human space suit rather than

Defining Cool through a Bricoleur's Studio Practice

i DIGITAL (USB) SUBMISSION ……………………………………………
   (front pocket of Report)
   i.   Report
   ii. Appendix
   iii. *1 2 3 (Unfinished)* – Part 4 Video
   iv. Scan of the Cool Mind Map
   v.   Animals in Space Graph ………. (hard copy also located in the back pocket of the Appendix)

ii LIST OF FIGURES

1	**INTRODUCTION**	4.3	Chronological Description
1.1	Research Context	4.4	Analysis
1.2	Key Terms		
1.3	Preliminary Hypothesis and Research Questions	**5**	**ARTWORK #2: *Lunar Salon***
		5.1	Introduction
1.4	Literature Review	5.2	Methodology: Marcus Coates' Functional, Non-Rational Processes
1.5	Methodology and Emergent Hypotheses/Research Questions		
		5.3	Design of Space and Object Inventory
1.6	Original Contributions to Knowledge		
		5.4	Analysis
1.7	Structure of Report		
		6	**ARTWORK #3: *Spacesuits for animals***
2	**APPROACHING COOL THROUGH BRICOLAGE AND PRACTICE**		
		6.1	Introduction
		6.2	R.U.S.S.E.L.L. Exhibition Report
2.1	Introduction	6.3	Browsing
2.2	Bricolage	6.4	Armatures
2.3	Cool	6.5	Tape
2.4	Approaching Cool Through Bricolage: Mapping and Preliminary Analysis	6.6	Joints
		6.7	Excess
		6.8	Mouse Units
		6.9	Deadlines/The Bodge
3	**NASA**	**7**	**CONCLUSION**
3.1	Introduction	7.1	Initial Findings
3.2	Project Apollo	7.2	Defining Cool Through My Bricolage Studio Practice
3.3	Spacesuits		
3.4	Astronauts	7.3	Future Discussion
3.5	Bricolage in NASA	7.4	Reflections on Practice-Led Research
4	**ARTWORK #1: *1 2 3 (Unfinished)***		
4.1	Introduction	**BIBLIOGRAPHY**	
4.2	Creation of a Differential-Like Methodology	8.1 Works Consulted	

Figure 7.2 Table of Contents of Fortais' (2018) Slade School practice-led doctoral report.

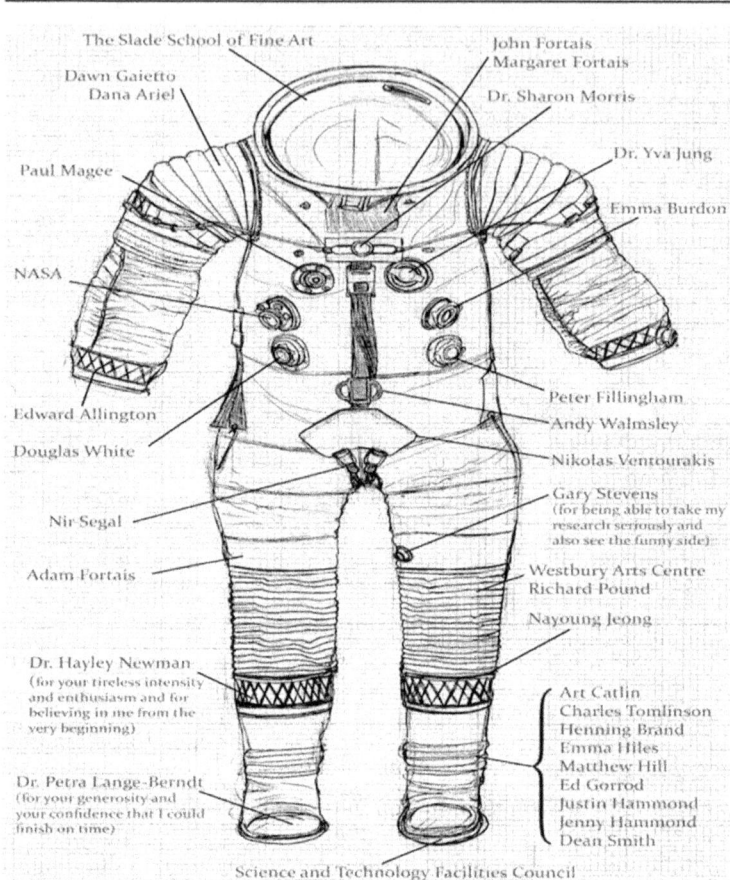

Figure 7.3 The acknowledgements page in Fortais' (2018: 5) doctoral report. Image courtesy of Sarah Fortais.

as conventional written text, echoing the theme of spacesuits for animals that was a significant component of her creative practice.

Chapter 1 of Fortais' report, the Introduction, is comprised of seven subsections all of which are the familiar components of a conventional PhD thesis (see Figure 7.2) such as hypothesis and research questions, literature review and methodology. Sarah stressed that her supervisors had focused on the 'set-up' or introduction to the report and impressed upon her that indicating the PhD's original contribution to knowledge had to be clear from the outset and that she needed specific research questions.

The word REPORT in large bold capitals appears centred in the middle of her title page, directly under the title of her study. However, despite the formal

40,000-word limit for a practice-based PhD, she estimated that her report was between 60,000 and 80,000 words in length, and probably longer than most of the practice-related theses; her literature review alone would have been more than the 15,000-word minimum. The report contains 336 figures many of which document her process of making the artworks while others reference work that has influenced her practice.

In her Table of Contents (Figure 7.2), she lists five items as being on a USB stick located in the front pocket of her report; while a PDF copy of the report is available on the UCL institutional repository (https://discovery.ucl.ac.uk/id/eprint/10052124/), not all the contents of the USB have been uploaded. A separate 161-page PDF document titled *APPENDIX* can be found in the repository as well as the *Animals in Space Graph* (a spreadsheet listing all the animals that have been sent into space). The Appendix contains eight separate appendices (A-H) and 233 figures. The report's word limit was the main reason for the size of the Appendix as Sarah explained that she had 'leaned out' chapters of the report, deciding to include the excised parts in the Appendix. She also explained that the large number of figures was due to a decision made with her supervisor that 'as many pictures as possible needed to be in the report, because that was, in itself, official argumentation for the methodology'. The images can thus be seen as evidence for claims and not simply as illustrations. As she writes in her report, her artwork, '*space suits for animals*, is concrete evidence demonstrating the potential for all 14 sensibilities of cool to form a network leading to a creative and coherent output' (p. 262).

Notably, the *Cool Mind Map* which forms a central part of Sarah Fortais' methodology is missing from the online repository and only available in the archived hard copy which we were, of course, unable to view. While there are several maps in the report itself, we discovered in the course of our interview that the *Cool Mind Map* listed as being on the USB stick was more elaborated and complex than these and considered by Sarah to be a studio output (see e.g. p. 29 of her report). She explained: 'Mapping by hand is a physical practice, drawing, and methodology to develop research' (Report, p. 91).

Sarah was later able to share the mind map with us via a google doc of three PDFs as the map is too large to be scanned as a single document. The hand-drawn map is at the core of her research process as she attempts to define the sensibilities of cool through her studio practice. Without talking to her, we would not have grasped what the *Cool Mind Map* was and the part it played in her creative output: 'Key to this refinement process was bringing my research into the studio and producing a mind map of cool, which allowed me to visualise and experiment with different connections between concepts' (Fortais 2018,

Report, p. 261). Another aspect of the presentation of the Report that the digital version failed to capture was the care Sarah had taken with the visual aspect, hand binding it and embossing letters on the cover.

Our interview enabled us to look beyond the written Report, to better understand the role of the creative components and also capture the enactment of the PhD genre through Fortais' exhibition of her work for the viva (oral examination) and its reception by the examiners within the studio space. She described her (successful) viva to us as 'very memorable' as somewhat unusually; it lasted for seven and a half hours and involved a performance/re-enactment of her Lunar Salon, two separate exhibition sites at different ends of the campus which the two examiners had to visit and then a lengthy 'forensic' discussion of the Report which they had received prior to the exhibition.

She also commented, as we noted earlier in this chapter, that for some of the students, writing was experienced as arduous and that this might have been a factor in the introduction of a written report which could be seen as more like an exegesis than a thesis. That writing was a concern at the Slade is suggested by the introduction of compulsory creative writing classes 'for first-year PhD students, every second Wednesday' (Sarah Fortais, interview, 2022). Sarah's Appendix H contains a twenty-five-page compilation of her creative writing in which she considers her relationship to the Stanley Kubrick film, *2001: A Space Odyssey*, which she had been very keen to include in her written component. Susan Collins explained that the writing course was called 'creative thesis' and aimed to enable students to be 'quite creative on the page; not feel like you have to follow a very strict academic route'.

In the conclusion to her report, in a subsection titled, *Ten Reflections on Practice-Led Research*, Sarah weighs up the complex interdependence of the relations between the written text and the creative work: 'I see my artworks and report functioning both independently and together. The report exists because of the artworks, but the artworks were also informed by my writing of the report' (p. 278). She writes: 'I found it helpful to think of myself as an artist first and a researcher second, … however, the reality is that these categories are bound together' (p. 279). At the same time, a caveat suggests that she remains somewhat unconvinced: 'The true conception of both the whole and its comprising parts is still best experienced through my artworks' (Fortais 2018: 37). When considering the practice-led PhD in the visual arts, it is clearly vital for writing researchers not to neglect the creative component and its intricate connection to the written text.

Dawn Gaietto's (2019) PhD from the Slade, 'What is happening here? [exploits of the nonhuman]', was also practice led; the Table of Contents (see Figure 7.4) of her Report was however quite different to Sarah Fortais' in that

What is happening here? [exploits of the nonhuman]

List of figures
The Situation
    A State of Mind
    Research Questions
    A Process
    Thinking Naturata
    Preparing a Space
    Art Histories and Presences
    Practical Presences
    Moving Forward
    Application
The Look
    Movement
    Reciprocity
    Slippage
    Modes of Non-Cartesian Representation – Critical
    Application
    Emerging
The State(s)
    Engaging with the Unfixed Perspective
    Un-defining the Un-fixed
    The Magik of Rats Run Amok
    An Airborne Assault
    Lucid Re-presentation
    The Function of Non-Cartesian Representation
    The Function of Non-Cartesian Representation – Critical Application (Take One)
    Translating On
The Frame
    Concentric Circles
    A Tale to Begin
    Defining Human
    Refining -or- Expanding
    A Brain + A Brain Intervened
    The Function of Non-Cartesian Representation – Critical Application (Take Two)
    Recovering Enchantment
The Furred
    Who Looks Back?
    Modes of Non-Cartesian Representation
    Potential States of Re-enchantment
    A|The
    Encounters with Her Presence
    Modes of Non-Cartesian Representation
    Potential States of Re-Enchantment
    Miss Maddie Dog performs *Being a Dog*
    Modes of Non-Cartesian Representation
    Potential States of Re-Enchantment
The Feathered
    The Loft
    Why the Pigeon?
    Expanding into Diagrammatic Relations
    Distributing through Constellations
    Modes of Non-Cartesian Representation
    Potential States of Re-Enchantment
    Concentric Agencies
The Consequence
    What types of representation are most revealing
    How can the practice of art-work Re-presentation
    Embarking
    Submerging
Bibliography
Appendices
    A.1 Expanded Case Studies
    A. 2 Critical Applications
        A.2.1 Cultural Narcissism in Two Acts of Artistic Practice
        A.2.2 Expanded Analysis: *The Feathered: an exploration of non-human labour*
    A.3. Institutional Relations
        A.3.1 Miss Maddie Dog
        A.3.2 The Pigeon

Figure 7.4 Table of Contents Gaietto's (2018) Slade School doctoral report.

it had no conventionally identifiable chapter numbering or generic section headings that referred to conventional components of a research thesis such as literature review, methodology or contribution to knowledge. She attributed her organizational and formatting choices to the written component's being:

> a report and not a thesis. I was able to make a lot of different decisions ... than a traditional thesis can make so I had a lot of freedom, so I really just was trying to use each element ... in a way that supported the project overall instead of it having to fit into a more traditional framework of a thesis. I had that freedom. ... My impulse was to take advantage of each of these decisions that I could make so it would be more in support of the content I was putting forward instead of it having to fit into that traditional framework.
>
> (Dawn Gaietto, interview, 2022)

Dawn also chose to lay her report out in a landscape format with the page divided into two columns with the written text of the Report on the left of the page on even-numbered pages and the right-hand side on odd-numbered pages. The columns are separated by a double rule and the column that does not contain the main text of the Report is used for references, for notes that would, more typically, be located as footnotes and, occasionally, images. She explained: 'I thought the layout was better for images to be laid out as such and, quite frankly, I just was more attracted to it as reading more like a storybook then a thesis.' She elaborated further on her choice, explaining how she had convinced her supervisors to accept it, 'because I like the kind of relationship to a textbook or unfolding a bit more like a story, like those ... physical associations that one would have to the layout versus the traditional, you know, portrait layout and ... so they were quite supportive after I was able to articulate why' (see Figure 7.5 for an example of her layout choice).

At the same time, Dawn was not able to argue against the 40,000-word limit on the length of the Report or convert her project to the practice-related stream which she had tried to do given the project's very theoretical focus. She was however able to add sixty-four pages of appendices which allowed her to include materials she would otherwise have had to exclude. Dawn said, 'I don't identify like as an artist. I identify more as the thinker-writer kind of position; I lean more heavily on the theory and the writing is just more how I think.' Her supervisors, however, 'had a continuous push for me to be more practical or to create more work'.

In a number of respects, Dawn's Report and the thesis (her creative project) are reminiscent of the new humanities theses discussed in Chapter 5. Her

Figure 7.5 Page 26 of Gaietto's (2018) PhD report showing landscape formatting. Image courtesy of Dawn Gaietto.

challenging of conventional layouts and formats, her choice of fairly opaque chapter titles, what she called her 'more gelatinous' framework, her use of theorists such as Deleuze and Guattari, Derrida, Bruno Latour and Jane Bennett, together with her interest in post-humanism and non-human agency, help to locate her work within this emerging paradigm.

The early chapters of Dawn's Report are titled 'The Situation', 'The Look', 'The States' and 'The Frame'; apart from a subheading "Research Questions" in the first chapter there are no further conventional headings; all these chapters help build her theoretical framework around non-Cartesian representation and as such contain elements of epistemology and literature review which a detailed reading reveals. In the two following chapters, 'The Furred' and 'The Feathered', she presents her artistic practice, a series of exhibition performances or experiments, inserting images from these into the chapters. The report's macrostructure is clearly topic-based; yet 'The Furred' and 'The Feathered' can be seen to function as two case studies in which she explores theories of what she names anthrodecentric art, that is, art that is not centred on the human and reveals non-human agency. In her concluding chapter, "The Consequences", she tells us that she "understands the works presented within this research to demonstrate the feasibility of anthrodecentric art as a practical methodology" (Gaietto 2019: 179) setting up a connection between the creative and written components similar to that of Fortais'.

Explaining the emergence of her report's structure, Dawn stressed how her 'supervisor was always most concerned with the last few chapters, 'The Furred' and 'The Feathered' which are the practice' but then added 'as I fleshed out how I was writing about the practice it actually became my argument for her [the supervisor] as to why I needed the additional theory to support those chapters'. 'The States' was thus 'a late emerging chapter' in which Dawn developed her argument for her supervisor as to why she needed additional theory to support her two practice chapters, 'so at the beginning I definitely had to push a lot to be able to write as much as I did on the theory'. She concluded her explanation saying, 'The Look', 'The State' and 'The Frame' all became chapters as they are, as they were necessary to support the discussion of the practice.'

It was, however, not possible to view a record of the performances which were listed on page 13 as being on the Portfolio Works on Drive as follows and which indicate a substantial body of creative work:

1. The Academy ~ Part One, compilation video, 6'46", 2015
2. Encounters with Her Presence, 26'21", 2016
3. Encounters with Her Presence, performance documentation, 4'23", 2017
4. Miss Maddie Dog performs Being a Dog, documentation of performance, 16'26", 2017
5. The Building of Homes, film, 16'28", 2016
6. The Rounds, sound compilation, 9'26", 2016
7. Speaking with …, sound compilation, 2'23", 2016
8. A Building of Homes, documentation of the spheres of function, 21'02", 2018

Dawn was surprised to find that the portfolio was not available in the UCL online repository where the PDF of the Report can be found as there had been quite an emphasis put on her producing it. This further underlines the challenges researchers in the visual and performing arts encounter as they attempt to demonstrate the integrity of their work and the often profound interconnections of the creative and written components which the transition to electronic and digital theses platforms does not appear to have satisfactorily resolved. In Vaughan's (2021: 334) terms this could be seen as an instance of the 'infrastructure default[ing] to, and to an extent privilege[ing], a traditional text-based model'.

The genre of the PhD in the visual and performing arts comprises what might be considered several part genres, with the written Report being one. Dawn's account of the viva or oral examination allows us to better understand the structure of the practice-led PhD at the Slade. She began by installing her three works in the spaces allocated to her: 'I installed the pigeon loft into an observatory; then I had the video work with the fox and the dog installed in a different location and then I had, outside of my examination room, Algernon, the mouse.' In addition, prior to the onsite meeting of Dawn, her supervisors and the examiners on the day of the viva, the examiners would have received a copy of the Report, the linked portfolio (see above) and the time-based work on a USB stick. In Dawn's words, there were 'a lot of moving parts … there are more parts that they have to take into consideration that just the report'. Without our interview with Dawn, we would not have fully grasped the complexity that students need to orchestrate to accomplish the practice-led PhD nor what is expected of examiners.

A further addition to the genre was the inclusion of an *Impact Statement* on pages 6–7 of her report, that her cohort was the first to be required to produce. Dawn explained that she had found drafting this short text the most challenging aspect of her writing as the expectation that a PhD student's work might have a significant impact was surprising to her and she had no idea of what form it should take.

Of the five 2019–20 theses in our Slade corpus, all but one contained an 'Impact Statement', similar to the UCL EdD theses discussed in Chapter 6. Susan Collins clarified that the inclusion of the impact statement was a UCL requirement that arose from one of the university's 2019 Research Strategy's key aims – 'to deliver impact for public benefit' (https://www.ucl.ac.uk/research/strategy-and-policy). Despite some ambivalence about such requirements, particularly for students, she acknowledged that they would need to know how to construct these statements: 'If they apply for any kind of research funding, they will have to write their pathway to impact.' Impact statement guidance notes for UCL research students and supervisors on the university's Doctoral School website (https://www.grad.ucl.ac.uk/essinfo/docs/Impact-Statement-Guidance-Notes-for-Research-Students-and-Supervisors.pdf) provide advice on how impact may be conceptualized and articulated. The impact statement should be no longer than 500 words and placed between the abstract page and the table of contents.

In her PhD 'On tangibility, contemporary reliefs, and continuous dimensions', Ausländer (2019), a slightly older student, discusses her work in terms of its impact on public art policies and the response it had received at workshops, roundtables, fairs, exhibitions and collections where she had discussed and shown her work. Her impact statement opens thus:

> My work has helped to shape recent public art policies in Canon de Vaud, Switzerland. It has facilitated an understanding of how public art can be simultaneously functional, permanent, innovative, and inspirational.
>
> My practical research has received a good response amongst my peers in terms of methodology. Practice-led PhD research in art still does not exist in Switzerland. My years of commuting, combining theoretical and practical research, collaborations, residencies, and commercial-based works have demonstrated the value of PhD research in art and its positive outcomes.
>
> (p. 5)

Interestingly, some of the PhD theses from the University of British Columbia's *Public Scholar's Initiative (PSI)* (which we discuss in more detail in Chapter 10) include a short text titled *Lay Summary* directly after the abstract which seems aimed at a broader readership than the traditional academic one and also arises from a concern with the wider societal impact of the PhD. Both innovations suggest how macro-level concerns, be they about funding or wider social impact, can influence the genre of the PhD thesis.

Another part genre that comprises the PhD at the Slade that we learnt about through the interviews is known as the upgrade exam which Sarah Fortais, Dawn Gaietto and Nir Segal (see below) all took part in. Susan Collins explained that this was the first major opportunity for students to gain detailed feedback from a panel on their progress. The upgrade takes place between nine and eighteen months from the beginning of the PhD and involves the submission of a portfolio of creative work, a public, timed presentation or viva on the student's work to date, followed by questions, as well as a 15,000-word upgrade report that contains components such as the introduction, a review of literature and art, a methodology section and a bibliography put together as the student chooses.

Lovett's (2019) submission 'Making a scene in London and Rio de Janeiro: Invisible theatre and urban performance after Augusto Boal (1931–2009)' is an example of a practice-related PhD from the Slade. Lovett's submission was in two parts. Part I was the written thesis and Part II contained a list of her creative work and extracts from the work on a USB. Thom's (2013) PhD, 'Embodied encounters: A performative, material reading of selected contemporary artworks by Santu Mofokeng, El Anatsui, Willem Boshoff and Johan Thom' followed the same format. In each of these cases, the written component had more prominence than in the practice-led PhDs we collected.

As mentioned earlier, the use of visuals to illustrate points being made in the report was a common feature of the Slade School PhDs. An example of this is shown in Figure 7.6 from Segal's (2020) 'The flat diamond: The role of intimacy in a collaborative practice'. This image is from a presentation titled 'The Whisper' in which the student went around the room and whispered in each person's ear 'I think you and I can make something great together'. He did this as a way of reflecting on his feelings about sharing his work with the PhD group at the Slade. He then looked each person in the eye for their response, hoping for their approval. The image in Figure 7.7 is of a performance piece titled 'The fabric of memory' in which Segal aimed to combine the daily ritual of ironing with people talking about memories of a piece of fabric related to a person or event in their life.

Figure 7.6 An image from 'The Whisper' in Segal's Slade School PhD (2020: 112). Image courtesy of Ellie Doney.

Figure 7.7 An image from 'The Fabric of Memory' in Segal's PhD (2020: 116). Image courtesy of Ioana Marinescu.

Canada

The ten Canadian visual arts PhD dissertations were from York University in Toronto. The PhD in Visual Art was inaugurated at York in 2008 and was the first of its kind in Canada. It is aimed at preparing artist-researchers to teach studio and theory courses and to supervise graduate students as well as to continue their careers as practising artists. Students undertaking the York PhD can work in areas such as video, performance, painting, drawing, printmaking, sculpture and digital media on their own or in combination. Elle Flanders' dissertation, which we discuss in more detail below, was amongst the first to be submitted as she joined the programme in its second year. As she told us, amongst her motivations for enrolling in the new degree was a sense that she 'would probably end up teaching …. And almost nobody had a PhD in visual art at that time'.

The York students undertake coursework in their first two years which has a focus on practice-based research. After this, they curate an exhibition which is a survey of their artwork plus write a twenty- to thirty-page paper which positions their work in relation to contemporary art theory and practice. This exhibition and the related writing serve as a comprehensive exam for the students. For Elle, the comprehensives were 'where all of the didactic needed to be … all the literature review', and this meant that 'afterwards the creation piece sort of kicks in. I felt the actual written piece needed to be as creative as the actual work itself'. The final phase of the degree comprises an exhibition plus a written dissertation which both amplifies and contextualizes the theme taken up in the student's studio work. The students' dissertation committee includes academic faculty plus a member of the art world community, such as an artist, curator or critic (York University Graduate Admissions nd; York University Faculty of Graduate Studies 2020).

All the York University visual arts dissertations in our corpus were topic-based. The dissertation by Elle Flanders (2014) titled 'What isn't there: Imaging Palestine' combined photography, film, sound and installation to examine the role images play in the making and unmaking of Palestine. The Table of Contents of her 136-page written component is shown in Figure 7.8. The inclusion of the map of 418 Palestinian villages which no longer exist is central to her dissertation which is a quest by Elle to locate the traces of these villages whose inhabitants were driven out during the establishment of the state of Israel.

What isn't there: Imaging Palestine

Map of Destroyed Palestinian Villages, 1948

Introduction

Chapter 1 (A personal history of Zionism)
    Tiyul
    The Arab (not) in the Landscape
    Lubye: Forest for the Trees

Chapter 2 (Photography and Aura)
    Vanishing Images and the Auratic Presence
    A Little History of Photography
    Conceptual Photography
    Isdud

Chapter 3 (Landscape)
    Space, Place and Landscape
    The New Topographics
    Dayr Al Hawa: Hunting the Mesopotamian Deer
    Sublime Landscapes

Chapter 4 (Archive)
    Reconstituting the Atlas: Redrawing the Archive
    The Quincunx
    Latrun: Shushan Purim
    Khirbet al Zahabida: Blinding Light, Looking at Looking

Chapter 5 (Index)
    Pointing East: The Indexicality of Palestine
    Al Shajara: Of Surrogates and Bitter Oranges
    Affect
    Al Majdal: Mary Magdalene's Hometown

Chapter 6 (Politics)
    Finding the Political
    Jammasin al-Gharbi: Hamakom Between Stillness and Movement

Conclusion
    Ramla
    Engaging Images

Figure 7.8 Table of Contents from Flanders' (2014) dissertation.

In the introduction to her written text, Elle describes her creative work, identifying the main themes of her dissertation:

> The film installation accompanying this dissertation is a four-screen film projection situated in an outdoor urban garden. The installation immerses the viewer in fifteen distinct landscapes that were once the locations of Palestinian villages. While these sites often contain little that reveal their origins, the placement of the installation, the repetition and juxtaposition of images all point to the imaging of Palestine.
>
> (p. ii)

She opens her written component with a photo of her mother and her aunt building her grandparents' home in Jerusalem in 1974, placing her own story at the centre of the text to follow in which personal narrative and poststructuralist theory intermingle as she lays out her project as inextricably bound to the histories of Israel and Palestine. She draws on the work of Judith Butler and, not surprisingly, on Butler's (2009) *Frames of War: When Is Life Grievable?* as well as that of photo theorist Ariella Azoulay, in particular on her work, *The Civil Contract of Photography*. The dissertation Introduction sits outside of the chapter numbering and displays many of the paratextual features identified in the new humanities theses (see Chapter 5), allowing Elle to introduce her complex researcher identity to the reader. As the Table of Contents (Figure 7.9) shows, Chapter 1 is titled (A personal history of Zionism) and further develops these themes.

As with the other visual arts theses discussed in this chapter, it is vital that we understand the thesis in its totality of written and creative components if we are to grasp the extent to which the practice-based or practice-led thesis signals the emergence of a new variant of the doctoral thesis. As researchers of doctoral writing, we do not yet fully have a means of understanding the challenges the student writer/researcher articulates as they explore their research questions in both creative and written modes.

In our interview with her, Elle captures her experience as a member of one of the earliest cohorts to enrol in the PhD in the visual arts in Canada of having to 'invent' the relationship between her creative and written components:

> I really decided to put my heart into it to create an installation and then write the dissertation. The dissertation was a struggle, not because I didn't like writing, I did. I think it was a struggle to try and find the right form and try and find the balance between the form of the dissertation and the form of the work. To understand what each one's function is and how they relate to one another.

---Isdud---

Illus.24

Mourning Dove (*Zenaida macroura*)

The flesh of these birds is remarkably fine, when they are obtained young and in the proper season. Such birds become extremely fat, are tender and juicy…These birds require good shooting to bring them down, when on wing, for they will fly with great swiftness, and not always in a direct manner. It is seldom that more than one can be killed at a shot when they are flying, and rarely more than two or three when on the ground.[74]

```
The daisy flock in the photo reminds me of a line from Palestinian poet-
laureate Mahmoud Darwish that he wrote for his father. As for my words
elle, I don't know what to say: That Israeli Poet Yehuda Amichai fought
there while my father at fourteen walked back alone in the night to
collect his school papers because his illiterate mother was not sure that
the new schools for refugees would recognize his schooling; while Amichai
rested, and fatigue rested in his memory for years in order to come alive
again in a poem about the three most exhausting times of his life. It
puts poetry to shame. He probably, or at least one would hope, would be
ashamed of himself and his poems had he known or even thought of the
child my father was that night.75
```

At the side of the highway, up on a hill, sits one single building—the boys' school of the Palestinian village, Isdud (PGR 118129). A few date palms were scattered around the site, while in front of us was a grassy hill laden with the yellow blooms of Bastard Cabbage. A black cat leapt from within the flowers and grabbed a Mourning Dove in mid-air.

---

74 John James Audubon. *Birds of America*. Online Version. http://web4.audubon.org/bird/BOA/F29_G3b.html
75 Excerpt from an email by Fady Joudah to me, May 9, 2011.

50

Figure 7.9 Page 50 from Flanders' (2014) dissertation showing Illustration 24 of Mourning Dove.
Image courtesy of Elle Flanders.

> I think what ends up happening is, because the university feels that they must have certain standards, they standardize aspects of the dissertation, forcing it into a traditional mode and/or a descriptive dissertation that simply describes the creative portion. Neither of those felt for me that they did justice to the actual PhD itself, to the creative work, and to what we were philosophically trying to understand: what is a PhD in visual art?

Without much to go on and without many examples, I found I was really just trying to invent it. I felt that the written portion needed to be creative in its writing and thinking; following the creativity of the form of the work itself rather than being descriptive of the work itself. I think that it felt to me that if I were descriptive of the work itself, it would kill the work.

And so that's sort of the balance, I tried to find with the dissertation. I felt it needed to be different from the actual creative work itself; they needed to march in step in terms of the creative aspect. I took the same relationship I had to the artwork to the dissertation. I think my supervisor was uncomfortable with the form for a long time. But I think the personal anecdotes and the choice of the form, was about creating a bestiary.

(Elle Flanders, interview, 2021)

Elle's written component contains fifty images which include photographs taken in Israel and Palestine, family photographs, stills from the installation, drawings of animals and reproductions of maps. The balance she sought to achieve emerges clearly through the intermingling of theoretical literature, personal anecdote, poetic writing and images. Many of the chapter subsections begin with an image of a bird or animal common to an area she has visited which is inserted into the text to resemble an illuminated medieval manuscript such as Illustration 24 of a Mourning Dove (see Figure 7.9) at the beginning of a passage on the village of Isdud which no longer exists. She writes:

> The chapters of this dissertation, like the installation itself, are meant to connect the reader to the landscape. Each chapter begins with a story that takes place in the landscape – in a village and the occurrences that happen there. But I add this: over the years, a miscellany of animals materialized in almost every village location I visited, from which I began to form a sort of bestiary.
>
> (p. 17)

In addition to the PDF version of her written component, the York University online institutional repository also links to a fifteen-page document in PDF format titled *What isn't there* which contains a version of the *Bestiary*, described in the written component. This document is part of the creative component. Each of the landscape formatted pages has an image of a hand-drawn animal found in the region on the left-hand side of the page with a short text about the animal underneath it from sources ranging from contemporary poetry to the Bible. The right-hand side contains a text about a specific village that no longer exists taken from *All That Remains: The Palestinian Villages Occupied and Depopulated by Israel in 1948* by Walid Khalidi (Beirut: The Institute For Palestine Studies, 1992).

In a footnote to her introduction, Elle makes it clear, as elsewhere in the text, and in our interview, through her use of the first-person plural possessive in 'our research' that the field research has been carried out jointly by her and her partner, Tamira: 'as a practiced-based PhD, the dissertation is composed of two components: An exhibition of our research and a supporting paper' (Flanders 2014: 14). She emphasized this in our interview:

> The other thing that was unique was the collaborative aspect of it. I did the work together with my partner, not the written work, but the film work. She filmed it. We were there at every village together so that was something that I think could have used more exploration in the actual dissertation. It started out as my own journey but then became very much a partnership.

The research carried out in Israel and Palestine and the movie/installation for the examination exhibition in Toronto are presented as the outcome of a collaborative process established prior to Elle's commencement of the PhD. While, as we discuss elsewhere, the PhD by publication may contain co-authored chapters, this is the first instance in our corpus of visual arts submissions of a creative component being jointly produced. In Chapter 10, we refer to a recent thesis from the University of British Columbia (Hallenbeck 2019) that has a jointly authored chapter and film as part of the thesis and we discuss the emergence of joint authorship in relation to the prototypical notion of originality. At the same time, we need to acknowledge that many visual artworks are collaboratively produced inasmuch as there may be editors, camera people and other creative collaborators involved in the realization of the work.

Although Elle does describe the installation in the written text and includes some stills in the text, we had not been able to view the film of the exhibition which had been submitted on a DVD but, in the course of the interview, she shared her screen and showed part of the installation *in situ* in Toronto, describing it to us thus:

> The installation was set up in a garden. These were the walls that we constructed for viewing. There were two, angled walls. You see them here at a 90-degree angle. The film was being projected. We had to wait until it got dark. As the sun set, you could see more and more. So imagine you're standing in the middle and one angle is in front of you, one angle is behind. It's meant to be very immersive.
>
> (Elle Flanders, interview, 2021)

The film can be viewed on https://www.publicstudio.ca/what-isnt-there.

Australia

The ten Australian visual arts theses were from the Sydney College of the Arts (SCA) at the University of Sydney. The SCA has been offering studio-based arts practice and education degrees since 1976. Once a stand-alone college, the SCA joined the University of Sydney in 1989 when Australian arts colleges were merged with universities. When it became part of the University, the SCA, like other art schools in Australia, was able to offer a PhD which it has done since then. Notwithstanding, there have been struggles for the visual arts to gain legitimacy within some Australian academic institutions. Fairskye, from the SCA, writing in 1993, stated that 'artists in the academy have felt like "gate crashers" at the University's dinner party [...] asked to show their I.D. before they're allowed to sit down at the table with everyone else' (Fairskye 1993: 2–3). Sone, a recent graduate, comments 'as a new form of degree, practice-based doctoral courses in Australia have not yet earned academic legitimacy' and that he sometimes felt he was seen as 'suspect' by theorists and artists alike (Sone 2005: 8). The visual arts have now, however, become more firmly established in the Australian academy with discussions at the doctoral level now turning to matters such as how visual arts students can become academic writers (Lowry 2014), how they can balance their research at the same time as continue to be practising artists (Vincs 2014) and how to best examine PhDs in this area (Webb, Brien and Burr 2012).

The SCA's visual arts PhDs in our corpus were in the areas of painting, digital media, printmaking, sculpture, photography and indigenous art. Until recently, PhD students at the University of Sydney were not required to undertake coursework for their degree but they are now required to include some coursework. Visual arts students work with a supervisor on the creation of their artwork and the writing of their accompanying text for the three to four years of their study. At the SCA, the students' examiners come to a final exhibition of the students' work. Students then participate in an oral examination at which their examiners are present and in which their creative work and their written submission are discussed (oral examinations are not normally held for PhDs in most universities in Australia).

Emma Robertson, whose thesis we discuss in more detail below, described the experience of her examination at the SCA to us. Her account again emphasizes the need for researchers of doctoral writing to understand the integrated nature of the practice-based thesis in the visual arts whether it be explicit as in the theses discussed in this chapter or more implicit as seen in some of our earlier work (see e.g. Ravelli et al. 2013). As discussed above, we also need to see the viva or oral examination and the exhibitions that may take place during the course of the thesis as part of the thesis genre. Emma gave a vivid description of her own oral examination:

> At the time, we still did *viva voce* where you defend your thesis. I had three examiners and you present for about half an hour or up to 40 minutes, and so you have slides as a summary. They've read your thesis in advance. And then you walk with those three examiners into the exhibition space. That was a really interesting experience because it's as though they asked you to position the academic, the thesis side of it first, then you walk them down into the exhibition. I could see the sort of sense of this breath, of wow, you know, it looks like something on a slide on a screen, but when you walk into the space, you walk around those three-dimensional objects, it's quite different. And I can remember thinking I'm fine. I could tell by their physical reaction in the space that they liked the outcomes, that they liked what I had done.
>
> (Emma Robertson, interview, 2022)

All of the SCA theses were topic-based. Figure 7.10 shows the Table of Contents from Emma Robertson's practice-based PhD thesis, 'Transitions: Biophilia, beauty, and endangered plants', which was submitted at the SCA in 2018. The thesis' main concerns are climate change, the anxiety it generates, its impacts on endangered plant species and the role of art and artists in responding positively to these impacts. In the one-page Preface which is located just prior to the Introduction, after the Abstract, she outlines her project in a very personal voice and identifies her art practice as a source of originality: 'Taking my artwork out of the frame, and then off the wall, into three dimensional installations, and ultimately short films and artist's books, allowed me to transition and actively explore more unique and original forms of artistic expression' (Robertson 2018: vi). In our interview, Emma emphasized the paratextual nature of the Preface in the thesis as well as the notion of transition in her art practice as signalled by her thesis title: 'A number of the PhDs I read had these one-page Prefaces and what they did is they made a bridge between the person that you were to the person you became.'

Emma's thesis has four chapters plus an introduction and a conclusion and two appendices. The thesis contains fifty-four figures, thirty-nine of which are of her own work, while the other images reference work that has influenced her practice. It is worth pointing out that during the course of her doctoral candidature, in addition to the final oral examination, Emma had several exhibitions of her work and images from these can also be found in the thesis

---

Transitions: Biophilia, Beauty and Endangered Plants

Acknowledgements	CHAPTER THREE: Mindfulness and Beauty
Table of Contents	
List of Illustrations	CHAPTER FOUR: My Work
Abstract	The First Year 2015
Preface	The Second Year 2016
INTRODUCTION: Context	The Third Year 2017
Plants	CONCLUSION: Transitions and Future View
Research Methodology	
Overview of Chapters	BIBLIOGRAPHY
CHAPTER ONE: Literature Review	Appendix A: Two Workshops
Four Key Books	Appendix B: Artwork Presented for Examination
Other Publications	
Exhibitions and Films	
CHAPTER TWO: Other Artists	
Eco Art and Transmedia Art	
Earlier Eco Artists	
Science and Drawing	

Figure 7.10 Table of Contents of Robertson's (2018) SCA PhD.

as evidence of her iterative progress. Appendix B of her thesis contains fourteen photographs of installations from the final exhibition of her work for her examination as well as embedded links to two short videos MICROGRAPHIA (https://vimeo.com/222003403) and DEPOSITION LINES (https://vimeo.com/222012367) (see also pp. 129–31 of her written component). In our interview, Emma explained that she had been allowed to add the photographic record of her examination exhibition as an Appendix, although this was contrary to usual practice in which only changes recommended by the examiners are allowed: 'Normally, they're very strict, your thesis is that thesis.' Contrary to the theses discussed earlier in this chapter, where access to the entirety of the thesis was restricted due to the limitations of the digital affordances, the inclusion of the photographs and the video links enable us to appreciate the three-dimensional sculptures Emma created, and how these were located and interacted with the projection of the video (see Figure 7.11).

Her thesis is largely topic-based, although chapter 1 is titled literature review and explores climate change and its relationship with endangered plants

Figure 7.11 Emma Robertson, Exhibition Overview (2017: 167).
Image courtesy of Ian Hobbs.

and art. The introduction, which sits outside the chapter numbering system, lists the subheadings research methodology and overview of chapters as do some of the other theses discussed in this chapter. Chapter 2, titled 'Other artists', is a critical review of the work of a number of artists working with climate change themes whose work she has drawn on and it includes images of their work. Chapter 3 discusses two influential texts on mindfulness that altered the trajectory of her work, resulting in her adding a late chapter (chapter 3) and how this deeply influenced her art practice in the final year of her PhD. In chapter 4, through a chronological presentation of her work over the three years of her PhD (2015–17), Emma discusses how her practice evolved through a series of 'experiments' (p. 114) leading to exhibitions that allowed her to create and show three-dimensional artworks. Figure 7.11 is a still from her final examination exhibition which illustrates how her video was displayed along with her three-dimensional globes. The written text also integrates images of her 'test drawings' as she charts the development of her creative practice and her 'research and writing' over the period of her study (p. 120).

In our interview, the centrality of Emma's art practice to her thesis became clearer. One of her initial motivations for embarking on a practice-based PhD after many years as an academic in an art school at an Australian university was her desire to 'transform her practice'. She also wanted to be able to supervise doctoral students and a PhD was a requirement for this. Reading twelve practice-based theses early on in her study (Robertson 2018: 53) was a confirmation of her choice of a practice orientation; 'they clearly recognized practice as … a valid way of doing research'.

Emma recalled a workshop she attended at the SCA in which ways of structuring the written component were discussed: 'You can have a literature review throughout, or you can have a literature review and a distinct chapter so there's a number of variables.' She added that they were asked, 'here's one structure of a PhD, here's another structure … which of these structures do you think yours currently fits in?', which she interpreted as meaning 'what they were actually suggesting to us was to keep our minds open to the fact that our own structures may in fact change and, of course, right at the end mine did'.

Emma is referring here to the late development of what became chapter 3 of her thesis which was shaped by two significant works on the brain and emotion that she read in the final third year of her candidature: 'Oh, my goodness that book is the PhD … the thing that is slightly missing, which is about how our brains react to stress. Why we become in denial about things like climate change.' At that point, she decided to remove the original chapter 3 on models of thinking and replaced it with a completely new chapter which investigated the brain and emotion. This transition in her thinking mirrored 'a transition in my work from being in a frame on a wall, being safe; it became very sculptural, very three dimensional, much larger scale'. It is worth quoting at some length Emma's account of how the structure of the written component developed and why she decided not to include the two new texts in the original literature review chapter:

> So the reason that those two are separate from the literature review is I read them in my final year. And they were partly my epiphany, that they really belonged in a separate section, because they spoke about something that was related to what came next, which was the actual work, the practice, if that makes sense. So in my structure, I was very deliberate and I did have a conversation with [my supervisor] and she's saying these two books that you're now talking about should we put them in the literature review? And I said no, there's this other thing that went on, if I'm taking somebody on a journey, that's where that belongs, because it really led to the final year of the work.
>
> (Emma Robertson, interview, 2022)

Emma's use of the journey metaphor and of a narrative and chronological structure for her written component appears very much motivated by her interest in transmedia storytelling and transmedia art. In the written component, she refers to 'the idea of combining scientific data and modelling in a visual way to tell a more powerful and accurate story, using drawings' (p. 59); later she talks about 'the need to more actively motivate audiences to connect with climate change' (p. 87) and suggests that the thesis's method of 'unfold[ing] a story progressively over a period of time' (p. 76) may be a way of doing this.

All of the SCA's written components were similar to Emma's in that they pointed to and discussed the student's creative works rather than being a text which 'stood beside' their artwork as we found in a number of cases in our earlier research into visual arts PhDs in Australia (see Paltridge et al. 2012a). Ann Elias, an experienced supervisor and PhD examiner at the University of Sydney, emphasized the need for the integration of the two components of the PhD. She described as problematic an examination of a doctoral thesis she had undertaken in which she saw 'no integration … at all in the dissertation [written component]' of the creative component and no images of the creative work were included. She added, 'I could not understand how I could examine that person easily unless they reflected on the connection between their practice and the body of work they'd made … and the dissertation that they had written' (Ann Elias, interview, 2022). For Ann, including images of the creative work in the written text, was 'quite fundamental really … if the person is doing a nice integration of the dissertation with the studio practice, they'll put examples of their work in the chapters, and then they have the images as the evidence of the work'. Most importantly, she stressed:

> That's what distinguishes the PhD in creative practice from other PhDs; in a sense, there are two bodies of work … dissertation and the studio practice. And the added area for the creative artist is to then do the reflection that brings the two together. Then studio practice becomes more imaginative through finding out about other artists and philosophers so it's two way or it's circular. It's one body of work in two different forms, you know.
>
> (Ann Elias, Interview, 2022)

We also did not find the variation in macrostructures in the SCA PhDs that we found in our previous research which examined visual arts PhDs in a larger number of universities in Australia (Paltridge et al. 2012b). In line with Ann's comments, the SCA theses all contained an explanation and discussion of the creation of the students' art works rather than a discussion of any particular research methodology in a more traditional sense. If the students did discuss methodology, they used this space, rather, to discuss the theory they would use in their thesis. The SCA theses, then, showed a sense of being 'stabilized for now' (Schryer 1994: 108) in terms of how they were written. This is not to say, however, that all Australian visual arts PhDs are necessarily the same as those we examined in this chapter. We only looked at theses within a single university. Our earlier research into visual arts theses in Australia showed that variation in the texts that students wrote was largely across universities, rather than within them. This, of course, may be the case in other parts of the world as well.

Conclusion

The practice-based doctorate, then, inasmuch as it is an alternate to the 'default' doctorate is surprisingly similar to more traditional doctoral degrees but, in some ways, quite different from them. The theses students write can be similar in that they might be topic-based or they might be simple traditional or occasionally complex traditional in terms of thesis-type. One key way in which the practice-based doctorate is different, however, is that the written thesis is not the only component that is required to display 'doctorateness'; the student's creative work needs to do this as well. These creative works, however, can take diverse forms and the texts that accompanies them can also be diverse. Indeed, the nature and structure of the text can be reconfigured, so long as the underlying functions of the text are still met, that is, that it must still display 'academicness' (Molinari 2021) and the qualities of a doctoral submission as they are understood by the particular discipline (Ravelli, Starfield and Paltridge 2021). And there are a number of different ways in which the relations between student's creative work and their written text may be presented. Our interview data helped us understand the extent to which, from the student's perspective, the two components are connected, even though at times the technological affordances fail to realize this interdependence. Our interview with Ann Elias offered an experienced supervisor and examiner's perspective on the relationship between the two parts. It is important too, from an analytical perspective, as argued by Ravelli et al. (2013), to 'extend the notion of text' to comprehend both written and creative components.

The theses we examined from visual art doctorates, further, had much in common with the new humanities PhDs we discuss in Chapter 5 of this book, particularly in relation to shared theoretical and methodological understandings and approaches and an, at times, disruptive approach to formal written conventions. As noted by Ravelli et al. (2013), writers tended to opt for a diversity of voice in their writing, often mingling a more conventional academic voice with informal, descriptive, autobiographic, narrative and poetic tenors which is a feature of some new humanities theses as well. The inherent multimodality of these theses is perhaps the area in which they have most innovated in the doctoral landscape and their influence can be discerned in the 're-imagined' theses and dissertations we discuss in Chapter 10.

Amongst all this, however, the doctoral thesis genre currently seems relatively stable in that there is largely a consensus for the need for a doctoral thesis in these degrees and what areas they should cover. At the same time, as our discussion with Susan Collins of the Slade indicated, local factors can work to stabilize the form the doctorate takes as the introduction of the practice-led PhD had clarified, if perhaps not completely resolved, issues of the relationship between the two components and the role of practice:

> One of the things I really wanted to do in 2010 was to get that practice-led PhD introduced and I felt very strongly about it; that we should have the confidence and the Slade's always been known primarily for its practice .... I felt that that we had the absolute confidence in all of our other programs ... whereas I think, at the time, a lot of art schools were kind of feeling slightly apologetic about academia and that they had to ... almost bend over backwards to be academic to prove that it was okay to have an art PhD.
>
> (Susan Collins, interview, 2022)

Clearly, in examining the development of the practice-based doctorate, it is important to understand the forces at play in the specific contexts being studied. The tensions referred to in Chapter 4 that shape both genre change and stability – that is, centripetal forces for unification and centrifugal forces for change – will play out differently in relation to the contexts in which practice-based doctorates are located as is the case for other kinds of doctoral degrees.

8

Practice-based doctorates in music

This chapter examines practice-based doctorates in music, specifically the Doctor of Musical Arts (DMA) which is on offer in the United States, Canada and Australia and the DMus which is available in the UK: both are relatively new arrivals on the doctoral landscape and as we shall see there is not necessarily consensus as to their structure at the current time or what is required for the award of the degree. The DMA and DMus are similar to the visual arts theses and dissertations discussed in the previous chapter in that they typically consist of a written and creative or practice-based component, be it a performance or a composition. As with other chapters in the book, doctorates are examined which have been awarded in the four different geographical locations referred to above: that is, the United States, the UK, Canada and Australia. We examine theses and dissertations that have been submitted in each of these locations and compare them with previous research into thesis types, such as that discussed in Chapter 4, as well as our own earlier research on this topic including the relationship between the two components that constitute the thesis or dissertation. In the course of our analysis, we draw on interview data from two recent DMA graduates.

One of the early universities in the United States to offer this degree was Yale University which first offered its DMA in 1968. We were not, however, able to locate any Yale DMA dissertations, even though a dissertation is referred to on their DMA website. A DMA has, however, been on offer at the University of California San Diego since 1966 and we were able to locate recent examples of these dissertations and discuss some of these below. Other US universities which offer a DMA include the University of Washington, the University of Rochester, Johns Hopkins University, the University of Michigan, Michigan State University, the University of Houston, Northwestern University, Stanford University, Boston University, the University of Florida, Claremont Graduate University, the University of Georgia, the University of Kentucky, the University of South Carolina, the Julliard School and City University of New York (Steinman 2019; Talley 1956).

In Canada, the DMA is offered by universities such as the University of Toronto, the University of British Columbia, the University of Alberta, the University of Western Ontario and McGill University (a DMus). Performance- and composition-based doctoral studies in music in the UK are offered as either a PhD, for example, in the degrees available at Goldsmiths University of London, the Royal Northern College of Music, the University of Nottingham, Cardiff University, the University of Edinburgh and the University of Birmingham, or a DMus as in the degree on offer at the Royal College of Music and the Guildhall School of Music and Drama. In Australia, the University of Sydney offers a DMA as do Griffith University and the University of Western Australia. Other Australian universities, such as the University of Tasmania, Monash University and the Australian National University, offer a PhD in music with a performance and/or composition component. The University of Melbourne, which has discontinued its DMA, now offers a PhD in fine arts and music which students can complete by creative work and dissertation.

When we asked Sang Kyun Koh, a DMA graduate from the University of Toronto, now teaching at a US institution, about the differences he saw between the DMA and the PhD in his field of music performance, he commented that, from his perspective, the difference was that the DMA has a heavy emphasis on performance. He went on to explain that what he did see as an issue with the DMA more broadly was a lack of standardization. He felt that the University of Toronto's written dissertation for the PhD 'did not seem significantly different than the DMA written component' as the

> DMA has a lot more performance and has a similar written component to it so it's a very intense program. But if you go to other institutions, University of Stony Brook in New York, for instance, they have a system in which recitals beyond the degree requirements can reduce the number of pages to be written for the dissertation and then you have institutions like Boston University that have a totally different program ... so there is no standardization. I think this creates the possibility of resentment amongst DMA graduates, since the same degree is not the same in value. It does depend on what program you come from.
>
> (Sang Kyun Koh, interview, 2022)

He also gave the example of the Eastman School of Music at the University of Rochester, which 'has arguably the strongest DMA program in the US; they have their written component [which] is not as long, but they have something called a comprehensive exam that students have to pass that is a very, very intense exam'. He added that whereas for his own DMA completed in 2017 there had been no such exams, the University of Toronto has now introduced a comprehensive examination. He concluded, 'So there is some trajectory of standardization but it's long and slow.'

While the inclusion of a professional dimension is seen as a distinguishing characteristic of the DMA, music education scholars have noted the diversity of DMA offerings in the United States and some have recommended greater standardization (see e.g. Jones 2009). Yale's approach, for example, is quite distinctive. The Yale DMA comprises a two-year residential component followed by a three-year, full-time dissertation period during which candidates 'develop and demonstrate professional and artistic excellence' and are then permitted to proceed to the final DMA recital and oral examination. During this time, the candidate compiles what is referred to as the 'Dissertation Component': a 'dossier of distinguished artistic and professional achievements' that must include 'letters from recognized individuals who are professionally qualified to evaluate the candidate's work' and supporting evidence such as programmes, compositions, reviews, articles, publications and recordings (information taken from the School of Music website https://music.yale.edu/degrees-and-programs). The portfolio-like Yale model of DMA may explain why we were unable to locate copies of the DMA dissertations online.

Data collected

A set of forty DMAs (Doctor of Musical Arts)/DMus (Doctor of Music) theses and dissertations was collected for this chapter. Ten music doctorates were collected from each of the University of California San Diego, the Royal College of Music in the UK, the University of Toronto and the University of Sydney. The US and Canadian dissertations were obtained through the ProQuest database and the UK theses through the British Library EThOS database. The Australian theses were obtained through a search of the University of Sydney's online thesis repository.

Findings

The United States

Latimer (2010: 19) refers to the DMA as having 'evolved and proliferated during the third quarter of the twentieth century, [to] become a mainstay for academic preparation of college and university professors in music performance areas'. It was conceptualized as providing professional musicians with a route to permanent appointment in the academy through a doctorate that combined original research and musical performance (Latimer 2010). One of our interviewees confirmed that it is still the case today that the DMA is a requirement for an academic teaching position in the United States. This 'new' Doctor of Musical Arts was discussed at a meeting of the Committee on Music in Colleges and Universities in 1956 in Indiana where a panel discussion was devoted to the topic. One of the speakers on the panel made the point that musical performance 'in the highest sense' – together with musical insights – was essential for the awarding of the degree (Talley 1956: 20).

The DMA is available in performance and composition in the United States, and also in music education (Jones 2009). There are now fifty-two institutions in the United States offering either a DMA or a Doctor of Music (DMus), although most universities use the title Doctor of Musical Arts for their degree (Steinman 2019). The US National Association of Schools of Music describes doctoral degrees in music as being

> intended for those planning to engage and participate at the most advanced academic and professional levels of musical endeavor. Students admitted to doctoral study are expected to achieve competencies that enable them to function consistent with their specializations as musicians, as scholars, and as teachers who can communicate effectively both orally and in written form.
> (National Association of Schools of Music 2021: 139)

The University of California (UC) San Diego DMA was chosen as the focus of this section of the chapter because of its long history in offering this degree as well as its high standing in the area of music education more broadly. The DMA at UC San Diego is in contemporary music performance. Students undertake core curriculum requirements as well as courses in their area of emphasis. DMA students give two or more recitals as part of the completion requirements for the degree or one recital with the option of either a thesis or research project – a concert or lecture recital that is innovative in design and/or content and which is supported by appropriate documentation or two chamber music concerts (UC San Diego 2021b). Some of the dissertations we examined did indeed refer to the written text as a document or a paper rather than a dissertation or thesis. Beetz (2017), in her Introduction, writes: 'This document will examine how my practice developed from one as an interpretive performer to a creator in The Winter Stars through a detailed discussion of and reflection on the creative processes involved' (p. 1). DMA students therefore have several options as to how they meet the completion requirements.

The UC San Diego DMAs examined in this chapter were in the areas of trumpet, percussion, sound, piano, guitar, drumming, voice, cello, conducting, opera and contrabass. The dissertations were all topic-based and, on average, about eighty pages long, much shorter than most typical PhD dissertations. While each dissertation was closely linked to the student's area of musical performance, in some cases the performed work was listed separately from the text, such as a list of recitals, sound recordings, supplemental files or music scores, while in others, as discussed below, there is greater integration of the performance or recital into the written text. One of the dissertations (Cano 2016) contained music extracts within the text that were not, however, linked to the student's performance but part of an explanation of particular guitar techniques. Supplemental files on the UC San Diego's online repository contain short audio recordings of the sixty-five guitar techniques.

Lander's (2017) dissertation, 'Coping mechanisms: An improvised opera for non-improvising opera singers', submitted in the field of contemporary music performance discusses the two-year development of her creative work, a one-act chamber opera for three singers accompanied by bass, cello and percussion. Four short video clips of the performers improvising have been uploaded to the university's online repository together with the written text and the *Proquest Dissertations and Theses* site includes a video recording of the performance. In her written component, she reflects on the experience of creating the opera and what it taught her about the intersection of her identities as an opera singer, a composer and an improvisor. In her composer notes for the performance programme, Lander describes her opera thus:

> *Coping Mechanisms* is an exploration of modern life interpreted as voluntary loneliness. I've met many people who react to hardship with various levels of retreat, only to find the pain exacerbated by the solitude. This piece attempts to highlight the frustration of this kind of coping mechanism, and explores the physical and mental relationships to stress, anxiety, fear, and grief.
>
> (Lander 2017: 38)

While there is no literal plot line to the opera, it takes place over three acts: 'Reckoning' in which the three characters experience shock and grief; 'Home' in which they avoid their grief through isolation; and 'Failure' in which they find they are unable to move past their trauma and flee the space which they are in. After the performance of her opera, a number of members of the audience

Coping Mechanisms: An Improvised Opera for Non-Improvising Opera Singers

Introduction

Chapter 1 – Narrative

Chapter 2 – Music

Chapter 3 – Fixed Elements

Chapter 4 – Reflections on Performance

Appendix

Figure 8.1 Table of Contents of Lander's (2017) DMA UC San Diego dissertation.

approached Lander to tell her how much they had been moved by the work, how they had identified with its characters and how the work challenged the way they viewed their own coping mechanisms.

Lander's dissertation abstract refers to the dissertation as a 'paper' stating: 'This paper describes the narrative and conceptual structures that gave this piece shape, the style of improvisation that resulted, as well as information about the process and success of the piece' (p. x). Her topic-based chapters (see Figure 8.1) are short, with none longer than ten pages. The dissertation is forty-four pages long and includes an eight-page Appendix of information about the performance itself. The connection of the written paper to the performance is amplified by the inclusion in the Appendix of detailed notes about the opera and its performance.

The dissertation did not contain reference to any published work or research on which her dissertation or creative work was based. This was unusual in that most of the other dissertations had a 'Works Cited' or 'Bibliography' section at the end of their text. Cano's (2016) dissertation, however, 'Modern guitar techniques: A view of history, convergence of musical traditions and contemporary works', was a further example of a text which did not cite other academic or creative sources. The dissertation lists four DMA recitals given during his candidature.

In the Introduction and through the chapters, Lander adopts a personal, narrative voice as do many of the other University of California San Diego DMA dissertations in our corpus. She writes:

> I have composed many improvised structures and performed many improvisations that experiment with this approach. In these works I express

emotion, neurotic thought, abstract sensations, stress, and excitement through visceral, musical, extroverted, intimate, and sometimes literal vocalizations. However, like an aria these improvisations are not typically treated as a part of a larger narrative, but rather removed from any context. Typically, these words are presented as unique moments in time that are being witnessed by the audience. I wanted to create an opera in this vein wherein the characters express their "interior state" with great emotional and personal detail, while allowing the performers freedom to develop their own character's stories in real time.

(p. 3)

In her final chapter, titled 'Reflections on performance', she says:

Through creating this piece I learned a lot about structuring theatrical, improvised pieces as well as what makes something a "composition" at all. Throughout the process and performance the performers never lost their need to be present, alert, engaged, and creative. I created a situation wherein Robert and Elisabeth were forced to develop their own music, their own characters, and develop a narrative for those characters and the audience without the aid of a score. Although throughout the creation of this piece I was essentially the "composer", I still feel as though the piece was made collaboratively, relying on and inspiring each performers' individual styles.

(p. 35)

As with Lander's text cited above, several of the DMAs from UC San Diego adopt an exegetical and personal tenor in that the written component largely recounts the development of the student's journey as they create the performances for their recitals. For example, Hepfer's (2016) dissertation 'Conducting, teaching, curating: Re-channelings of a percussive education' begins with the words 'This dissertation examines the ways that my formal training and education as a percussionist have provided a logical foundation for three separate vectors of activity in my professional life: conducting, teaching and curating' (p. 1) and contains descriptions of and his reflection on each of his three DMA recitals integrated into the third section of his dissertation. The majority of the UC San Diego dissertations that have a practice or performance component clearly linked the written and creative components in the written text as did Nestor (2018), who commented that his multimedia work, 'This is not a Drill', is a 'synthesis of my work as a percussionist and researcher. The piece embodies concepts from my dissertation, my background as a contemporary percussionist and interpreter, and interest in the history of the use of sound in warfare' (p. 36). Nguyen (2016) goes a step further, explicitly connecting the personal and the academic:

> How these ideas evolved from the humble germination of an idea to public performance is told with both an academic voice, as well as a deeply personal one. Perhaps this is a slight risk to take for an academic paper, but considering the subject matter it seemed impossible to discuss the topic of my work with any degree of depth without also delving into what is deeply personal.
>
> (pp. 2–3)

A number of the UC San Diego DMAs dissertations contained interviews as data which were appended at the end of the text as well as referred to in the dissertation itself. Allen (2020) in her dissertation 'An adaptable approach to expertise: The application of Ivan Galamian's violin pedagogy to trumpet practice and teaching', Bowden (2018) in her 'Max Roach and M'Boom: Diasporic soundings in American percussion music' and Beauton (2020) in 'Systems of value: Societal influences on, and the mediation of, the classical interpreter percussionist' did this. Interviews are also used as a method in the two Canadian and Australian theses we discuss in more detail below.

Beetz (2017), Blair (2018) and Lander (2017) were the only students who submitted recordings of their performances that have been uploaded to the UC San Diego online repository, although there were several others who list performances and recitals. In Nguyen's (2016) written text he sets out how each of the four main chapters is 'dedicated to the four concert programs I presented during this time' [during his DMA] (p. 1). There are, thus, a range of possibilities for what the UC San Diego DMA students can include in their dissertations as well as what they can omit.

The UK

While there are a number of practice-based research degrees in the UK that offer music as an area of specialization, there still seems to be some uncertainty about the written text that supports the portfolio of practice that students submit at the end of the degree. Key to all this is the achievement of 'doctorateness' and how this is displayed by students in their work. Beyond this, students undertaking a practice-based doctorate in music have to 'satisfy academic demands as well those relating to professional practice' (Burland, Spencer and Windsor 2017: 115) as they produce work/performances that are both novel and contribute to knowledge in the field.

The Royal College of Music in London which is the focus of this section of the chapter was founded in 1882. It is a music conservatoire with a worldwide reputation, training performers, conductors and composers (QAA 2012). DMus students at the Royal College of Music have a supervisory team of at least two for their studies. This team is made up of both practitioners and scholars (Pearson 2014). There is no formal coursework at the Royal College DMus. Students instead attend group tutorials and seminars in their particular area of research. At the end of their degree, students submit a portfolio of practical work in performance or composition and a commentary on that work. The commentary is between 20,000 and 50,000 words and contextualizes the student's research (Royal College of Music in London nd). The portfolio and commentary are examined by a panel which includes a practitioner in the student's area of specialization who is external to the College (Pearson 2014).

Four of the ten Royal College of Music DMus theses collected for this chapter were in performance and six were in composition. Of the four performance theses, only Yahav's performance had been uploaded onto the *EThOS* platform. The performance submissions were in the areas of piano and performance preparation. The composition submissions included original works for piano, acoustic instruments and electroacoustic media, pre-recorded electronics, live electronics, bass clarinet, chamber opera, music ensembles and orchestra. Some of the compositions also included dance, video and video animation.

Yahav's (2018) performance submission, 'From text to sound: Revisiting some performance indications in Chopin's works', was titled a DMus Portfolio and Commentary. The written component was ninety-seven pages long (24,000 words) and was topic-based as were the other performance submissions. His submission also included three recorded one-hour concert programmes of his performances of Chopin's work for piano which can be downloaded from the EThOS website and a statistical survey of Chopin's worded performance indications as an Appendix. His project aimed to explore how he could use the notations that Chopin had made on his scores 'in order to draw conclusions that could be useful to performers of the music of Chopin' (p. 9). He describes his methodology as aiming to explore this question through his own performance. Chapter 1 of the written component contains the prototypical components of a research thesis: research questions, research methodology and review of the literature (see Table of Contents in Figure 8.2). The survey findings referred to in his first chapter are the results of an analysis Yahav did of Chopin's notations on his scores, not a survey in the research methods sense. His written commentary is multimodal in that it contains many instances of extracts from piano scores.

From Text to Sound: Revisiting Some Performance Indications in Chopin's Works

Abstract

List of Musical Examples

List of Recorded Material

Chapter 1: Introduction
   Summary
   Research Questions
   Research Methodology
   Review of Literature
   Contents
   Survey Findings

Chapter 2: Indications of Tempo Modification

Chapter 3: Indications of Dynamics

Chapter 4: Indications of Expressivity

Chapter 5: Conclusions

Bibliography

Web Resources

Selected Discography

Appendix A: A Survey of Chopin's Worded Indications

Figure 8.2 Table of Contents of Yahav's (2018) performance submission.

Liu's (2019) DMus composition submission, 'An exploration towards the enrichment of a personal musical language in musical composition', related to three of her works for piano: *The Passage, Rain Air II* and *Rain Air III*, works inspired by the sound of the rain. She describes her commentary thus:

> The following commentary details ways in which I have enriched my own compositional language by exploring the integration of elements from Chinese musical culture within the context of Western Contemporary music. This commentary accompanies a portfolio of compositions and sets out to articulate the means by which I have attempted to develop and to enrich my personal musical language through the integration of certain, in my view, key elements from Chinese musical culture within the context of Western contemporary musical thought. My focus is on three elements which are shared between both Chinese and Western cultures, used in each with very different effect and intent: glissandi, modality and micro-tonality. The commentary explores the role each of these plays in my own work, how their practice and use derive from Chinese

musical traditions and how I have set out to re-think that practice in terms of a musical language derived from a contemporary 'Western' art-music context.

(p. 2)

Her submission is also topic-based, as were the other composition submissions. Liu's Table of Contents (see Figure 8.3), however, provides more detail on the content of her submission than Yahav's (2018) submission described above. She analyses the work of other Chinese and Western composers and reflects on elements from their work which are important for her own compositions. As with many of the Royal College of Music submissions and with the University of California San Diego DMA dissertations, her commentary adopts a personal, reflective voice. She begins Chapter 1 by locating her musical development in relation to her Chinese cultural background:

> As a composer, it is important to me to explore the role of my Chinese heritage in the development of my own musical language. For this to evolve, I feel that it

---

An exploration towards the enrichment of a personal musical language in musical composition

1. **Introduction**
2. **Compositions before 2014**
   2.1 An exploration of contemporary classical music in Chinese and Western cultures
   2.2 A selective collection of elements from contemporary music
   2.3 Analysis of my own music
3. **2014–2015 Compositions**
   3.1 The horizontal writing in traditional Chinese music
   3.2 Glissando: my own reflection on the traditional Chinese music
4. **2015–2016 Compositions**
   4.1 Micro-Polyphony and Macro-Polyphony
   4.2 He Xuntian's SS (stream of structure) Method of Musical Composition in *The Image of Sound – FuSe Pattern*
   4.3 My own reflection on Macro-Polyphony
   4.4 Macro-Polyphony in my own music
5. **Compositions after 2016**
   5.1 Explorations of other Chinese composers' approach to Chinese modes in contemporary music
   5.2 My own reflections on the works in the previous section
   5.3 Analysis of my own music
   The Passage
   Rain Air II
   Rain Air III
6. **Conclusions**

Figure 8.3 Table of Contents of Liu's (2019) composition submission.

is crucial that I remain open to all different possibilities which may materialize in the course of composing.

(p. 6)

Liu's composing process is often related as grounded in a personal story too:

The Other Side (2014) and *Broken Connection (2015)* are both written for solo violin and electronics. ... I chose violin and electronics because I want to explore the glissando as the main material of the linear movement in a single melodic line. The inspiration for this piece came from the classic film *The Exorcist* (1973), because I am fascinated by the idea of an exorcism and of making contact with the dead.

(p. 32)

While most of her submission analyses the work of others and her own work, her personal voice returns in her conclusion chapter:

Throughout my research I have been constantly surprised and reassured by how two different cultures, which may seem to share little in common, complement each other. By integrating different approaches and techniques in order to explore different tools for composition I have been able to focus on both similarities and differences which, as a whole, create a well-balanced approach in which neither culture imposes on the other. This means that I can focus on aspects of composition which are not dependent on culture but which remain universal: the changes that take place within material over time, and how we as composers can create structures from balancing similarities and differences in personal ways.

(p. 88)

Her submission, further, is highly multimodal in that it contains numerous notated examples of extracts from her own and other people's work within her text. In addition, a series of supplementary PDF files on the *EThOS* website contain the scores of her compositions with notations for performers.

Canada

The University of Toronto is Canada's oldest and largest university, having been established in 1827. Its Faculty of Music offers a wide range of music programmes from undergraduate through to postgraduate coursework and research degrees. The DMA at the University of Toronto has two streams: performance and composition. Students in both streams undertake coursework as part of their studies. Performance students give three DMA recitals and composition students present a recital of original works in their third and fourth years of study. Students in the composition strand of the DMA submit the score for an original composition as their end of their programme of study while performance students submit a research thesis or a performance guide, also titled a 'thesis'.

Sang Kyun Koh, a graduate of the performance stream whose dissertation forms part of our Canadian corpus and who we introduced at the beginning of this chapter, described the structure of the performance component:

> Our school, University of Toronto, had an option of doing three full, just performance-only recitals or two performance-only recitals and a lecture recital, so I opted for the second option, and so my dissertation ['Spaces-in-Between: A Swing-Informed Approach to Performing Jazz – and Blues-Influenced Western Art Music for Violin'] was the main subject for my lecture recital where I performed the music that we talked about, and then I discussed the points.
>
> (Sang Kyun Koh, interview, 2022)

He elaborated on his choice saying, 'It's a necessary step because I'm talking about how to create swing and performance; I should be able to at least demonstrate that knowledge in practice so I think for what I wrote about it was necessary.' However, as he explained to us, the performances were not of his own work; in the case of the first two they were works by classical composers such as Beethoven and Brahms and for the lecture recital he performed some of the jazz-influenced works discussed in the thesis. Without interviewing Koh, we would not have fully understood the nature of the performance components, the options available to students and their relationship with the written component: 'The written component is the one that everyone gets to see on the web and the performance components, I have videos of them, but I don't make it public.'

Ten University of Toronto DMA submissions were collected for this chapter, six in the area of performance and four in composition. Three of the performance submissions were in the area of cello and electronics, guitar and jazz violin and were accompanied by a research thesis. A further three of the performance submissions were performance guides as in Dong's (2020) 'A performance guide to Tan Dun's *Elegy: Snow in June*', a concerto for solo cello and percussion quartet. The composition submissions were works for soprano and modular orchestra, cello and chamber orchestra, and orchestral compositions.

In terms of thesis types, the performance submissions were either topic-based or simple traditional. The Table of Contents for Ascenzo's (2020) simple traditional DMA submission, 'Digital landscape: An annotated list of works

---

Digital Landscape: An Annotated List of Works for Solo Cello and Electronics

Chapter 1: Introduction
   1.1: Research Positionality
   1.2: Background, Research Rationale, and Existing Literature
   1.3: Context, Definitions, and Limiting Factors

Chapter 2: Performing with Live Electronics
   2.1: Elektronische Musik and Musique Concrète
   2.2: Recording Technology
   2.3: Performance Technology
   2.4: Competences and Music Technology
   2.5: Obsolescence and Evolving Technology

Chapter 3: Methodology
   3.1: Locating and Collecting Repertoire
   3.2: Framework and Terminology
   3.3: Developing a Difficulty Rating System

Chapter 4: Annotated List of Works

Chapter 5: Discussion

Chapter 6: Future Directions

Figure 8.4 Table of Contents of Ascenzo's (2020) simple traditional DMA performance submission.

for solo cello and electronics', is shown in Figure 8.4. The first two chapters of his dissertation are analogous to the Introduction and Literature Review chapters of a simple traditional dissertation. These are then followed by Methodology, Results (his Annotated List of Works) and Discussion chapters.

As mentioned above, Koh's (2017) topic-based DMA, 'Spaces-in-between: A swing-informed approach to performing jazz – and blues-influenced Western art music for violin', was an exploration of swing in relation to jazz violin submitted through the performance stream. His written thesis is an exploration of his research topic rather than a reflection on or an analysis of his own musical performance. This was also case with the other Toronto DMA performance-oriented submissions.

Koh describes his study thus:

> The purpose of this dissertation is to examine how several significant classical music composers have tried to incorporate music that swings, particularly jazz and blues, into compositions that showcase the violin. It also aims to offer performers insights into how they might interpret these compositions and others like them through attention and informed approaches to several vital aspects of swing – namely rhythm, timing, and articulation.
>
> (Koh 2017: 1)

He explained to us that rather than publish academic papers, 'for performers our research is performances like concerts so we do a lot of concerts'.

Koh's dissertation comprises six chapters plus an introduction. As mentioned above, the dissertation contains no mention of the performance component and the two can be seen as quite separate; the dissertation's focus is on the work of other composers, performers and scholars and how they have defined the 'very elusive concept' of swing (Koh 2017: 8). The first three chapters essentially review literature, performances and musical notation. Chapter 1, 'What is swing', is a review of previous research into swing and attempts to define its constituents; Chapter 2, 'Towards understanding Ravel's, Copland's, and Bernstein's conceptualizations of swing', reviews works by these three composers that incorporate elements of swing, attempts to trace jazz and blues influences on their work and includes short sound clips embedded within the PDF of influential jazz performers from the 1920s to the 1950s to supplement the discussions and illustrate influences on the works discussed.

Chapter 3, 'Notations of swing by Western art music composers', reviews and analyses the musical notation used by the three composers, attempting to identify a swing-informed approach to performance. Chapter 4, 'Steps towards developing a swing-informed approach', is based on interviews with three jazz violinists who are asked to select recordings of performances of the work of the three composers that 'they felt best conveyed a sense of swing' (2017: 96) and also includes links to sound clips for analysis. Chapter 5, 'Techniques of swing', examines video clips of performances by three well-known jazz violinists to identity playing techniques that may provide evidence of swing being performed. Chapter 6 is a short conclusion that focuses on the implications of the study for performers.

The inclusion of sound and video recordings through short clips linked to *YouTube* within several of the chapters is an innovative feature of the dissertation that Koh explained to us he had devised rather than having to provide a separate CD or USB which can be mislaid or difficult to access as we noted in our discussion of the visual arts theses in Chapter 7. The inclusion of the sound and video clips and examples of musical notation contributes to the multimodal nature of Koh's doctoral thesis which is a feature shared with other theses discussed in this chapter and the practice-based doctorates in the visual arts discussed previously.

While Koh's written dissertation bears no trace of the performance component, it can nevertheless be understood as animated by Koh's desire, as he explained it to us, to change his playing style and therefore his practice:

I wanted to write about what the American school of violin playing was …
and then, through that research of trying to … define what American music

and the school of violin playing was, I discovered jazz and then kind of just started researching it and then I also, at the same time was going through some issues with my own playing, and my biggest issue with playing was that I tended to play very 'square' so like not much emotion … square playing … everything is there, everything is correct, but it doesn't have that emotional component, doesn't have that quality, that X factor that draws you in as a listener, and I didn't know how to recreate that. When I listened to jazz musicians, I felt like they had it. They had it innately so that's how I got sucked in, maybe there's something that jazz musicians do fundamentally or how they approach music that better allows for their artistry to come through in the way that I would like my playing to come through so that's what I started researching … that's how it all started.

(Sang Kyun Koh, interview, 2022)

At the same time, the main topic of the lecture he gave as part of the performance component was the topic of the dissertation and the recital was of jazz violin compositions. There is therefore a mutual influencing occurring rather than a total separation of the two components. As Koh said, it was important for him to be able to demonstrate the connection.

The composition submissions were all scores for the student's original work which followed a pattern of Abstract, Table of Contents, Notes on Instrumentation (in some cases) and the Score. Wright's (2020) 'Dimensions of perceived reality for soprano and modular orchestra' shown in Figure 8.5 is an example of this. The 'Text' referred to in his Table of Contents are the poems by William Wordsworth that were the basis for his composition.

The performance DMA students, then, wrote topic-based or simple traditional dissertations for their submission. It is not clear, however, from publicly

---

Dimensions of Perceived Reality for Soprano and Modular Orchestra

Instrumentation

Text

Movement I – Humanity

Movement II – Environment

Movement III – Space and Time

Movement I – Existence

Figure 8.5 Table of Contents of Wright's (2020) DMA composition submission.

available information on the degree what the relationship is between their dissertation and the recitals they give as part of the degree. Our interview with Koh does however offer insight into his conceptualization of the relationship. None of the composition students, however, wrote a dissertation-type text for their submissions but, rather, presented the score of their original work for examination.

Australia

Doctorates in the practical study of music are a relatively recent phenomenon in Australia, with most appearing after the higher education reforms of the late 1980s (Hannan 2008). The Sydney Conservatorium of Music, which was founded in 1915, joined the University of Sydney in 1990 as part of these reforms. The Sydney Conservatorium offers postgraduate degrees in music in a wide range of areas of specialization, including a DMA which is described as a research-based doctorate in music performance, conducting or composition. While a central feature of this degree is a written thesis as part of the student's final submission, Joanne Heaton, whose recently submitted DMA we discuss below, writes that 'an Australian Doctor of Musical Arts degree requires a significant final recital that has a strong relationship to the research questions of the thesis' (Heaton 2020: 32).

At the University of Sydney, DMA students undertake coursework in their initial year of study. At the end of their degree, it is through the public presentation of their work (for example, through a recital or recording), or a composition folio, in addition to a 25,000–30,000-word thesis, that students display their original contribution to research in their area of specialization (University of Sydney nd). Forbes (2014) writes that this contribution to knowledge

> can take the form of realisation of new musical works (premiere performances), new interpretation of existing musical works, or investigation of specific performance practices through the performance of historic or avant-garde repertory, just to give a few examples.
>
> (p. 267)

Ten DMA theses from the University of Sydney's Conservatorium of Music were collected for this chapter. Eight of the theses were in the area of performance and two were in composition. The performance submissions were in the areas of flute, viole, conducting, saxophone, piano, cello and opera. The composition theses were in the areas of improvising orchestra, and a set of works for flute, viola, vibraphone and piano, clarinet and string orchestra, music for dance and an opera.

Six of the performance submissions were topic-based theses and two were simple traditional. Lim's (2018) 'Unsuk Chin's Piano Music: 6 Piano Etudes (1995–2003) and Piano Concerto (1996–1997)' is an example of a Sydney Conservatorium performance thesis (see Figure 8.6). Lim's first chapter, the Introduction, has components that would be expected of a simple traditional thesis, that is, the background to her study, and the aims and significance of her research. Her thesis contains a short Conclusions chapter which is also typical of a simple traditional thesis. The other chapters in her thesis are topic-based

---

Unsuk Chin's Piano Music: 6 Piano Etudes (1995–2003) and Piano Concerto (1996–1997)

Abstract

Acknowledgements

Table of Contents

List of Examples

List of Figures

List of Tables

Chapter 1: Introduction
- 1.1 Research Background
- 1.2 Aims of the Research
- 1.3 Research Significance

Chapter 2: Overview
- 2.1 Biography
- 2.2 Unsuk Chin's *6 Piano Etudes*
- 2.3 Unsuk Chin's *Piano Concerto*

Chapter 3: An analysis of Unsuk Chin's *6 Piano Etudes*
- 3.1 No 1, *in C*
- 3.2 No 2, *Sequenzen*
- 3.3 No 3, *Scherzo ad libitum*
- 3.4 No 4, *Scalen*
- 3.5 No 5, *Toccata*
- 3.6 No 6, *Grains*

Chapter 4: An analysis of Unsuk Chin's *Piano Concerto*
- 4.1 First Movement
- 4.2 Second Movement
- 4.3 Third Movement
- 4.4 Fourth Movement

Conclusion

References

Appendix 1: List of Unsuk Chin's work

Appendix 2: Letter of Permission

Figure 8.6 Table of Contents of Lim's (2018) Sydney Conservatorium performance thesis.

(see Figure 8.6). In her Introduction, Lim explains her reasons for studying Unsuk Chin's work and outlines the recital she gave of Chin's work as part of the requirements for her doctoral degree. Personal accounts were a feature of the Sydney Conservatorium of Music submissions. Lim explained the reason for the focus of her thesis:

> My curiosity regarding Korean contemporary piano music began when I came to Sydney in 2010 to study with Associate Professor Stephanie McCallum at the Sydney Conservatorium of Music, the University of Sydney. During the first lesson, which I still vividly remember, Stephanie and I discussed my first semester recital repertoire and she suddenly asked me, "Since you are from Korea, have you played a lot of pieces written by Korean composers like Isang Yun?" The question made a very strong impression, because although I am Korean, I had never played a Korean composer's piece, or even thought about Korean composers and their piano pieces.
>
> (p. 1)

Joanne Heaton's (2020) thesis 'Beyond the Baton: An investigation of the intangibles of conducting' submitted at the University of Sydney was submitted in the specialism of conducting. The thesis involved a substantial performance of her conducting a wind band repertoire of works by Ravel and other well-known composers. In order to do this, she formed her own ensemble of fifty-six players of various wind instruments. A video of the hour-long recital is included with her 126-page written submission in the University of Sydney online repository and can be downloaded and streamed at https://ses.library.usyd.edu.au/handle/2123/22420.

As she explained in our interview, the recital took place before she began the bulk of the research and writing for her empirical study and as the examiners would not have been selected at that point, they would have only seen the performance via the video in May 2020 when they would have received it together with the written component. The link between the recital and the written thesis is made clear through the inclusion in Appendix D (see Figure 8.8 for Table of Contents) of the fourteen-page recital programme in which Joanne states, 'This performance project has been launched as the cumulative practical activity for the fulfillment of [the] Doctor of Musical Arts, specializing in the area of Wind Band conducting.' She goes on to add, 'Data collection begins next month, with the assistance of some of the musicians from today's performance. Stay tuned for the findings of the completed research!' (Heaton 2020: 114). Figure 8.7 is the cover page of the Recital Program from Appendix D of her doctorate. In

Figure 8.7 Front cover of Heaton's DMA recital programme.
Image courtesy of Joanne Heaton.

this sense, her DMA differs considerably from Koh's where the performance component is not explicitly connected.

For all but three of the eight performance-based DMAs from the University of Sydney a video of the final recital is available in the online repository, although two can only be viewed with a university login. Kay (2019) and Meurant's (2019)

Beyond the Baton: An investigation of the intangibles of conducting

Abstract

Acknowledgements

Chapter 1 – The Motivation for this Research
  Preamble
  Outline and Aims of the Investigation

Chapter 2 – A Review of the Existing Body of Thought

Chapter 3 – The Methodological Journey
  The Research Method
  Design and Procedure
  My Reflective Portfolio

Chapter 4 – Primary Findings: The Interview Data
  Description of Data
  The Situation
  Individual Agency

Summary

Chapter 5 – Findings from Other Perspectives
  The Conductor's Perspective
  The Recital

Chapter 6 – Critical Considerations

Chapter 7 – Conclusion and Implications of this Study

Bibliography

Appendix A – Excerpts from the Reflective Diary
  Sample Lesson Notes
  Rehearsal Preparations
  Sample Phrase Analysis

Appendix B – Recital Repertoire Energy Graphs

Appendix C – Ethics Approval

Appendix D – Recital Program
  Program Bibliography

Figure 8.8 Table of Contents from Heaton's (2020) DMA submission.

composition DMAs have the scores, video recordings and relevant texts available in the repository.

Heaton's thesis sought to explore what she calls the 'the intangible forms of communication' (Heaton 2020: 10) between conductor and orchestra that make for a successful performance. To do this she interviewed eleven musicians who were part of the ensemble and two experienced conductors using a methodology known as phenomenography which seeks to understand how individuals attribute meaning to specific phenomena and situations. Her investigative approach draws therefore from the social sciences and it is perhaps not surprising that the chosen thesis macrostructure is a simple traditional one (see Table of Contents, Figure 8.8 for an overview of the thesis macrostructure).

Joanne spoke to us about her reasons for choosing to enrol in a DMA after a lengthy career teaching music and conducting school bands:

> I just really wanted to have a performance practice degree. I felt I already had two education degrees. … I wanted to do something for me and I wanted to better my conducting and that was an opportunity to have lessons. … I just

> really wanted to immerse myself and better my own musicianship I think was the reason for choosing the DMA over a PhD, which to me was kind of a little more of a solitary experience.
>
> (Heaton, interview. 2022)

Enrolling in the DMA also gave her the opportunity to study with a leading conductor who had just arrived from the United States to teach at the Conservatorium. At the same time, Joanne acknowledged the importance of the written component in the DMA and how it needed to connect with the practice-based component:

> But then of course when you do a DMA you have to make the writing match the performance in some way and that's incredibly difficult to do; to find a subject that you really want to tease out, but then link it to the content of the performance. So you know a lot of people end up analyzing a certain composer or something like that and will delve into the development of some repertoire, and then their performances is that repertoire. ... The basic premise is the content of the thesis must be linked to the performance or the performance must be linked to the content of the thesis, whatever your major is. Therefore a composition major might not actually be performing for theirs, but have a group perform their works.
>
> (Heaton, interview, 2022)

She then explained the challenge that this presented for her own thesis:

> For me it was tricky because on the one hand, you could look at it very loosely and say well I'm studying conducting, therefore, if I conduct it's relevant but there had to be more substantiation between the content of the thesis and the actual content of the performance, which is where the players in my ensemble that I conduct became the subjects of the research. They became the data and that's where the link grew from.
>
> (Heaton, interview, 2022)

Joanne recounted that in the early stages of her DMA, she must have downloaded 'a couple of hundred theses' as she sought an orientation for her own study and how to present it. Returning to academic study after a number of years, she then, in her first semester, took a methodology course which 'really gave me an overview of, okay, these are the hundred ways that we can write theses now', eventually settling on phenomenography as her chosen approach. Studying the methodological choices of others is described in the written component as 'invaluable' (2020: 29).

Similarly, an interaction with three exemplars of previously submitted theses helped her find her 'writer's voice'. After referring to herself as 'a reasonably verbose writer', she described how her supervisor encouraged her to write in 'more plain speak'. Her supervisor asked her to read three theses focusing on the writer's academic style. One of the theses was particularly important in the development of her writing as the author had adopted 'an incredibly plain speak, like ridiculously plain speak, … type of conversational writing'. Joanne found writing in a more narrative, personal voice challenging but was ultimately happy with the outcome, saying, 'When I'm in the literature review, I might be getting a bit verbose but by the time we're getting into working with the data it's very, very storylike, I think.' In the written component she reflects on the experience of examining the style of another thesis writer as a learning experience: 'His writing approach also gives the impression of the writer's honesty, and prompted me to consider what my writing "voice" should sound like. I suspect that my writing style falls more formally than Holgate's [the writer], however the experience of analysing his research has provided a sense of permission to write more plainly' (Heaton 2020: 29).

As is the case with several of the DMAs discussed in this chapter, Joanne's personal voice is evident in much of the thesis as she recounts the development of the musical project and her research. Chapter 1 starts with a fairly lengthy 'Preamble' which recounts Joanne's musical journey from her childhood to her becoming a conductor (see Table of Contents, Figure 8.8). In the section of the written thesis titled, 'Recital' (see Figure 8.8), she begins: 'A doctoral recital is a significant milestone in any musical journey and the preparation of this event took on great personal significance for me' (p. 78). Her use of a 'reflective diary' (see Figure 8.8, Appendix A) as a data source 'trying to pin down the electricity that happens between the conductor, and the performer' contributes to the sense of the connection between the written and performed components as do the interviews with band members.

As the Conservatorium requires that 'both components are expected to be an original contribution to the candidate's field of creative research' (https://www.sydney.edu.au/courses/courses/pr/doctor-of-musical-arts0.html), we spoke to Joanne about how she perceived her original contribution. She explained that, from her perspective, each performance is 'unique' inasmuch as 'if somebody else even did the same repertoire I did it would be completely different output', however,

> The need for the written to be original thought is critical and was expected. Particularly when I started to investigate and try and find previous writing

exactly on my topic there was almost none. There was a lot that danced around it, so that I think we had no problem with. As far as original work for the performance I don't recall it being measured to the same extent.

(Heaton, interview, 2022)

Both the Sydney University composition theses provided a research context to their work and support for the student's compositions. In this way, the composition theses were similar to the 'two part' model of PhDs by publication (Nygaard and Solli 2021) discussed in Chapter 9 of this book. That is, the thesis commenced with an overview and theoretical discussion of the student's work which both contextualized and supported their composition/s. Kay's (2019) 'Spectralism decomposed: An exploration of process and transformation through the improvisational network' is an example of this kind of thesis (see Figure 8.9). The Table of Contents of his thesis contains no mention of the prototypical constituents that might be found in the simple or traditional complex thesis and it can therefore be considered to be topic based. The twelve-page Introduction chapter however reads very much like a review of previous research in the field to introduce the key concept of spectralism in music and the work of its founders: 'Spectral composers followed a modernist agenda developing

---

Spectralism Decomposed: An Exploration of Process and Transformation through the Improvisational Network

Abstract

Table of Figures

Acknowledgements

Introduction

Instrumental Transformations
1. Sound to Image to Sound
2. Becoming Gong
3. Improvised Approximations

Metaphorical Transformations
4. Virtual Ensembles
5. Chaos
6. Cybernetics
7. Autopoietic Improvisers
8. Rhizome

Psychological Transformations
9. Morphing Trajectories
10. Territories of Oblivion
11. Fuzzy Periodicity
12. The Future Past
13. Perceptual Presence
14. The Edge of Continuity

Eclectic Emergences
15. Lehman's Liminality
16. Notational Recessions
17. In the Deep

Conclusions

Composition Portfolio

Bibliography

Figure 8.9 Table of Contents Kay's (2019) composition thesis.

during the late 1960s and early 1970s, identifying with the revolutionary zeitgeist occurring within society and science, seeking paradigmatic shifts within their musical agenda through a rethinking of form and experience' (p. 2). Elements of reviews of previous work are also found through the remaining chapters of the thesis as the processes of composition are analysed. The chapter titles are reminiscent of some of the new humanities theses we discussed in Chapter 5 and indeed some of the theorists whose influential work undergirds those theses are drawn on by Kay.

The final section of his thesis was titled Composition Portfolio in which he listed the performances he had given of his work. The scores for his compositions were also included with his submission and a video of the performance itself can be viewed on the University's digital theses platform.

When asked about the thesis in this kind of doctorate, one of the supervisors we spoke to in our earlier study explained its role as being

> to contextualize the performance or composition folio, by explicating the research that is underpinning the professional practice and how that research has informed the contents, creative philosophy, techniques etc represented in the folio (and examination recital). This also allows the candidate to argue for the originality of the contribution to the discipline and to position their work in the body of existing knowledge.
>
> (Supervisor survey, Academic writing in the visual and performing arts project, 2009)

In a follow-up interview, she added that while each doctoral project is individual, the thesis provides a space for students' scholarly reflection on their practice. When we asked a student about his thesis, however, he said 'I loved the research, I just hated writing it', reflecting the challenge writing a thesis is for many students doing practice-based doctorates.

Conclusion

The DMA or DMus is in some respects similar to a professional doctorate in that the authors of many of the submissions we examined are performers or composers with significant careers. This did somewhat hamper our ability to interview former students as many were extremely busy and hard to contact. For many, the DMA/DMus offers a route to an academic career in addition to that of a performer. At the same time, the doctorate is strongly reminiscent of the practice-based theses and dissertations in the visual arts that we examined in the previous chapter in that there are two distinct components, a written text and a practice or creative component (sometimes referred to as a portfolio) which may be linked in a variety of ways depending on the specific context and choices made by the individual student. Multimodality is also a strong feature of the written texts as musical scores are frequently included. Access to the creative components was not straightforward and it is unclear why recordings of performances had been uploaded in some instances but not in others.

The length of the written component varied considerably according to institutional settings with the DMAs from UC San Diego being noticeably shorter. The explicitness of relationships between the two components also varied, with many of the written submissions adopting what Vella (2005: 2) calls an 'exegetical perspective', taking the reader on the author's personal creative journey in a narrative, fairly descriptive mode. Burland, Spencer and Wilson (2017: 13) allude to this, noting that practice-based doctorates in music are individualized according to the needs, goals and current practice of the students and that it is the interaction of practice, self-reflection and identity that 'underpin the shape and progress of the project'. In their view, the need for individualization may contribute to a lack of standardization of the expectations for the doctorate in music, in particular the relationship between the creative portfolio and the written text. This may go some way to explaining that while the DMA/DMus appears to be fairly stabilized within particular institutional contexts we surveyed, there appears to be a degree of cross-institutional variation that it would be interesting to explore further.

9

Doctorates by publication

While common in the sciences, engineering and medicine, doctorates by publication – a compilation of journal articles either previously published or destined for publication – are a relatively new form of doctoral degree in the humanities and social sciences (Cayley 2020). Increasing pressure on students to publish during or immediately after their candidature is reshaping the doctorate in these fields. This version of the genre shares features of both the prestigious research article and more conventional features of the doctoral thesis. This chapter draws on a textual analysis of recently submitted theses by publication in the United States, the UK, Canada and Australia and interviews with students and supervisors to investigate the choices students make in their writing in what is relatively uncharted territory. University rules for the submission of doctorates by publication and related policy documents are also discussed.

Doctorates by publication

The doctorate by publication is variously called a thesis by publication (Nygaard and Solli 2021), a thesis with publications (Mason 2018), a publication-based thesis (Cayley 2020; Sharmani, Sproken-Smith, Goldman and Harland 2015), an articles-based thesis (Nygaard and Solli 2021), a manuscript-style dissertation (Anderson and Okuda 2019), a compilation thesis (Gustavii 2012), a PhD by published work (Smith, S. 2015) and a journal format thesis (Rigby and Jones 2020). The range of names given to this kind of doctorate reflects the unsettled and emergent nature of this variant of the doctoral thesis genre, especially in the social sciences and humanities, where it 'has not yet found its form' (Nygaard and Solli 2021: 2). As Nygaard and Solli (2021) explain, there are fewer shared conventions for how this type of doctorate might be written in the social sciences and humanities, compared to the fields of science, technology, engineering, mathematics and medicine where the doctorate by publication is more firmly established. There are also institutional differences in that a social sciences and humanities doctorate by publication in one area of study in one institution might look very different from a doctorate by publication in another area of study in the same institution or in a different institution in another part of the world (Nygaard and Solli 2021).

The doctorate by publication is a doctoral thesis that is not a monograph, but rather, a thesis that contains a number of articles or papers that have already been published or are aimed for publication with an accompanying text 'that explains how the papers or articles together form a larger coherent project' (Nygaard and Solli 2021: 4). The doctorate by publication (in nearly all cases a PhD) may be undertaken during an extended period of study as with other types of doctorate, that is, it may be *prospective* in that the student writes research articles during their enrolment in the degree with the intention of including them and having them evaluated as part of their doctoral submission (Nygaard and Solli 2021). The doctorate by publication may also be *retrospective* in that it may be a collection of already-published pieces of work that have then been submitted as a PhD, typically called a PhD by published work (Badley 2009; Smith, S. 2015). Although less common than the prospective PhD by publication, the retrospective PhD by publication is an option in some parts of the world. This is especially the case where, in the words of Nygaard and Solli (2021: 5), 'individuals who have been teaching and conducting research in higher education without a PhD are awarded a PhD degree by submitting a certain number of published texts without going through a formal PhD programme'.

The number of papers contained in a doctorate by publication is generally from three to six, although this varies across disciplines (Guerin 2016). A key feature of the doctorate by publication is that it has what Nygaard and Solli (2021) term a 'narrative text' which explains how the pieces of work relate to each other. This text involves the student 'writing *about* the articles, the research that took place behind them, and the relationship between the articles and the overarching doctoral project' (Nygaard and Solli 2021: 7). It also requires students to show how their thesis as a whole demonstrates doctorateness, that is, how it 'demonstrates research competence, higher-order thinking skills and mastery of disciplinary knowledge' (Nygaard and Solli 2021: 72–3) as well as the qualities of originality and publishability.

The doctorate by publication is particularly suited to someone who is aiming for an academic career as it means they will already have research publications when or soon after they complete their degree which will enhance their competitiveness and employability in the academic job market (Freedman 2018; Guerin 2016; Huang 2020; Liardet and Thomson 2020; Mason and Merga 2018a; O'Keeffe 2022; Thomson 2021). This kind of doctorate can also help students develop important research skills, such as managing the peer-review process (Jowsey, Corter and Thompson 2020), as well as help them develop confidence and their sense of themselves as scholars (Guerin 2016; Thomson 2021). Not every doctoral project is suited to this kind of PhD, however, as some projects may not be easily divided into separate pieces of work which they need to be if they are to be published as research articles that stand alone in their own right. And, of course, this kind of doctorate may not suit people who are wanting a degree that will help them advance in their professional lives rather than in an academic career (Nygaard and Solli 2021), although it may prepare them better for the kind of advanced-level writing they will do in professional settings than they might with a more traditional style PhD (Mason 2018).

Some universities encourage students to undertake a doctorate by publication as a way of increasing the institution's research outputs in a time when universities are facing more accountability for what they do as publications are one way in which university performance is measured and by which they are ranked. In addition, universities are often under pressure to take on doctoral students and to see that they complete on time. The doctorate by publication can help with this in that there are measurable steps and milestones for students to meet along the way. Students, further, can benefit from the reviews of their work in progress. They can also, however, be obstructed by this process, especially if the papers that will form part of their submission are 'pulled apart while going through the various review processes and journal pipelines' (de Lange and Wittek 2014: 391). A further problem is the time it takes for journal articles to be reviewed and accepted for publication (Cowden 2013; Jowsey, Corter and Thompson 2020). This may lead to students taking longer than expected to submit their thesis for examination (Nygaard and Solli 2021). The time it takes for articles to be accepted for publication may also explain why some of these doctorates include articles that have been submitted but have not yet been accepted for publication at the time the student submits their thesis for examination. There is, further, the danger that the research article/s may be rejected by the journal they have been sent to (Mason and Merga 2018a), meaning the student will have to try another journal in order to meet the requirements for the submission of their thesis. This can also add to the time it takes for them to complete. Another complication is if the university requires the student to submit their articles only to high-impact factor journals (Rahman and Jahan 2020) which typically have very low acceptance rates. And, of course, examiners need to be chosen who are familiar with and accepting of this kind of doctoral submission, especially where some of the chapters that make up the submission are co-authored, rather than just the student's work (Finkelstein 2022). This may be less of a problem in parts of the world where this kind of thesis is increasingly common but more so where it is not (Pretorius 2017). The doctorate by publication thus is not, in the words of Niven and Grant (2012: 110), an 'easy way out' to the award of a PhD.

A number of universities give explicit guidance to students on what to include in a doctorate by publication and how to arrange the submission. An example of this is Texas A&M University's guidelines for students doing a doctorate by publication in their College of Education and Human Development (Texas A&M University nd). Their guidelines for organizing this kind of dissertation are shown in Figure 9.1. Beyond this, however, the Texas A&M guidelines discuss matters such as the purpose of the Introduction and Conclusions chapters in a doctorate by publication, strengths and weaknesses of a doctorate by publication, the types of study that are best suited for this kind of submission, dealing with overlap and redundancy, authorship and requests for changes from journal editors and reviewers when writing this kind of dissertation. In answering the questions as to whether this format is easier than a traditional dissertation, their very clear answer, echoing the words of Nevin and Grant (2012), is 'Not at all', saying it may be more difficult to write this kind of dissertation given page restrictions laid down by academic journals. In addition, writers of this kind of dissertation need to take account of multiple readers who will assess the quality of their work, the journal editors and reviewers where they will send their articles as well their university's examiners of their dissertation.

---

1. Chapter 1 – Introduction
2. Chapter 2 – Manuscript #1
3. Chapter 3 – Manuscript #2
4. Chapter 4 – Manuscript #3
5. ….. [further chapters]
6. Chapter X – Conclusion
7. References
8. Appendices

Figure 9.1 Texas A&M guidelines for organizing a doctorate by publication.

Thesis types and the doctorate by publication

Anderson, Saunders and Alexander (2022) describe the overall organizational structure of the doctorate by publication as commencing with an Introduction section followed by each of the manuscripts which make up the thesis, followed by a Conclusion section, as in the Texas A&M model described above. Each of the manuscript chapters typically contains Methods, Results, Discussion and Conclusions sections. In addition, there may also be separate Literature review, Methodology, Discussion and Conclusions chapters in the thesis. Anderson, Saunders and Alexander (2022) found the dissertations in one of their studies which contained previously published work were largely from the one university suggesting a preference for this type of dissertation at particular institutions. They suggest the blending of more traditional types into hybrid dissertations might 'demonstrate an increasing move towards the acceptance of more flexible conventions with respect to dissertation writing' (19), at least within the context of the area of study focused on (Education) in their study. They also point out how these hybrid dissertation types were likely guided and influenced by the students' supervisory teams, showing 'the pervasive role of social factors in shaping genre decisions by writers' (19). In addition, Anderson and Okuda (2021) observe, in a subsequent study based on a corpus of 1,254 doctoral dissertations from a single Canadian university submitted from 1966 to 2018, that the PhD by publication had increased in popularity from 1999 when the first manuscript-style PhD appeared through to 2018 when the manuscript-style PhD had become equally as common as the traditional-simple PhD. The PhD, thus, had increasingly become manuscript-based and/or contained published sections at the particular university, many of which were co-authored with the students' supervisor (Anderson and Okuda 2021).

An example of a manuscript-style dissertation from Anderson, Saunders and Alexander's (2022) data set is shown in Figure 9.2. Each of the chapters in this dissertation is structured like a standard IMRD article. The thesis follows very closely the structure outlined by Anderson, Saunders and Alexander (2022) in that it commences with an Introduction chapter which is followed by article-type chapters, Chapters 2–5, which are then followed by a Conclusion chapter, Chapter 6. Each of the article-type chapters was laid out as they would be as journal articles. The articles had not, at the point of examination, been submitted to journals, although they were subsequently submitted and accepted for publication (Okuda 2018, 2019a, 2019b, 2020). In a sense then, this thesis (and other manuscript type PhDs by publication) has a structure which is similar to a complex traditional thesis.

The Writing Centre as a Global Pedagogy: A Case Study of a Japanese University Seeking Internationalization

Chapter 1: Introduction

Chapter 2: Policy Borrowing in University Language Planning: A Case Study of a Writing Center in Japan

2.1 Introduction
2.2 Policy Borrowing and Language Planning
2.3 Borrowing the Idea of the Writing Center
2.4 Research Site and Method
2.5 Language Planning Process of the MLU Writing Center
2.6 Discussion
2.7 Conclusion

Chapter 3: Generalist Tutoring at a Japanese University

3.1 Introduction
3.2 International Writing Centres: A General Review
3.3 Writing Centres in Japan
3.4 Role of Non-Specialists in Language Education
3.5 This Study
3.6 Findings
3.7 Discussion and Conclusion

Chapter 4: Perceptions of Non-native English Speaking Tutors at a Writing Center in Japan

4.1 Introduction
4.2 Non-Native Writing Center Tutors
4.3 Motives, Stances, and Roles: Insights from Peer Feedback Research
4.4 Methodology
4.5 Findings
4.6 Discussion and Conclusion

Chapter 5: The Writing Center and International Students in a Japanese University: A Language Management Perspective

5.1 Introduction
5.2 An Overview of Writing Centers and International Students
5.3 Bringing the Discussion to Japan
5.4 Re-examining the Intuitional Role of Writing Centers: A Language Management Perspective
5.5 Methodology
5.6 Findings
5.7 Discussion and Conclusion

Chapter 6: Conclusion

Figure 9.2 An example of a manuscript type dissertation (Okuda 2017).

The thesis shown in Figure 9.2, further, fits with the narrative framework proposed by Nygaard and Solli (2021) in that it commences with an Introductory narrative, presents the individual articles and ends with a Concluding narrative.

Gustavii (2012), referring specifically to the sciences, describes two ways in which PhDs by publication may be written. The first is what he terms the *Scandinavian model* because they are common in Scandinavian countries. This is sometimes called the *two-part model* of PhD by publication (Nygaard and Solli 2021). In the two-part model, there is an introductory section, often made up of several different chapters, followed by the articles or, in many cases, summaries of the articles. In this model the articles are 'sectioned off' and placed after the narrative rather than being placed inside it (Nygaard and Solli 2021).

McGrath's (2015) PhD 'Writing for publication in four disciplines: Insights into text and context' is an example of the two-part model of PhD by publication. Her thesis was submitted at Stockholm University and is based on four research articles, one that had been published, one that was under review at the time of submission, one that been submitted to an academic journal and one that was in press and was co-authored with her supervisor. Figure 9.3 shows the Table of Contents of McGrath's two-part thesis. The first of her chapters, the Introduction, provides the background to her studies and her second chapter the theoretical

Writing for Publication in Four Disciplines: Insights into Text and Context

1	**Introduction**	12
	1. ESP approaches to the investigation of writing for publication	15
	2. The use of English in writing for publication	16
2	**Theoretical framework**	20
	2.1 Discipline	21
	2.2 Disciplinary discourse	23
	2.3 ESP genre theory	24
3	**Methodology**	27
	3.1 Ethical considerations	27
	3.2 Methods and procedure	28
	3.2.1 Study I	28
	3.2.2 Study II	31
	3.2.3 Study III	35
	3.2.4 Study IV	36
	3.3 Concluding remarks	38
4	**Discussion and conclusion**	40
	4.1 Contribution to ESP genre research	40
	4.2 Contribution to ERPP research into publication practices	42
	4.3 Contribution to EAP research methodology	44
	4.4 Significance for EAP provision and pedagogy	45
	4.5 Limitations and future research	46
	4.6 Conclusion	47
5	**Summary of the studies**	49

Figure 9.3 An example of the two-part model of PhD by publication (McGrath 2015).

framework she is working with. Chapter 3 discusses methodological matters and Chapter 4 discusses her studies in relation to previous research. The published articles are not included in the thesis but are summarized in her final chapter, Chapter 5.

The other format proposed by Gustavii (2012) is the *sandwich model* in which the articles appear in their entirety as individual chapters between substantial Introduction and Conclusions chapters, as in the theses described by Anderson, Saunders and Alexander (2022) and the model proposed by Texas A&M University described above.

Stevenson's (2005) PhD 'Reading and writing in a foreign language: A comparison of conceptual and linguistic processes in Dutch and English' submitted at the University of Amsterdam is an example of the sandwich model of PhD by publication. She commences her thesis with an Introduction and preview chapter and ends it with a general conclusions chapter, between which she places four research articles. One of the research articles in her thesis is an adapted version of a paper that had already been published, and three were articles that had been submitted for publication and have subsequently been published (see Figure 9.4 for her Table of Contents). There are a number of authors on the articles as she did her PhD as part of a larger government-funded research project. She is however lead author on each of the articles.

Reading and Writing in a Foreign Language: A Comparison of Conceptual and Linguistic Processes in Dutch and English

1	Introduction and preview	1
2	Inhibition or compensation: A multi-dimensional comparison of reading strategies in Ll and FL	15
3	The relative importance of word-processing skills and strategy use in Ll and FL reading	59
4	Revising in two languages: A multi-dimensional comparison of on-line writing revisions in Ll and FL	95
5	Fluency and inhibition of higher level processing in L1 and FL writing	135
6	General conclusions	177

Figure 9.4 An example of the sandwich model of PhD by publication (Stevenson 2005).

Challenges in writing a doctorate by publication

Beyond the matters raised at the start of this chapter, a further challenge in writing a doctorate by publication is determining and agreeing on the authorship and level of contribution to the published work that will go in the thesis (Mason and Frick 2022), especially when students are publishing with their supervisor or as part of a broader research team. This can present challenges for examiners who are making a judgement on the quality of the student's work and need to have a clear understanding of which parts of the work are the student's and which parts are not. Also, as mentioned above, the turnaround time in the peer-review process can create a problem for timely completion, especially if the articles require substantial revisions (Merga, Mason and Morris 2019) or if the student sends their articles out for review close to their submission date. In addition, publication of the students' submissions is far from guaranteed (Kamler 2008), adding another level of stress and uncertainty to the process. Rejection of an article, further, can have a negative impact on the student's confidence and motivation, as well as their ability to complete on time (Mason 2018).

The breaking up of the student's research into publishable parts can also make it hard for them to see their work as a single and cohesive study. The relationship between the stand-alone articles and the thesis as a whole and creating coherence between the two can also be a problem for students. The different purposes and audiences for the research articles and the thesis can also be a challenge for student writers (Solli and Nygaard 2022). There is also the problem of the amount of overlap and repetition that may occur in the articles which can become apparent when the articles are brought together for the final thesis (Cayley 2020; Merga, Mason and Morris 2019). Different writing styles and expectations for each of the journals may also create problems for students when they are trying to bring the chapters together in their thesis.

Another challenge is if the focus of the study changes during the student's candidature and articles they submit early on do not have an easy fit with where the research ends up and the work it eventually contributes to. There is also the issue of whether the student produces enough papers during their period of study to meet their institution's submission requirements. And even if all the articles in the thesis have been accepted for publication, there is still no guarantee that an examiner will not ask for further revisions to the sections of the thesis that have already been published (Mason 2018). Beyond this is the challenge for students of finding a supervisor who is familiar with this kind of doctorate and who will agree to taking on supervising them writing a thesis in this way (Solli and Nygaard 2022).

Data and analysis

We collected 101 PhDs by publication for this chapter, the total number of theses of this kind that we were able to locate. These were from the United States (forty two), the UK (twenty seven), Canada (twenty) and Australia (twelve). The theses were analysed to see to what extent they fit, or not, with the macro-structure patterns described in previous research into the doctorate by publication. Interviews were also conducted with students and supervisors in order to explore the challenges they face in writing and guiding the production of PhDs by publication. We also examined University rules for the submission of PhDs by publication and related policy documents.

The US theses were located through ProQuest Dissertations & Theses (proquest.com) and the UK theses through the British Library EThOS site (ethos.bl.uk). We searched for the theses by using the key terms 'manuscript-style dissertation' in ProQuest and 'by publication' and 'by published work' in EThOS. The theses in Canada were much more difficult to locate, however, and were finally obtained through a colleague who had done research on a similar topic to that of this chapter. This colleague also reported having difficulty in finding PhDs by publication through Canadian university library searches and, finally, had to engage a research assistant to download all the PhDs submitted in the discipline he was interested in at each university and go through them to find which, amongst them, was a PhD by publication. The Australian theses were also difficult to locate and were mostly obtained through reference to specific theses in journal articles and book chapters written by students in Australia who described their experience of undertaking a PhD by publication. When we did find the Australian PhDs by publication, some, however, were only available for view in the university libraries and were thus not available electronically. The theses from Sweden, the Netherlands and Norway referred to above were obtained through personal contacts as well as through reference to theses by publication in published work on the topic. There was no special mention that the theses were by publication in this latter data set as they are by and large considered the norm for writing a PhD in these contexts (Gustavii 2012).

Findings

The United States

All of the US PhDs by publication, or as they are termed in the United States manuscript-style dissertations, were in the area of Education. Twenty-six of the PhDs were sandwich-style dissertations in that the dissertations followed the model presented earlier in this chapter. These were in the sub-areas of Urban Education, Science Education, Educational Counselling, Environmental Education, Gifted Education, Teaching, Higher Education, Human Development, Literacy Education, Teacher Education and STEM Education. Four of the sandwich-style dissertations were from New York University, four from the University of Georgia and four from the City University of New York. The others were from different universities in the United States.

Sixteen of the US PhDs by publication, however, were two-part dissertations which commenced with a section which showed the conceptual links between the papers that were included in the dissertation. The manuscripts which made up the dissertation were then presented. The two-part dissertations were all from the School of Education and Human Development at the University of Virginia. They were in the areas of Gifted Education, Special Needs Education, Teacher Education, STEM Education, Mathematics Education, Literacy Education, Online Learning, Early Childhood Education, Classroom Interaction and Student Behaviour. Two of the University of Virginia dissertations however simply presented the research articles which made up the submission. In one of these dissertations, there was an opening section, but it was extremely brief, only two pages. The introduction was a word for word repeat, however, of the abstract provided with the dissertation. The dissertation ended with a one-page summary which was, in essence, a paraphrase of the introduction. The merit of the degree then was the four manuscript chapters which made up the submission. Two of the articles contained in this submission had been published in high-ranking journals at the time of examination, one article was published after submission and the final chapter was accepted for presentation at an international conference. The other dissertation just included three research articles without the theoretical and methodological overview which was a feature of the other dissertations in this group. This submission included a letter from the student's supervisor pointing out that one of the chapters had been accepted for publication, one had been submitted for publication and the other was about to be submitted for publication. The letter also clarified the level of contribution the student had made to one of the papers which was multi-authored. There is, then, a clear preference for two-part dissertations in Education at the University of Virginia.

Figure 9.5 is an example of a sandwich-style dissertation from the US data, from the University of Idaho. The dissertation commenced with an Introduction which was followed by Literature Review and Methods chapters. Three papers were then presented, with each of the papers having very similar sub-section headings to each other. The dissertation ended with a general Conclusions chapter.

An example of a two-part dissertation from the US data is shown in Figure 9.6. The dissertation commenced with a section which showed the conceptual and theoretical links between the papers which were included, in their entirety, in the second part of the dissertation. Thus, the opening chapter is titled 'Conceptual Link' and the second chapter 'Three Manuscripts' where the student's papers are presented.

A number of the two-part dissertations also contained an overview statement which showed how the dissertation followed the university's guidelines for submission and a statement of authorship. One of the students said in her overview statement that the School's guidelines

> require the student to take a lead role on two research papers, contribute to a third research paper and submit an additional document that articulates the conceptual link among the manuscripts. I am the lead author on all three of the studies described here. Additionally, the first study has been accepted for publication in *Early Education and Development*, and the second two studies will be submitted to refereed journals upon completion.
>
> (Haak 2012: 2)

The School's guidelines also indicate the number of papers to be included in the submission, as well as point out that revisions may be requested on the papers, even if they have already been published.

A student we interviewed who had submitted her PhD at another US institution found there were no guidelines for this kind of PhD. As a result, she had to search for guidelines from other universities to help her structure her work. She found the Texas A&M guidelines shown in Figure 9.1 through an internet search and worked with these as she planned her writing, finding the concrete nature of the guidelines extremely helpful. In terms of authorship of her published papers, she was required to provide a written statement signed

What is Negentropy? A Manuscript Dissertation on "Negentropic Leadership" for Innovation and Change in Higher Education

Chapter 1: Introduction

Background
Purpose of The Study
Research Questions
Procedures
Definitions
Significance
Limitations
Organization

Chapter 2: Literature Review

Higher Education Organization Theory
Faculty Motivation
Effective Academic Leaders
Negentropy as Theoretical Framework

Chapter 3: Methods

Research Design for Manuscripts 1 and 2
Research Design for Manuscript 3

Chapter 4: Good Energy: Fostering Faculty Leadership and Innovation for Institutional Change (Manuscript 1)

Abstract
Introduction
Research Questions
Background and Literature Review
Theoretical Framework: Negentropy
Methods
Findings
Discussion
Implications for Policy and Practice
Future Research
Conclusion

Chapter 5: Rethinking Hiring and Socialization in the Selfie Era: Building a Faculty of "Negentropic Actors" (Manuscript 2)

Abstract
Introduction
Research Questions
Background and Literature Review
Theoretical Framework: Negentropy
Methods
Findings
Discussion
Implications for Policy and Practice
Future Research
Conclusion

Chapter 6: "Knowledge-Rich, Relationship-Poor": Online Doctoral Education for Faculty Career Preparation (Manuscript 3)

Abstract
Introduction
Research Questions
Background and Historical Context
Theoretical Framework
Methods
Findings
Discussion
Implications for Policy and Practice
Future Research
Conclusion

Chapter 7: Conclusion

Background on study
Summary of Findings
Contributions
Future Research
Conclusion

Figure 9.5 An example of a US sandwich-style dissertation (Thacker 2020).

Understanding Teacher Effectiveness: Theory and Measurement of Teacher Skills, Knowledge and Beliefs

Conceptual Link	1
Understanding Teacher Effectiveness: Rationale and Conceptual Link …	
Three Manuscripts	
Study 1: Assessing Teacher's Skills in Detecting and Identifying Effective Interactions in the Classroom: Theory and Measurement … …..	24
Study 2: Teacher Reflection in the Context of an Online Professional Development Course: Applying Principles of Cognitive Science to Promote Teacher Learning … … … … … … … … … … … … … … … ….	72
Study 3: Exploring Developmental Changes in Teacher Expectations and Associations with Children's Academic Achievement … … … … … …	120

Figure 9.6 An example of a US two-part style dissertation (Jamil 2013).

by her co-authors confirming the percentage of the contribution they had made to her publications. When asked however why she chose to do a PhD by publication, she said:

> It didn't intend to start that way. The project that I designed was a longitudinal mixed methods study of a whole cohort. I wanted to follow the students through their teacher education program and then into their first jobs but the data became so enormous, it was just easier to process the data in smaller chunks.
> (US PhD by publication student interview, 2022)

She found this chunking however challenging as the article chapters were constrained by size. An ethnographic chapter in her dissertation was about 20,000 words but the journal she was planning to submit the article to had an upper limit of 10,000 words. She didn't however submit the article until after she had completed her PhD. She had to, nonetheless, cut back the article to meet the word limit of the journal. Beyond this however she felt that, even in the dissertation, she hadn't been able to 'tell the whole story', commenting that this is still a challenge she faces in writing for publication.

There were features of the new humanities thesis in a number of the US doctorates by publication we examined. Ali-Khan (2011), for example, in the abstract for her City University of New York doctorate by publication 'In these bones the economy of the world: A multi-logical, multi-representational cultural study', provides a reflexive statement which is typical of new humanities PhDs. She lays out her theoretical position at the same time as she represents herself in the writing:

> In this work I offer critical interpretations of street skaters, images in schools, collaborative writing and discourses on Muslims in schools. Employing a phenomenological, hermeneutic approach, I have thought back on my experiences, made claims and supported them hermeneutically.
>
> (p. iv)

She then, in an account titled 'A personal introduction to really bad theory', makes connections between her life and her research in a way that provides a paratext for her dissertation:

> Some knowledge is "good for something" and some is quite the opposite. In 1989 Shahrazad Ali wrote *The Blackman's Guide to Understanding the Blackwoman*. It quickly made her famous. I do not know if my sweetheart at the time ever actually read the book of if he just watched her on The Sally Jesse Raphael Show, but when her theory met his life, my life changed dramatically.
>
> (p. 14)

Later, in a section titled 'Reflexivity and connections', she returns to race and other matters as she outlines the focus of her work:

> Positionality, or the intersection between race, class, gender, age, location (and other social categories), as well as the ability to belong to dominant groups and the fluidity with which we can pass between categories, defines what we are able to see and care about both in research and in life.
>
> (p. 24)

Ali-Khan's chapter titles (see Figure 9.7) play with words, are often metaphorical and draw on particular cultural references. The subtitle 'Shaken and stirred' in Chapter 1, for example, is a reference to 'Shaken not stirred', how Ian Flemings' fictional secret service agent James Bond likes his cocktails. 'I skate, therefore I am', a sub-heading in Chapter 2, references a song with the same title by Jimmy Bean and the Playground Revolution as well as the theme of skating which she threads throughout her text. Her dissertation, thus, is similar in many ways to the new humanities theses discussed in Chapter 5 and subsequent chapters of the book.

In These Bones the Economy of the World: A Multi-logical, Multi-representational Cultural Study

Chapter 1
The whole and the parts
Shaken and stirred: On coming to critical praxis

Chapter 2
Go play in the traffic: Skating, gender, and urban context
I skate, therefore I am
Half awake and half dreaming
Skating in toyland
Go play in traffic: Sport versus play
Access to a good drug
Life is elsewhere
These streets are home
Skateway

Chapter 3
Seeing what we mean: Visual knowledge and critical epistemology
Looking to see more
Halos, horns, and bog wallets: The visual construction of childhood
Re-loading the Matrix
She taught me to walk this way: Advertising images in schools
Seeing by the book: Visual literacy in schools
Seeing others
Closing thoughts on the meeting of visual and critical pedagogies

Chapter 4
Common sense, uncommon knowledge and fighting words
Teaching against
Teaching from
Teaching about
Other view of others
Afterword – Words to chew on

Chapter 5
Writing We: Collaborative text in educational research
Meeting
No bystanders: Constructing knowledge together
Kyle * Caroline * Marisol * Chris
Framing the collaborative production of knowledge and text in historical and ideological contexts
Bodies and hearts in schools
Students as coauthors
Coconstructed text and community – knowledge across difference
Towards a more equitable "we"

Chapter 6
To sea in a sieve
A world always already there
A world at my fingertips
Worlds awaiting

Figure 9.7 Table of Contents for Ali-Khan's (2011) dissertation.

The other US doctorates by publication that we collected, however, were not the same as Ali-Khan's dissertation in terms of reflexiveness or reflectiveness, making her dissertation somewhat of an outlier in the US data that we collected for this chapter. There was also little playfulness in the chapter titles in the other dissertations, perhaps because the articles had been written for publication and the student authors anticipated a certain level of conservatism on the part of journal editors and reviewers in this regard.

The UK

The PhD by publication was first introduced in the UK in 1966 at Cambridge University (Peacock 2017) and has, since then, slowly been accepted by other UK universities (Wilson 2002). A study published by the UK Council for Graduate Education (Christianson, Elliot and Massey 2015) found that 83 per cent of the fifty universities that took part in their research allowed the submission of a PhD by publication, or its equivalent. A subsequent study carried out by Rigby and Jones (2020) which examined the PhD by publication in Sociology and History found that eight of the twenty Sociology departments and fifteen of the thirty-three History departments they contacted allowed a PhD by publication. It is not clear, however, from higher education statistics data, how many PhDs by publication have actually been submitted in the UK (Peacock 2017), in part because there is no publicly available information on this and there are few, if any, organizational records kept on numbers of PhDs by publication being submitted in academic departments (Rigby and Jones 2020). Thomson (2021), in fact, points out that this type of PhD is still rather uncommon in the UK, at least in the ways it is seen in the United States and in Scandinavia. While some of the submissions for this type of PhD are called PhDs by publication in the UK, most frequently, however, they are what (Smith, S. 2015) terms 'PhDs by published work', that is, a collection of pieces of previously published work which, together, make a significant contribution to scholarship in the field. In some cases, there are very specific requirements for the submission of this kind of PhD, such as at the University of Cambridge whose guide for applicants states that

> the evidence in support of an application for the PhD Degree under these Regulations should comprise of a list of the published works submitted, two copies of those published works, and a short introductory summary of between 1,000 and 5,000 summarizing the rationale behind the work submitted, the extent to which the works constitute a consistent body of research and the original contribution to knowledge they make.
>
> (University of Cambridge 2017: 1)

In addition, the guidelines state:

When a candidate submits work published jointly with others, he or she should use the introductory statement to elaborate on his/her own contribution to such work.

(1)

The Quality Assurance Agency for UK Higher Education (QAA 2020) describes PhDs by published work as being

> normally awarded on the basis of a thesis containing a series of peer-reviewed academic papers, books, cited works or other materials that have been placed in the public domain as articles that have been published, accepted for publication, exhibited or performed, accompanied by a substantial commentary linking the published work and outlining its coherence and significance, together with an oral examination at which the candidate defends his/her research.
>
> (7)

Twenty-seven of the UK doctorates in the data we collected for this chapter were PhDs by published work and one was by publication (Kirchherr 2017). This is not to assume, however, that there are not more humanities and social sciences PhDs by publication (that is, prospective PhDs by publication) being submitted in the UK. We found it difficult however to locate them. Steven Day (2020) who is currently doing a doctorate by publication (an EdD) in the Faculty of Education at the University of Cambridge had the same difficulty when looking for previous examples of doctorates by publication, finding only one that had been awarded in his Faculty at the time he did his search. We were not, however, able to locate that thesis.

The PhDs by published work in the UK data set were in the areas of Education (seven), Visual Arts (three), Social Work (two), Music (two), Social Policy (two), Fiction (two), Media Studies (one), Art History (one), Film (one), Religious Studies (one), Archaeology (one), Law (one), Sport and Leisure (one) and Library Studies (ones). These PhDs were submitted between 1993 and 2019. The published works included in the UK submissions were journal articles, books chapters and papers from conference proceedings. However, published work also included books (in the areas of Education, Fiction, Media Studies, Art History, Social Work, Music and Visual Arts), music scores and recordings (Music), photographic works (Visual Arts), exhibition catalogues (Visual Arts) and sculpture (Visual Arts).

The submission by Black (2016) in the area of art history at the University of Glasgow was noteworthy in that it contained five books and seven journal articles. Black, like most of the authors of the PhDs by published work in the UK data set, was a very established scholar with the work in his submission dating from 1986 to 2016. Jackson's (1993) PhD in religious studies from the University of Warwick was based on work that had been published over five books and seventeen journal articles. The work he drew on in making his case for the award of the degree had been published between 1976 and 1993. Of the submissions that contained just journal articles and book chapters, Shibili's (2016) submission contained sixteen pieces of published work and Town's (2016) PhD eight published works. Some of the submissions, however, had generic titles such as 'Integrative chapter in support of the award of a PhD by publication' (Town 2016) and 'Explanatory essays and seven articles' (Black 2016), rather than titles which reflected the content of the work.

In terms of thesis type, all the UK PhDs by published work were similar to the Scandinavian two-part-style PhD referred to earlier in this chapter. They contained many more pieces of published work, however, than is the case with the Scandinavian submissions or the US two-part submissions described earlier in this chapter. In all cases, the UK submissions started with a review (and in some cases a critique) of the candidate's published work followed by a list of the publications that made up the submission and, in some cases, summaries of the publications. Hirst's (2019) PhD, 'Early childhood studies as a site for education for sustainability, eco literacy and critical pedagogy' awarded by Middlesex University is an example of this. The Table of Contents from her submission is shown in Figure 9.8. Her thesis was sixty-three pages long.

Early Childhood Studies as a Site for Education for Sustainability, Eco Literacy and Critical Pedagogy

Table of contents

Chapter 1: Autobiographical context for the portfolio of evidence
Chapter 2: Chronological description and development of the work
Chapter 3: Main methodological approaches
Chapter 4: Originality and evaluation of outputs
Chapter 5: Critical synthesis
Chapter 6: Critical reflection of self as a researcher
Chapter 7: Final reflections
References

Appendices
1: Curriculum Vitae
2: Visual flow of connections within communities of practice
3: List of refereed publications with confirmed contribution

Figure 9.8 Table of Contents of Hirst's (2019) Middlesex University two-part PhD by published work.

The first section of Hirst's (2019) submission is what (Smith, S. 2015) terms a 'synthesis' in which the candidate discusses the originality of her thinking, connections between her pieces of work and how the work made a contribution to knowledge over the time of its production. In some submissions (e.g. Brown 2001), this first section was titled a 'Context Statement'. Other titles are also possible for this part of the submission such as 'Doctoral Statement', 'Portfolio Summary', 'Cover Story', 'Exegesis', 'Summary of the Work' or 'Reflective Summary' (Smith, S. 2015) each of which also captures what Brown had done in this part of her thesis (see Chong 2021 for other possible labels for this section of a PhD by published work). The opening section of a PhD by published work, thus, is a commentary which links the published work and outlines its coherence and significance. The commentary can vary in terms of length and content, however, depending on university requirements (Chong 2021, 2022; Smith, S. 2015).

Beyond this, however, it is clear that the PhDs by published work met the typological requirements for the PhD referred to in Chapter 2. That is, they were all successful examples of the PhD in that they represented a significant, coherent and original contribution to scholarship in their particular area of study (Smith, S. 2015) and the examination committees which assessed the work and discussed it with the students in their oral examination (or viva) were in agreement about this due to the fact that the degrees had been awarded to the candidates.

Chong (2020) discusses his experience of having undertaken a PhD by published work in the UK. One of the most valuable experiences for him of doing a PhD this way was the opportunity it gave him to write up a commentary which demonstrated a 'golden thread' (Smith, S. 2015;: 95) of his publications and which enabled him to reflect on how his published work had contributed to his field of research. He does however point out that some people are sceptical of the value of doing this kind of PhD because of its short duration (from six to twelve months) and its lack of research training and supervision compared to a more traditional PhD in the UK (see Campbell 2022; Solli and Nygaard 2022 for further discussion of this).

A student we spoke to who was an established academic in a UK university and who had done a PhD by published work commented that she thought the PhD would push her to publish and 'keep her on track', even though she did have publications before she enrolled in the degree. She was fortunate, she said, that her supervisor had himself completed a PhD by published work, although not in the same area as her. He simply said 'Look at mine. It's not the same but it will help' which indeed it did. When she went to examination, she was asked to make only minimal changes to her submission, not to the published works, but to her reflections where she was asked to provide a little more detail and explanation of things. What she did find challenging however was that kind of PhD was still quite new at her institution. When she first expressed interest in doing a PhD by published work, the University had very little information to provide her with about what would be expected of her. This changed relatively soon after, however, and she was able to move ahead with it (UK PhD by published work student interview 2022).

While most of the UK doctorates by publication we examined were largely descriptive, there were some instances of submissions which were both reflexive and reflective. For example, Brown (2001) in her PhD from Middlesex University says:

> The researcher's biography is relevant to the research endeavor, not just in that it may impact on the research subject orientation but is also likely to impact on methodological approaches chosen as well as interpretation of the research data.
>
> (p. 20)

She then goes on to provide an extended account in which she shows how her personal life and her professional and academic experiences impacted on her research, all the while making connections between these experiences and the research approaches she employed in her work.

Reflective accounts of the writer's experience in relation to their research also occurred in several of the other UK submissions such as in Jackson's (1993) 'The interrelationship between religious education and religious studies' and Williams' (2018) 'Embers in the ashes: Apocalyptic horror and the creative process'.

Canada

Anderson, Saunders and Alexander (2022) carried out a study in which they examined doctoral submissions in the area of Education at five major Canadian universities over a ten-year period, between 2007 and 2017. They looked at the universities' writing guidelines and analysed the submissions in terms of thesis type, length of the submissions, co-authorship of thesis chapters and research design. Of the 1,373 dissertations that made up their data set, 184 of the submissions (13.4 per cent) were manuscript-style, that is, PhDs by publication. The manuscript-style dissertations averaged 52,000 words in length and contained an average of 5.5 chapters. Sixty-one per cent of the manuscript-style submissions drew on quantitative methods, 23 per cent mixed methods, 15 per cent qualitative methods and one of the dissertations contained no study design at all. In most cases the papers that were included in the submissions were collaboratively written; that is, they were co-authored. This was particularly the case with dissertations which employed quantitative and mixed methods study designs. Only eight of the twenty-eight qualitative dissertations however were co-authored. The longest manuscript-style dissertation in their data set was 120,000 words, whereas the shortest was made up of just three chapters. Two of the universities' writing guidelines gave an upper word limit of 100,000 words for submission, and three did not state a word limit. There was no minimum word limit in any of the university's guidelines. One of the universities said there must be more than one paper in their manuscript-style submissions, whereas the others did not specify a number.

A study by Anderson and Okuda (2021) which examined doctoral submissions in one research university in Canada over a period of fifty-two years (1966–2018) found that manuscript-style dissertations have become much more common in that university's Faculty of Education and that traditional-simple style dissertations have fallen in popularity by a considerable amount. They also found co-authorship was becoming common in manuscript-style submissions at that university with 25 per cent of submissions in the final six years of their data collection listing co-authors of the manuscripts contained in the dissertations with a statement of authorship being required by the university in a preface to the submission.

In a jointly authored paper, Anderson and Okuda (2019) discuss their experience of writing, defending and preparing material for publication from a manuscript-style dissertation. They make the important point that students writing this kind of dissertation need to consult their university's guidelines in terms of rules regarding co-authorship and using previously published manuscripts (as opposed to *publishable* manuscripts) in their dissertation. They also point out that tensions could arise if an examiner makes a condition that a previously published manuscript be revised for the degree to be awarded. For this reason, they held off submitting the core chapters from their dissertation to academic journals until after the examination of their dissertation.

The PhDs by publication in the Canadian data set were all sandwich-style dissertations and were all in the area of Education. They were from the University of British Columbia, the University of Toronto, McGill University, Simon Fraser University and the University of Alberta. Three of the dissertations contained only one previously published paper while one of the dissertations contained eight. Mostly, however, the dissertations contained from three to five published or about to be published papers. Figure 9.9 shows the table of contents from one of the manuscript-style dissertations in the Canadian data set (Jackson, P. A., 2013). This dissertation included one published paper and two that were being prepared for submission to academic journals. Each of the journal article chapters, Chapters 2, 3 and 4, contained components that would be expected in published articles, that is, an overview of the theoretical

---

Better Late than Never? Identity Work, Trajectories and Persistence of Latecomers to Science

Chapter 1: General Introduction

Overview of Theoretical Framework
Context
General Methodology
Overview of Chapters 2–4

Chapter 2: Science Identity Trajectories of Latecomers to Science in College

Abstract
Theoretical Framework
Methodology
Findings
Discussion
Conclusion
Acknowledgments
References

Chapter 3: Identity Work in the College Science Classroom: The Cases of Two Successful Latecomers to Science

Abstract
Theoretical Framework
Methodology
Findings
Discussion and Implications
Conclusion
Acknowledgments
References

Chapter 4: I am Smart Enough to Study Postgraduate Science: A Critical Discourse Analysis of Latecomers' Identity Construction in an Online Forum

Abstract
Theoretical Framework
Methodology
Findings
Discussion
Conclusion
Acknowledgments
References

Chapter 5: Conclusion

Summary of Findings and Original Contributions to Knowledge
Implications for Practice: Providing New Resources for Identity Work
Directions for Future Research

Bibliography

Figure 9.9 An example of a Canadian sandwich-style manuscript dissertation (Jackson, P. A., 2013).

framework employed in the study, followed by Methodology, Findings, Discussion and Conclusions sections.

A number of submissions also contained a section titled 'Statement of authorship and remarks on style' in which the student clarified her level of contribution to the dissertation chapters, as in the following example from (Jackson, P. A., 2013: viii) thesis:

> This thesis follows a manuscript-based format. As is expected in this format, there is some repetition in the text. As primary author of every chapter, I conceptualized and carried out all aspects of the research and also wrote the current dissertation in its entirety. Chapter 2 is co-authored with Dr. … …. and has been published in the *Journal of Research in Science Teaching*. Chapters 3 and 4 are in preparation for submission to peer-reviewed journals. As my doctoral supervisor, Dr. … … has served in an advisory capacity during the conceptualization of this research, formulation of the research questions, and writing of the dissertation. She has provided guidance, feedback and critique throughout the project. For Chapter 2, Dr. ….. contributed to the initial drafts and to the publication revision process, working closely with me to address reviewers' comments.

Only eight of the twenty Canadian PhDs collected for this chapter, however, contained such a statement. This could, of course, be because the authors of the other dissertations were sole authors of the work and there was thus no need for a co-authorship statement (see Anderson and Okuda 2021; Gross, Alhusen and Jennings 2012 for further discussion of co-authorship in doctoral dissertations).

A student who had done a PhD by publication at one of the Canadian universities in our data set said his university was extremely flexible in what they expected a student to submit for this type of PhD. There was a submission that contained only one paper and was thirty-five pages long through to submissions that were much longer than his (his PhD was 200 pages). He did however get 'blowback' from other PhD students in his department who felt he had taken the easy way out in his PhD, which of course was not the case. He, in fact, said he found the writing of his dissertation, especially in the very early stages of his study, a 'trial by fire' and that it was far from easy. One thing he found especially challenging was bringing together the density involved in writing research articles with the more extended expectations of dissertation writing. He did however find the experience of having done a PhD by publication set him up for getting the tenure track position he later went on to, which he didn't think he would have obtained had he not done his PhD this way.

In his thesis from the University of British Columbia, Anderson (2016), after describing personal, professional and academic reasons for carrying out his research, describes his positionality thus:

> The above-described cumulative interests and experiences, combined with the lack of research in the area, have therefore been the primary drivers for my decision to research this topic. These experiences and positionalities have also provided me with both an insider and outsider perspective to guide this research process, particularly being a PhD student myself and experiencing many of the same pressures, challenges, and successes learning and adapting to the rigours of academic life during my PhD. I also, however, recognize my own involvement in subjectively shaping, interpreting, and representing the stories and experiences of the seven participants in this study – indeed the inevitable *situatedness* of the qualitative research process.
>
> (p. 11)

MacEntee (2016), similarly, in her UBC thesis 'Can participatory visual methods make a difference? Responding to HIV and AIDS in rural South African schools', explains her connection to her research:

> In 2008, following my master's degree, I had the opportunity to visit South Africa as an intern with the Rural Teacher Education Project. My role was supporting preservice teachers during their four-week practicum at two schools in a rural region of KwaZulu Natal. During this time, I was introduced to some of the complexities of addressing HIV and AIDS in schools. The setting of the resource-deprived school was quite different from any of my schooling experiences in Canada or in Europe and was also a new experience for many of the practicum teachers who had grown up in comparatively affluent urban settings in South Africa. I facilitated the preservice teachers' day-to-day activities, including daily debriefing sessions of their practicum experiences. I integrated participatory visual methods such as collage and drawing into these sessions to encourage self-study on how we saw ourselves in this context. I also encouraged the teachers to integrate issues of HIV and AIDS into their classroom practice.
>
> (pp. 237–8)

In a section titled 'Positionality', Okuda (2017) does something similar as she writes about her experiences and motivations for carrying out her study. None of the other Canadian PhDs by publication, however, contained reflective comments of this kind.

Australia

A study by (Jackson, D., 2013) into PhDs by publication in thirty-four Australian universities found there are three main kinds of PhDs by publication available there. The first, a 'PhD by prior publication' (that is, a PhD by published work for established academics), was available in nine of the universities which took part in the study. Applicants for this kind of PhD were required to submit their thesis within three to twelve months of enrolling in the degree. The second was a 'PhD by publication' which is basically the same as the manuscript-style dissertations discussed earlier in this chapter. Twenty-three of the thirty-four universities offered this kind of PhD. The third kind of PhD by publication was a hybrid thesis type which combined the two other models and which allowed students to include papers in their thesis that they had published prior to the commencement of their candidature. This was offered by five of the thirty-four universities.

The PhDs by publication in the Australian data set were in the areas of Education, History, Linguistics, Environmental Studies, Urban Geography, Music and Social Work. Eight were sandwich-style theses and four were two-part theses. Swapan's (2018) PhD, for example, was a two-part thesis in that the articles were summarized in the first part of the thesis and the articles were attached in a second part to the thesis, separate from his argument for their inclusion in his submission.

Three of the PhDs, further, were retrospective, that is, they were PhDs by published work. The PhDs by published work were in the areas of History, Music and Visual Arts. Clarke's (2004) PhD by published work focused on six previously published books about women in nineteenth-century Australia. It was a two-part thesis in that the first section of the thesis provided a thirty-six page overview of the books which was then accompanied by copies of the books. Savage's (2008) PhD in Music was an autoethnographic account of his public activity as a musician. Recordings of his performances were appended to the submission which was also a two-part thesis. The performances in his submission, thus, were his publications, in a way that is similar to the practice-based PhDs discussed earlier in this book.

Di Mauro's (2015) PhD by publication was a reflection on his art practice over twenty years in which he drew connections between his creative works and his Italian heritage. He did this over an Introduction and two chapters titled 'Receptions to my art practice, 1995–2015' and 'Connections between my work and other selected artist's work', respectively. The thesis ends with a Conclusion chapter (see Figure 9.10). This section of the submission is eleven pages long. The Conclusion is followed by References and Bibliography sections followed by Appendices which include his CV and accounts of his art works. The thesis was accompanied by a DVD which documented his creative work which, similar to the submission by Savage (2008), presented his creative work as the publication component for a PhD by publication.

Stories in Search of a Perfect Home: Sebastian Di Mauro's Visual Arts Practice 1995–2015

Table of Contents

Introduction	Questions Framing the Thesis
	Art Education Cultural Policies and my Developing Visual Arts Practice
	Contemporary Australia: Various Contexts
	Notions of Home
	A Human Presence
	Chapter Outline
Chapter 1	**Reception to my Art Practice, 1995–2015**
	Nature
	Suburban Dreams
	Being Australian
	Commissioned Public Art
	Growing up with an Italian Heritage
Chapter 2	**Connections between my Work and Other Selected Artists' Work**
	Links between Arte Povera and my Practice
	Context and Comparative Analysis: Selected Contemporary Artists
	Hossein Valamanesh
	Mona Hatoum
	Do Hu Suh
	Anigh Kapoofr
	Roxy Paine
Conclusion	
References	
Bibliography	
Appendices	
	Chronology
	Curriculum Vitae

Figure 9.10 An example of an Australian two-part PhD by published work (Di Mauro 2015).

An example of an Australian sandwich-style PhD by publication (Cowden 2012) is shown in Figure 9.11. The thesis commences with an Introduction which describes the aim and structure of the thesis, then summarizes each of the papers that make up the submission. The papers are then presented. The thesis ends with a Conclusions and Future Directions chapter.

Do Children Have Rights? Five Theoretical Reflections on Children's Rights

Table of Contents

Chapter One: Introduction
1.1 Introduction
1.2 Thesis Aim
1.3 Thesis Structure
1.4 Summary of Papers
    1.4.1 Paper One
    1.4.2 Paper Two
    1.4.3 Paper Three
    1.4.4 Paper Four
    1.4.5 Paper Five
    1.4.6 Concluding Chapter
1.5 Conceptual Clarifications
1.6 Children's Rights so Far
1.7 Conclusion
1.8 References

Part One: Theoretical Basis

Chapter Two: Capacity, claims and children's rights
2.1 Abstract
2.2 Concepts and Definitions
2.3 Theories and Functions of Rights
2.4 Realising Rights and Imposing Duties
2.5 Conclusion
2.6 References

Chapter Three: 'Capacity' and 'Competence' in the Language of Children's Rights
3.1 Abstract
3.2 Part One

Part Two: Cases and Application

Chapter Five: What's Love Got to Do with it? Why children have a right to be loved?
5.1 Abstract
5.2 Introduction
5.3 Liao's argument and empirical nonsense
    5.3.1 Maternal Deprivation
    5.3.2 Acute Distress
    5.3.3 Experiential/nutritional privation
    5.3.4 Bond privation and antisocial disorder
    5.3.5 Is this lack of love?
5.4 Loving is not a duty
    5.4.1 The command problem
    5.4.2 What does love add?
5.5 Some alternatives
    5.5.1 Love as a manifesto right
    5.5.2 Non-interference and architecture
5.6 Conclusion
5.7 Notes
5.8 Refences

Chapter Six: No harm, no foul: donor conceived children and the right to know their genetic parents
6.1 Abstract
6.2 Introduction

3.3 Part Two
    3.3.1 The case of capacity and competence
    3.3.2 A conditional analysis of competence
3.4 Part Three: External conditions and Ableness
3.5 Part Four
    3.5.1 The Series Problem
    3.5.2 The objection from 'constant competence'
3.6 Part Five: Application to the rights of the child
3.7 Part Six: Conclusion
3.8 Reference List

Chapter Four: Children's Rights and the Future Interest Problem
4.1 Abstract
4.2 Introduction
4.3 The Future Interest Problem
4.4 Potential Solutions
    4.4.1 Feinberg
4.5 Reconciling Rights and Future Interests
    4.5.1 Capacities and Competencies
4.6 Positive Duties
4.7 Constraints on these rights
4.8 Some objections
    4.8.1 Deafness as a Disability
    4.8.2 Protecting Core Capacities
4.9 Conclusions
4.10 Notes
4.11 Reference List

6.3 Australia and Anonymous Donor Conception
    6.3.1 History of Anonymity in Australia
    6.3.2 Legislation in Australia Today
6.4 A Child's Right to Know
    6.4.1 Genetic and Medical History
    6.4.2 Consanguinity
    6.4.3 Psychological Harm
6.5 No Harm, No Foul
    6.5.1 Inadequacy of Arguments from Harm
6.6 Risk of Harm and Respect
    6.6.1 Risk of Harm
6.7 Respect
    6.7.1 Two Claims – Two Rights?
6.8 Conclusion
6.9 Notes
6.10 References

Chapter Seven: Conclusions and Future Directions
7.1 Conclusions and Future Directions
7.2 Children Have Rights
7.3 Capacity and
7.4 Duties
7.5 Children's rights as special claims
7.6 A strong theory
7.7 Future Directions for Research
    7.7.1 Hohfeld
    7.7.2 Capacity
    7.7.3 Duties
7.8 Conclusion
7.9 References

Figure 9.11 An example of an Australian sandwich-style PhD by publication (Cowden 2012).

Only two of the Australian PhDs by publication had a reflective component to them. Savage (2008) explained how his life connected with his research and Di Mauro (2015) made connections between the creative works he submitted for examination and his Italian heritage. Both these theses were from the same university, Griffith University in Queensland, but from different departments, the Queensland Conservatorium of Music and the Queensland College of Art, respectively. Further, while they were submitted as PhDs by publication, they were both in the visual and performing arts and bore similarities to the submissions described in Chapters 7 and 8, rather than those described in this chapter.

There are, then, various types of PhDs by publication in Australia. That is, they may be sandwich-style theses or two-part theses, especially if it is a PhD by published work. Beyond this, both prospective and retrospective PhDs by publication were seen in the Australian data collected for this chapter.

Cowden (2013) writes in a reflective piece titled 'A PhD by publication or how I got my doctorate and kept my sanity':

> I did my PhD in a department [Politics and International Relations] which was still sorting out its policy towards this format. As a consequence I needed the strong support of my supervisor and head of department to make this work (which I was lucky enough to have). You shouldn't expect a clear set of instructions here; guidelines and policies seem to vary between departments, disciplines and universities.

The biggest advantage, however, with doing this kind of PhD, she argues, is that she came out of her doctoral studies not only with a PhD but with a healthy publication record which would help her when taking the next step in her career.

Nethsinghe and Southcott (2015: 167), also writing in Australia, discuss writing the doctoral thesis by publication as a 'juggling act between maintaining coherence and focussing on publishable segments' of the work. It is also 'a dialogue between supervisor and candidate involving the resolution of sometimes conflicting demands'. They also discuss the 'inbuilt risks' (p. 180) of producing a thesis by publication, saying that students need to be strategic in their journal selection, 'always have a back-up plan, keep the overall frame of the topic and methodology in mind, and work hard' (p. 180). They also say that the thesis by publication, on occasion, required steady nerves. The active support of the student's supervisor, Robins and Kanowski (2008) argue, is central to the enabling of publications for this kind of thesis as well as the broader achievement of the PhD by publication.

A study carried out by Liardét and Thomson (2020) in Australia explored the factors that influenced students' choice of writing a PhD by publication versus a 'monograph' style thesis. The students they surveyed were in the humanities, science, medicine, the arts and business and economics. Liardét and Thomson were especially interested in whether language background, in terms of being a first or second language writer, influenced the students' choices. They found that the second language writers at their university were more likely to do a PhD by publication than first language writers. They asked both students and supervisors about this. Some supervisors, they found, advised against writing a thesis by publication. One of the supervisors they spoke to said:

> I really try to share with them that [a thesis by publication] might sound that it's easy but it's actually really hard to do because you are constantly riding a rollercoaster: you write a paper, you submit a paper; you get the rejection … so it's actually cognitively very difficult for them to do these two tasks at the same time … and of course some projects will never really work that way … it really depends on the project. Does it lend itself to a thesis via publication?
>
> (Liardét and Thomson 2020: 7)

Some students, however, viewed this choice very differently, with one student saying:

> It just made sense … and it's beneficial to me and the university … You often hear about people doing a thesis-by-monograph and then having to turn around and re-form the papers into chapters and how hard it is to do and half the time they don't get to do it.
>
> (Liardét and Thomson 2020: 9)

In addition, there was the case of departmental expectations, with a Psychology student saying, 'I decided to do the thesis-by-publication because that's generally what the department does' (p. 9). Liardét and Thomson also found some second-language students saying that they found the idea of writing up research articles easier, and more manageable, than writing a full-length monograph-style thesis, suggesting a reason why so many second-language students at their university did their thesis by publication.

One of the students we spoke to for our book who had done a 'PhD with publications' (the University of Sydney name for a PhD by publication) said she chose that route because her supervisor had suggested she might want to do it. She liked this idea as she was already doing casual academic teaching and wanted to go on to become an academic. Writing her thesis with publications meant she could publish along the way and would, as Cowden (2013) mentions above, increase her list of published papers before she completed her PhD. Beyond this, however, she said the studies in her project lent themselves 'to being written about individually more than just as one collective whole'. She found it difficult, however, to find examples of what a PhD with publications should look like as they seemed to be different across Faculties. She did, however, attend workshops in her Faculty which gave advice on what a PhD with publications might look like which she found very beneficial. One thing she especially liked about the PhD with publications was that she wrote early and often and got feedback from peers on her work. She also found the process of submitting papers to academic journals introduced her to the world of academic peer review, although, she said, sometimes the harshness of it was upsetting and, as she said, 'I'm still learning to deal with that' (University of Sydney student interview, April 2022).

A supervisor we spoke to at the University of Sydney found it difficult to find university guidelines for writing a PhD by publication and consulted colleagues who she knew had supervised this kind of PhD for advice. One of the examples she looked at had inserted the articles that had been published into the thesis in the exact same pdf format in which they had been published. She advised her student to do this as it presented the completeness of the articles as well as discouraged examiners (she hoped) from asking for changes to them. A challenge however she felt this kind of PhD presented for students was dealing with the succinct and focused nature of research articles in contrast with the more expansive discussion of research that is typical of a more traditional PhD. She described writing the thesis as

> a little bit like building a brick wall, the journal articles are the bricks, and the cement is the other chapters in the thesis.
> (University of Sydney supervisor interview, April 2022)

Conclusion

This chapter has examined the doctorate by publication in the humanities and social sciences in a number of different countries, and in particular the United States, the UK, Canada and Australia. It has found that the doctorate by publication is available in each of these countries, but there seems to be a preference for different types of doctorate in each of the countries. In the United States, where the doctorate by publication is referred to as a manuscript-style dissertation, they were all prospective PhDs with the work being especially written for the thesis. In terms of dissertation types, however, there were examples of both sandwich and two-part dissertations in the data that we collected from the United States. In the UK, by contrast, retrospective PhD, the PhD by published work, seems to dominate and all of the UK doctorates were two-part theses. They however, by and large, included many more pieces of work than did the US PhDs by publication. Canada was found to be similar to the United States, at least in the area of study where the data were collected for the chapter, Education. All the Canadian PhDs, however, were sandwich-style theses as opposed to the United States where they were both sandwich- and two-part-style dissertations. In Australia, both prospective and retrospective PhDs were found, although it was the former, the prospective PhD, which dominated. The prospective PhDs were sandwich-style theses, whereas the retrospective PhDs were all two-part theses. In addition, while the US and UK PhDs by publication had features of new humanities PhDs, this was much less prominent in the Canadian and Australian PhDs by publication we collected.

A further aim of the study was to see to what extent the theses in the collection fitted with previously published research on thesis types. The theses that were collected, to a great extent, fitted with Nygaard and Solli's (2021) work on sandwich and two-part thesis types. Thus, from a taxonomic perspective the theses fitted well with previous descriptions of thesis and dissertation types. From a typological perspective they were all successful texts in that they all met their university's requirements for the award of the PhD.

A matter we weren't able to address however is what happens when an examiner is not happy with the published work and requires revisions to it. None of the students we spoke to had had this experience. That is not to say however that it cannot happen. There is also the matter of guidelines for examiners for this kind of PhD. Most universities that we are aware of send their general PhD examination guidelines to examiners, regardless of the thesis type. Advice to examiners as to how to treat the published work would be helpful to them, we have been told, especially when they are uncertain of the quality of this work. This brings us to the question of what indeed is 'publishable quality' in relation to the work included in a PhD by publication? Nygaard and Solli (2021) point out that this is difficult to assess. They add, further, that including articles that have been published does not in itself constitute doctorateness, making it especially important that this is shown in the narrative sections of the text which accompany the published work.

There are further limitations to the work presented in this chapter. One is the size of the sample on which the chapter is based and the uneven number of theses in each of the country groups. We could, of course, have made the number of theses in each group more even by just choosing ten PhDs from each of the countries. In doing this, however, we felt, we would have limited what we might have seen in our analysis. The Canadian theses, further, were only from a single study area, whereas the areas of study for the UK and Australian data sets at least were wider. This was the result of the difficulty of identifying doctorates by publication in university libraries and thesis and dissertation databases (see Data and analysis above). Another limitation is the disciplinary areas in which we examined doctorates by publication. There may well be doctorates by publication in other humanities and social science areas of study that we are not aware of which would be useful to examine as well. It is, thus, not possible to generalize our results to other humanities and social science areas in universities other than the ones we examined. A further matter that could be explored in more detail than we have been able to here is the comparative reputation of PhDs by publication and the institutional weight of these kinds of PhDs compared to more traditional PhDs. This is something that would benefit from being examined, perhaps by large-scale survey, which examines the views of not only students and supervisors but also other stake holders such as university and other kinds of employers as well as committees tasked with the overall process, procedures and award of doctoral degrees. Notwithstanding, our study has implications, we feel, for the teaching of thesis and dissertation writing and the supervision of theses by publication. Often doctoral writing guides and handbooks offer generic descriptions of doctoral theses but few have provided analyses of the PhD by publication in the humanities and social sciences in different parts of the world in the way that we have in this chapter, an instance of the doctoral dissertation genre which, while having some local instances of stability, has not yet reached a level of stability, overall.

10

Genre evolution in thesis and dissertation writing

Earlier in this book we discussed Carolyn Miller's (2016) work on genre evolution in which she considers how genre change over time involves the inheritance of genre features from earlier exemplars of the genre. We have seen just this in our book where the earliest PhDs at the four English-medium universities where we collected our data had features which have become more formalized in subsequent examples of the doctoral dissertation. An example of this is the traditional simple dissertation type which has extended to the traditional complex form which takes the earlier form which is based on a single empirical study and re-works it when the dissertation presents more than a single study. We have also seen the continuation of topic-based dissertations, from the earliest submissions to the present day. We have also seen the dissertation types we have discussed being employed in professional doctorates, such as the EdD, and in the PhD by publication. In addition, alternate forms of submission are now being accepted as part of the dissertation genre category in particular areas of study, for example, the visual arts and music. And we have seen features of new humanities dissertations appearing in areas of study such as the visual arts, music and education in addition to fields such as sociology.

The notions of typology and taxonomy (see Chapter 2) have been useful for helping us understand variation in doctoral submissions, that is, the formal structures (taxonomy) and expected characteristics (typology) of doctoral submissions. Some of the submissions we examined were examples of the dissertation genre from a taxonomic point of view, whereas other relied more on a typological view for us to see the dissertations as successful examples of the doctoral dissertation.

Prototype and family resemblances (see Chapter 2) are also important notions for discussions of doctoral submissions. According to prototype theory, people categorize items and concepts according to a prototypical image they build in their mind of what it is that represents the particular item or concept. This, plus the notion of family resemblances, allows language users to see instances as being more or less typical of a particular category, but still be members of that category (see Chapter 2 for further discussion of this). This is in contrast to a defining features view which holds that items which exhibit all the defining features of a category are members of that category and those which do not are not. A prototypical view of categorization, thus, allows for the inclusion of less typical instances of a doctoral dissertation within the same genre category rather than a view where entities are classified into sets with clear-cut boundaries and where instances are seen as belonging to a genre category, or not.

Patrick Stewart's (2016) PhD 'Indigenous architecture through indigenous knowledge', referred to in Chapter 2, illustrates how the notions of prototype and family resemblances allow less typical (and alternate) doctoral submissions to be considered as examples of the doctoral dissertation genre. Stewart, a First Nations scholar, wrote his dissertation as 'a form of grammatical resistance' (p. xvi) to the acceptance of English language conventions in the academy. He describes his submission as 'one long, run-on sentence, from cover to cover. There's nothing in the (UBC dissertation) rules about formats or punctuation', he said. Some people 'thought it was great', he said and others most certainly didn't. He was both cautioned and warned. Some people, he was told, just wouldn't get it. The first draft of his dissertation was in Nisga'a, his own indigenous language. The professor who had the role of signing off on his dissertation told him this was not acceptable and that he had to translate his dissertation into English which he did. After a long dissertation defence, which included two hours of questions, the examiners retired to vote on whether to accept the dissertation or not. Stewart was called back and told the vote had been unanimous. He had passed his defence (Hutchinson 2015).

And of course, notwithstanding the challenges that Patrick Stewart faced, the dissertation does not always need to be written in a language of the academy. An example of this is a PhD that was awarded to Roxana Quispe Collante in 2019 by the University of San Marcos in Lima where the student wrote and defended her dissertation entirely in Quechua, the language of the Incas and not the language of the academy, in this case, Spanish. This was the first time in the university's 468-year history that this had been done (Simon 2019). It was a long road, she said, 'but it was worth it' and 'I hope my example will help to revalue the language again and encourage young people, especially women, to follow my path' (Collyns 2019).

We have, thus, seen both change and stability in thesis and dissertation writing, the title of our book. The points we now need to consider are, what are the forces for change that have been behind this evolution and how might the PhD be re-imagined for the future? These are matters that we turn to in this, the final chapter of our book.

Forces for change

When we first conceptualized writing a book about the evolution of the doctoral thesis/dissertation, the world had not yet heard of Covid, and the term 'variant' did not have the connotations it has today. In the early 2000s, Chris Park, a British academic, in a paper titled, 'New variant PhD: The changing nature of the doctorate in the UK' (2005), identified contextual challenges to the traditional PhD and the emergence of several 'new forms' of the doctorate. Pursuing the 'evolution' metaphor, Park wondered whether we might be witnessing the doctorate's 'adaption to changing circumstances in order to survive' (p. 189). The new forms he identified are depicted as variants on the traditional monograph-style 'big book' format whose evolution we have attempted to trace over three continents and four educational contexts in the Anglosphere. The three main variants he pointed to: the PhD by publication, the professional doctorate and practice-based PhDs in the visual and performing arts are the subject of several of the chapters of our book. In addition, we considered disciplinary variation in a study of a small corpus of twenty recent sociology and history PhD theses from one university, examining claims to the emergence of a 'new humanities' PhD identified in an earlier study. We now consider in more detail some of the contextual factors shaping changes in the doctoral landscape and examine some doctoral theses and dissertations that have attempted to 're-imagine' the PhD.

In the later years of the twentieth century and over the first two decades of this century, there has been much discussion of the future of doctoral education and, more specifically, on the future of the dissertation/thesis in the humanities and social sciences. Some of the concerns articulated stem from macro-level structural changes in the university sector. The impacts of neoliberalism, in conjunction with an overall decline in state funding for higher education, further exacerbated by the global financial crisis, have in turn affected the academic job market. These factors have contributed to increased pressure for timely completion and to greater competition for fewer tenure-track positions post-PhD. As is often pointed out, the PhD is no longer a guarantee of a permanent academic appointment and this is undoubtedly one of the reasons for the diversification of the PhD. For example, Deem and Dowle (2020) estimate that 'well under 10% of all doctoral graduates in the UK find a permanent [academic] post' (p. 169) while Bentley and Meek (2018) estimate that fewer than half of all Australian PhDs work in higher education. Doctoral education is thus no longer conceived of as solely producing future academics who would become 'stewards of their discipline' (Golde and Walker 2006) and this too may affect both the form and content of the thesis or dissertation. Park (2005: 198) questioned whether 'the traditional notion of the magnus opus – a piece of research that could have a lasting impact on a discipline – has over the last decade or so been replaced by a more pragmatic notion of a manageable piece of work, of a scope and size that a student could reasonably expect to complete within three years'. A related set of concerns centres on the nature of the doctorate and whether its chief purpose is to contribute to knowledge creation as in the past or to certify the researcher as competent to conduct independent research.

Over the last twenty-odd years, there have been calls to 're-envision the PhD' (see e.g. Nyquist and Woodford 2000), and numerous conferences and workshops have been devoted to the future of the PhD and the dissertation. One of the key recommendations of the *Report of the Modern Languages Association (MLA) Task Force on Doctoral Study in Modern Language and Literature* (2014) was to 'reimagine the dissertation'. The task force clarified that while an extended research project should remain the defining feature of doctoral education, departments should 'expand the spectrum of forms the dissertation may take' (p. 2). The motivation for the task force's report was the future of the PhD in modern languages and literature which is perceived to be under threat from *inter alia* the forces described above including poor completion rates and excessive time to completion (median time to degree for 2012 humanities degree recipients in the United States was nine years from entry into graduate school); declining university funding; dwindling of traditional academic career paths; the demise of university presses and consequent declining opportunities to publish the PhD thesis as a monograph.

The National Endowment for the Humanities in the United States set up a Next Generation Humanities PhD Planning Grant in 2017 to support efforts by institutions to bring together faculty, graduate students and administrators to produce plans that aimed to transform scholarly preparation in the humanities at the doctoral level. Most grants appear to be oriented to ways of preparing candidates to consider careers outside of the academy given the decreasing numbers of humanities PhD graduates obtaining tenure track positions on graduation. Although the project has now officially ended, a record of its discussions can be found at *The New PhD: A Renaissance of Public Engagement* https://nextgenphd.commons.gc.cuny.edu/proposal/ and more information on the *Next Gen* consortium can be found at https://nextgenphd.commons.gc.cuny.edu/consortium/.

In 2018, the Canadian Association for Graduate Studies (CAGS) produced a *Report of the Task Force on the Dissertation: Purpose, Content, Structure, Assessment* which was the outcome of a consultative process aiming to develop 'strategies to ensure both quality and relevance of doctoral research and the dissertation for the 21st century' (p. 2). Noting that most graduates are now employed outside academia, the report recommends broadening doctoral education and the scope and intention of the dissertation. While not shying away from the potential difficulties involved in promoting expanded conceptions of the dissertation, the report provides examples of dissertations that include creative works, lay communication materials, policy papers, websites and syllabi that may be entirely digital or in the form of a graphic novel. Some of these theses will be discussed below in our discussion on re-imagining the PhD.

Similarly, the Council for Graduate Schools (CGS), a North American body, has hosted several meetings on the future of the dissertation (e.g. https://www.humanitiescareers.pitt.edu/sites/default/files/CGS%20Future%20of%20the%20Dissertation%202015.pdf) discussing topics such as 'Toward a Twenty-First Century Dissertation and 21st Century Doctoral Dissertations in the Humanities'. In 2015, the University of British Columbia launched the *Public Scholar's Initiative (PSI)*, an initiative set-up to support doctoral students who embark on research 'beyond the academy, and beyond traditional disciplinary approaches, to have a tangible impact for the public good through collaborative, action-oriented, and/or creative forms of scholarship in their dissertation work' (https://www.grad.ubc.ca/psi). In profiles on the PSI website, graduate students outline their project and the ways in which they propose to broaden doctoral scholarship. Max Chewinski, a PhD candidate at the time of writing, describes his sociology PhD's contribution to public scholarship as 'focused on knowledge mobilization through public presentations and writing op-eds, which I believe are important for making academic knowledge more accessible. My dissertation research continues this work with the added value of writing and presenting a policy brief to decision-makers' (https://www.grad.ubc.ca/campus-community/meet-our-students/chewinski-max). We discuss dissertations submitted by some PSI scholars below.

When we consider the future of the PhD thesis/dissertation from the perspective of our study, we can make no definitive claims. While the MLA report (2014: 14) identifies the dissertation as 'the pivot point for change in doctoral education', much will depend on the future of the universities themselves and the extent of disruption they experience. At the time of writing, the global context looks increasingly unstable. Will we continue to see the fairly slow evolution of the genre witnessed to date or something more akin to a Kuhnian revolution or paradigm shift (Kuhn 1962; Park 2005 and Chapter 5)? In what follows, we point to several themes that have arisen in the course of our study and tease out how they may shape the doctorate in the future within our four contexts.

The pressure to publish

A number of factors can be seen to be contributing to the growth in the PhD by publication and will likely ensure its continued popularity into the future (see Chapter 9). Graduating from the PhD with several publications already in hand, produced as part of the doctoral submission, has come to be seen as highly desirable when applying for one's first academic position. Thacker (2020), author of one of the theses in our corpus, endorses this view in explaining his choice, 'The MDIS [manuscript dissertation] format is recommended for individuals pursuing an academic career by encouraging opportunities for article development' (p. 8). In a study of the publication profiles of recent PhD graduates across four social science disciplines at US universities who were employed in academic positions, Hatch and Skipper (2016) found that the average number of publications (journal articles or book chapters) per student was 4.3. While they do not report on the format of the doctorate submitted, the authors highlight the importance of publication during candidature for future employment. Dissertation supervisors who co-author papers with their students can increase their own publication outputs and citations and thus enhance their own opportunities for promotion. Larkins (2019 cited in Burns and Rajcan 2019) estimated that Australian PhD students contribute two-thirds of university outputs across all disciplines and Burns and Rajcan (2019) point out that the 'allocation of funding within universities is being more and more tightly tied to the rate of research outputs and PhD completions that a given unit or faculty achieves' (p. 54).

Another outcome of these processes which could be seen to favour the PhD by publication is the decline in university presses which traditionally published humanities PhD theses as monographs, due to the funding cuts and changing priorities referred to above. The 2014 MLA report cited above notes a 'crisis in academic publishing in literary studies [that] also calls into question the traditional book-length print dissertation as the exclusive capstone for graduate study' (p. 14). Greg Britton, the editorial director of the Johns Hopkins University Press, writes that 'scholarly presses have already pulled out of entire fields of Humanities simply because the market could not support books in those subjects' (2015: 15). University libraries that were once the main purchasers of research monographs based on doctoral theses have themselves been severely impacted by financial cutbacks and are not purchasing the number of volumes required to sustain university presses. Journals and journal articles however continue to grow. Paré (2014: A-88) notes 'The collective effort to transform the doctoral thesis into a more publishable document' shows that the genre of the thesis as monograph is 'not immutable'.

While Britton makes a strong case for the need for doctoral students to consider the article-based thesis and for writing for a broader audience than that of the traditional thesis, we noted earlier that five of the ten recent history theses in our 'new humanities' corpus (see Chapter 5 for details) have been 'turned into' books published by university presses or by more generalist publishers. This could be specific to History as a discipline or perhaps to Australian history more particularly but the two published authors we interviewed in Chapter 5 both emphasized the personal significance of publishing the thesis as a book for them despite neither having embarked on an academic career at that point. As we point out in our chapter, apart from the two oral history theses in the corpus, the others take the form of the traditional research monograph. Further research into disciplinary norms and traditions in academic publishing in cross-national contexts would certainly be worth pursuing.

The Lean PhD (Kirchherr 2018) almost reads as a parody of the many books in the self-help genre offering thesis writing advice. The author, Julian Kirchherr, is however deadly serious. His book is perhaps the clearest articulation of the logic underlying the PhD by publication as a response to a number of the pressures outlined here. The book is an argument for how the principles of efficiency, quality, impact ('lean methodologies') which characterize successful 'start up' businesses can be optimized to produce a successful PhD thesis through a strategy of publication and join authorship.

Adopting these principles, Kirchherr submitted his social sciences DPhil at Oxford University twenty-one months after enrolment. It is a DPhil by publication that consists of four papers plus an introduction, literature review, methods and discussion and conclusion chapters. Three of the four papers are co-authored with his supervisors and other researchers; he is the lead on all papers. In the preface to his thesis, he acknowledges the co-authorship, stating, 'I herewith confirm that I designed the research presented in these papers, drafted the various papers, and managed the submission and revision process' (2017: viii). Two chapters are the pre-print versions of papers accepted for publication, while the other two are unpublished but have each been submitted to a journal.

The entry of the journal article, a genre with its own exigencies, into the thesis genre raises issues not only of authorship of the thesis but also of readership. Whereas in contexts such as Australia the primary readers are the two or at most three examiners of the thesis, a thesis by publication may contain multi-authored papers, often previously peer-reviewed and published, thus altering the relationship between examiner and student. Can the examiners then request changes to a paper that reviewers have accepted?

In the section that follows, we discuss emerging issues of authorship that arise primarily with the growth of the PhD by publication in the social sciences and the humanities but also with increasing collaborations between student authors and others in the research process as advocated by the PSI and others (see above).

Authorship

Sole authorship has been, until fairly recently, one of the inviolable constituents of the doctoral dissertation, particularly in the humanities and social sciences, but as we have shown in our discussion of the PhD by publication above, this is now open to change largely due to the pressure to publish as early as possible and the influence of the sciences. The MLA Taskforce concluded that 'the paradigm of the isolated research scholar is losing its sway' (2014: 8).

Doctoral authorship has certainly not always been as straightforward as we might assume. As Chang (2010) pointed out, early modern European dissertations evidence a type of joint authorship between supervisor and candidate as the student publicly defended the thesis prepared by the supervisor. Both names would appear on the title page of the dissertation with the supervisor's name often having greater prominence. Both student and supervisor benefitted from this arrangement as the student gained authority from association with the professor and the professor gained a financial benefit through an honorarium and the right to distribute copies of the printed thesis. Student authorship only became common practice in the nineteenth century (Sugimoto 2015).

In contemporary PhD theses in the social sciences and humanities, where the emphasis is on an original contribution to knowledge and the monograph has traditionally predominated, so has the notion of the student as sole author under supervision. The supervisor's name can usually only be found in the acknowledgements, in some instances in the digital thesis metadata in the university repository, and in the authorship of previously published papers. In the sciences it is standard to see multiple joint authorship on papers included in the thesis and joint authorship is considered a form of mentoring and disciplinary socialisation (see e.g. Matzler 2022), and this practice is evident in the PhDs by publication in our corpus. Larivière, Gingras, Sugimoto and Tsou (2015) however argue that the pattern of collaborative research that is now dominant in the natural and medical sciences in doctoral research is becoming more visible in the social sciences and humanities. As noted in Chapter 9, Anderson, Saunders and Alexander (2022) reported that of the 184 manuscript-style dissertations in their corpus of Education doctorates across five Canadian universities between 2008 and 2017, most contained co-authored publications.

Joint authorship at the doctoral level is felt to better prepare graduate students for the post-doctoral world and the practices of disciplinary scholarly communication. In its 2014 Report, the MLA Taskforce notes that 'collaboration and teamwork are the norm in large swaths of the social and natural sciences and that doctoral study in the modern languages and literatures must equip students with the skills to collaborate effectively' (p. 8). 'Collaboration is being enabled', it observes, 'by digital technologies, which facilitate more robust forms of scholarly communication. It has become much easier than in the past to share texts, provide comments, and engage in coauthorship' (p. 8).

In the theses by publication, we can see emerging signs of what has been called the 'contributorship' model of publication now common in the sciences and medicine in which clear roles other than 'authorship' are assigned to contributors to specific papers. Certainly, in the journals in our own field we are now asked to allocate contributor roles to multiple authors. Quite what these changes might signify for future dissertations is hard to discern. Are they further evidence of the neoliberal pressure on outputs at all costs in a shrinking job market or do they perhaps suggest a desire to acknowledge the work that academic mentors contribute to their students' theses?

As we noted in Chapter 9, the care taken in many of the theses by publication we examined to clarify authorship suggests that agreement has not been reached on genre expectations. We see features that would appear anomalous or marked in monograph theses. For example, Kathryn Accurso's (2019) PhD by publication from the University of Massachusetts Amherst contains two chapters prepared for publication and one that has already been published. A footnote tells the reader: 'This chapter appeared as a co-authored article in the 2017 *International Journal of Mathematics Teaching and Learning*, 18 (1), 84–108. Kathryn Accurso is the lead and primary author; second author Meg Gebhard served as faculty advisor for the project, and Stephanie Purington provided statistical support. Reprinted with permission' (p. 105). Accurso further notes that, as the chapter is reprinted from a co-authored publication, the pronouns 'we' and 'our' are used rather than the first-person singular, as is used in the other chapters of the dissertation. She also points out that the paper [not chapter] follows the spelling conventions of the journal in which it was first published, and that these may thus differ from those used in other chapters and that the only changes that have been made are to the numbering of headings, figures and tables.

Outside of the PhD by publication, we have noted some developments that may suggest the potential for future changes to sole authorship in the thesis genre. As discussed in Chapter 7, Elle Flanders' PhD drew on research carried out jointly with her partner, particularly for the creative component, and this is acknowledged in the written component itself. As we note in that chapter, creative works may have a number of contributors such as camera operators and editors. Chapter 7 of Jessica Wynne Hallenbeck's (2019) geography thesis from the University of British Columbia is co-authored with Rosemary Georgeson, who is also the subject of the thesis (see further discussion below), suggesting possibilities for collaborative authorship may emerge in qualitative studies in the social sciences. In the Preface to her thesis which was also part of the Public Scholars' Initiative (PSI), Hallenback writes:

> The published article is co-authored with each author contributing approximately half of the research and writing to the publication. Each author's contribution is clearly identified within the text of the publication. The work also includes a film entitled "In defiance of all that" directed by Rosemary Georgeson and filmed and edited by Jessica Hallenbeck. The rest of this dissertation is unpublished. It is an independent work by the author, Jessica Hallenbeck.
>
> (p. v)

The examples cited above illustrate the care that needs to be taken to define authorial roles when joint authorship emerges as an option for doctoral candidates.

Authorial voice

In addition to changing conceptions of authorship in the doctoral thesis, a related area in which we have noted change is authorial voice. The MLA Taskforce encouraged experimentation with 'different kinds of scholarly voices; trying different modes of dissemination; working alone and collaboratively' commenting that 'students require the ability to speak in different scholarly voices to different audiences, including publics outside the academy' (MLA 2014: 9). The PSI has responded to the desire for the PhD to embrace a broader audience by including a 'lay summary' in doctoral submissions directly after the traditional academic abstract. Anne Williams' thesis as podcast (see below) includes a 'public abstract' which is written in a less academic tenor than the abstract which precedes it. The Slade School of Art now asks students to include an impact statement in the written component of the PhD that reflects on the wider societal impact of the research (see Chapter 7). Different genres such as policy papers and essays, as well as digital and multimodal media may also require the adoption of a range of voices other than a conventional, impersonal academic voice.

Academic prose is slow to change but the use of a more personal voice through the deployment of the first-person singular as well as the creation of a more reflexive researcher self and the introduction of a 'lay' voice from the lifeworld as noted in our discussion on the new humanities theses, in particular sociology PhDs with a qualitative orientation, and practice-based theses in the visual arts, suggest some disruption of the traditional academic voice. A. D. Carson's PhD, 'Owning my masters: The rhetorics of rhymes & revolutions' (2017) referred to in Chapter 2, mounts a challenge to the traditional voice of academia as the entire dissertation is a rap recording. It breaks so decisively with tradition as to be revolutionary rather than evolutionary.

With the expansion of possible readerships or audiences for the PhD in the social sciences and humanities through some of the changes we have identified, we may see the emergence of the phenomenon known as 'context collapse' (Pérez-Llantada 2021) as doctoral students need to imagine multiple readers of their theses and dissertations and adapt their work to manage differing reader expectations. The increasing uptake of digital dissertations may accelerate change in this regard. For example, Edminster and Moxley (2002) noted that electronic theses and dissertations 'provide a means for graduate students to successfully reach more diverse, perhaps more interdisciplinary audiences' (p. 96).

Re-imagining the PhD in the social sciences and humanities

Earlier in this chapter, we noted the many calls to 'reimagine' the doctorate in the course of the twenty-first century. The MLA Taskforce signalled that 'alternative modes of scholarly communication challenge the priority of the dissertation as proto–print book' and floated the notion of a 'nontraditional dissertation' (2014: 14). They encouraged consideration of 'an expanded repertoire' of dissertations that might include 'a suite of essays on a common theme; Web-based projects that give evidence of extensive research; translations, with accompanying theoretical and critical reflection; public humanities projects that include collaboration with people in other cultural institutions and contain an explicit dimension of research; and the treatment of texts in terms of their pedagogical value in classrooms' (p. 14).

In the UK, several British universities held a seminar series from 2008 to 2010 with similar ambitions. Titled *The nature and format of the doctoral thesis in the digital and multimodal age*, presentations examined 'the turn to digital in the conception, design, supervision, production and examination of dissertations and theses' (p. 9) and the implications of multimodal formats in the arts, humanities and social sciences culminating in the publication of the *SAGE Handbook of Digital Theses and Dissertations* (Andrews et al. 2012). While the online deposition and storing of theses is now commonplace and has, for example, greatly facilitated this study (notwithstanding limitations identified in the course of our research), the impact of the digital on the conception and production of multimodal theses using the affordances of the digital and the consequent impact on the genre of the thesis have been less well studied. In our earlier study on the practice-based thesis in the visual and performing arts, while focused on the written component, we were able to collect some records of performances and exhibitions on CD or DVD through correspondence with the author or view still images inserted in the written text. The initial study of PhDs in the New Humanities (see Chapter 5) required regular trips to the Library basement to photocopy pages from the archived hard copies. Now, to an increasing extent, the multimodal is moving 'out of the appendix' or the back cover of the printed thesis and reshaping the thesis' structure and organization (Andrews and England 2012: 37).

In some instances, particularly with regard to technologies and multimodalities, students may be the drivers of genre change. In his Doctor of Musical Arts (DMA) Sang Kyan Koh (see Chapter 8) devised a solution to some of the problems besetting creators of multimodal theses. His suggestion that embedding sound and video clips that he had edited and uploaded to *YouTube* into the PDF version of his dissertation via a hyperlink would be the most convenient way to make these available to readers and examiners was initially met with scepticism by his supervisors. He explained their resistance as 'a generational thing … I thought it was so obvious. I know how to edit audio files. I uploaded to *YouTube* and linked it to the document. I don't think many advisors think about it that way. They think are you going to have a CD with a track list?'

The Academic Book of the Future Project (2014–16) https://academicbookfuture.org/ was funded by the British Arts and Humanities Research Council (AHRC) and the British Library (BL) in response to widespread concerns about the future of academic books, publishing and libraries. The decline in monograph sales, funding issues and rapidly changing new technologies, amongst other factors identified earlier, all contributed to concerns about the academic book in the arts and humanities in the UK. While not specifically focused on the PhD thesis, the published report (Deegan 2017) does discuss topics directly relevant to the changing nature of the PhD in the social sciences and humanities such as multimodality, creative practice and the ability of online repositories to handle multimedia and non-text research outputs submitted as part of the thesis. Problems of access, storage and long-term survival are identified in the report similar to some we have noted in Chapters 7 and 8 and below. Deegan highlights the challenges posed by the digital and the multimodal: 'At the moment, the system can offer new style PhDs as a kind of novelty; but to repurpose graduate training in line with new, non-print ecologies will require major change and investment' (2017: 31).

In a blogpost linked to the project, Manton (2016) commented that 'many PhD students and supervisors are showing a desire to rethink the traditional thesis to include multimedia research including video, audio, data, games, apps and web pages' but that 'for many recording multimedia outputs, in the way they would choose, is not possible and compromises must be made'. In a related post, Foxton (2016), a PhD student, reports on a meeting on the multimodal thesis she attended as part of the project in order to discuss how multimodal (mixed media) methods can be used to develop an argument within PhD research and the subsequent difficulties in submitting non-textual work. Archaeologists such as herself, for example, 'make use of such technologies as 3D models, digital photographs, and virtual realities' in their research which may be challenging for an online repository to make available and store adequately.

The last decade or so has seen the emergence of a slowly growing body of humanities and social sciences PhDs that have 'expanded' the dissertation, many embracing digital technologies to do so. As Macleod and Holdridge (2004) argued in relation to the emergent doctorate in the fine arts, theses and dissertations such as these can play a vital role in providing exemplars of the diversity of non-traditional doctorates and suggest possible modes of future evolution. As yet, these 'broadened' doctorates exhibit few signs of standardization and are located on the fringes of what is possible in a PhD. At the same time, they offer a version of what is possible for students, supervisors and administrators and may be the inspiration for theses currently underway. In the section that follows, we overview some recently submitted PhDs in the humanities and social sciences that could be understood as 'risky' or 'brave' or both.

One of the challenges that the authors of non-traditional doctorates face is the presentation, dissemination and storage of their work as a coherent form. That going digital is not without its challenges is made clear in 'We rock long distance: Manifest and the circulations of diasporic hip-hop', Justin Schell's (2013) PhD thesis from the University of Minnesota. In the PDF version in the university's online repository, he provides a link to a fully digital version https://sites.google.com/a/umn.edu/wrld/, telling us that in the 'conventional dissertation PDF, the only media will be photographs' (Schell 2013: 7). In the Preface, he outlines his rationale:

> I have incorporated media (photos, audio, and video) directly into the text, rather than solely as supplemental material attached afterwards. Moreover, the media is integral to the text itself. Sometimes the media illustrates a point, sometimes it serves to introduce a story, sometimes it tells a story in itself. But in all cases, it vivifies the voices and images inside its frame far better than a block of text could. This dissertation is not an argument that audio-visual media are inherently better than text as a source of knowledge, but rather an exploration of the intersections of written and audio-visual knowledge.

> Yet with all of the technological possibilities available to scholars to create different formats of their work, or combine existing formats of work (as I'm doing here with text, photo, audio, and video), the form of the dissertation still suffers from technical limitations. Due to these limitations, there is no way to embed the media directly into the dissertation PDF and have it be the official dissertation document. To do so would require embedding actual audio and video files into the PDF itself, and while this is certainly easy to do, the resultant PDFs would be too large to archive with the amount of video that is part of this dissertation. In order to work around these limitations, I have created an online

version of the dissertation, with all of the media embedded from the University of Minnesota's Digital Content Library, a secure, long-term storage site for the media files resulting in a much smaller chance of broken links.

Nick Sousanis' (2014) EdD, 'Unflattening', is a comic book about visual thinking. It is cited fairly regularly as an example of a successful non-traditional PhD and may well have encouraged more recent forays into multimodal representation. Sonia Estima, in her dissertation, 'Multimodal meaning making and the doctoral dissertation – An exploration of academic forms' (2020), credits his dissertation as the inspiration for her own study and, in the PDF and online version of her thesis (https://www.soniaestima.com/), links to a video of Sousanis talking about his work on visual thinking. His dissertation was published by Harvard University Press (Sousanis 2015) and won a prestigious award for excellence in the humanities (https://proseawards.com/winners/2016-award-winners/) which was encouraging news for proponents of alternative dissertations. That Sousanis now has an academic position at a North American university is also cited as evidence that multimodal dissertations do not rule out tenure track positions.

A. D. Carson obtained his PhD in Rhetorics, Communication and Information Design at Clemson University in 2017. His dissertation, which we have referred to earlier, won an award for the 2017 Outstanding Dissertation from Clemson's Graduate Student Government. The dissertation, 'Owning my masters: The rhetorics of rhymes & revolutions', is an album of original rap music and spoken word poetry that is the primary feature of a digital archive at https://phd.aydeethegreat.com. The dissertation is a complex, multimodal digital text comprised, according to Carson, 'entirely of digital sounds' (https://phd.aydeethegreat.com/lyrics/) that takes full advantage of the affordances of the digital.

The Clemson online repository links to a thirty-eight-page multimodal text which contains a link to the digital archive as well as text and images and a list of all the numbers performed. The text consists of a mix of academic writing, lyrics and reference to scholarly works. The final page of the text has links to the songs composed and performed by Carson through his time at Clemson. Carson describes the dissertation as a 'hip-hop album [that] is a critical-theoretical reflection on personhood vis-à-vis Black bodies and Black lives. Rather than theorizing about hip-hop, the project "does" this work through the genre of hip-hop'. The digital archive houses performances of the lyrics and additional text.

Subsequent to the dissertation submission, Carson has published an ebook with the University of Michigan Press titled *I Used to Love to Dream*, billed on the publisher's website as 'a mixtap/e/ssay that performs hip-hop scholarship using sampled and live instrumentation; repurposed music, film and news clips; and original rap lyrics' (https://www.fulcrum.org/concern/monographs/m900nw52n). The publication is open access at https://doi.org/10.3998/mpub.11738372.

Anna Williams' 'My gothic dissertation: A podcast' (2019) is a next-generation PhD available in open access through the University of Iowa's library (https://iro.uiowa.edu/esploro/outputs/doctoral/My-Gothic-dissertation-a-podcast/9983777133102771?institution=01IOWA_INST). She presents herself as following 'in the footsteps of A.D. Carson and Nick Sousanis' (p. v). The thesis is described in the abstract as 'an intertextual analysis of Gothic fiction and modern-day graduate education in the humanities' that adopts 'a nontraditional format – the podcast' (p. v). She mixes voice, music and sound to dramatize scenes from the novels and incorporates analysis throughout her narration. The podcast 'chapters' can be downloaded from the *Proquest Dissertations and Theses* database from the supplemental files tab (https://about.proquest.com/en/dissertations) along with the 137-page thesis which is the text of the podcast. Williams stresses that the dissertation was produced *for the ear* (our emphasis) and is designed to be heard rather than read. She also emphasizes her choice of authorial voice: a 'creative/journalistic style of reporting [that] is heavily influenced by programs such as *This American Life*, *Invisibilia*, and *Serial*, with the dual aims of engaging a broad audience and expanding our modes of scholarly communication beyond the page' (p. v). In line with the Next Gen approach to the dissertation, Williams interned at a radio station during her doctoral study and learned how to podcast.

Jesse Alan Merandy produced The City University of New York (CUNY)'s first entirely digital PhD dissertation, submitted to the Department of English. 'Vanishing leaves: A study of Walt Whitman through location-based mobile technologies' (Merandy 2019) is a location-based mobile experience (LBME) that takes players to Brooklyn Heights to learn about the poet, Walt Whitman, and his connection to the neighbourhood where he lived, worked and published the first edition of *Leaves of Grass*, in 1855. An online White Paper details the development and theory behind the mobile experience of following Whitman though Brooklyn as he composed his poetry. Components of the White Paper resemble those of the more traditional dissertation such as literature review or methodology but are not named as such. Merandy used gaming technology and mobile devices to build the experience in which the reader is assigned the role of a secret agent working to protect the works of writers from forces which threaten them. It can be experienced on a phone while walking through the neighbourhood or solely on a mobile device. While the CUNY online repository does not provide direct access to the white paper, a link to a separate dissertation website https://vanishingleaves.com/ comes with instructions on how to download the technology needed to access the game and the White Paper as well as an online version of the traditional dissertation acknowledgements.

Kathryn Coleman is an art educator at the University of Melbourne. Her PhD thesis, 'An a/r/tist in wonderland: Exploring identity, creativity and digital portfolios as a/r/tographer' (2017), is entirely digital and can be found at http://www.artographicexplorations.com/. On the homepage she states: 'This digital PhD Thesis and a/r/tographic study is a multimodal living inquiry, curated as a digital collection of images, essays and ethnographic video, and situated within embodied praxis.' A number of dropdown menus allow access to the content she has curated and the viewer/reader may enter the site where they wish as there is no linear chapter structure. The web-based thesis disrupts conventional linear argumentation, allowing for the development of what Andrews and England term 'multimodal argument' (2012: 35). Unlike the visual arts theses discussed in Chapter 7, in Coleman's 'thesis as eportfolio', the artwork and the written text are entirely digital. Her authorial voice is a mix of the intensely personal and reflective and the more conventional scholarly argumentative, citing the work of other scholars. Her methodologies are presented as autoethnographic and are influenced by the theoreticians of the new humanities (see Chapter 5).

'Graphic violence: Representing conflict and migration through visual narratives' consists of a 55,000-word anthropology thesis accompanied by a 110-page graphic novel titled *Memories of the Vanni* submitted to the University of Sussex by Benjamin Dix (2016). The topic of the study is the lengthy, violent conflict in Sri Lanka between government forces and Tamil nationalists seeking liberation for the Tamil inhabitants of the Vanni or northern part of Sri Lanka. The graphic novel draws on narratives collected during the ethnographic research that are presented as a fictionalized account of a Tamil family during and after the conflict. The thesis is available in PDF format on the university Library website; the first five chapters follow a topic-based macrostructure with chapters that include literature review and methodology components followed by *Memories of the Vanni* which comprises the remainder of the thesis. The Table of Contents lists Dix as author and Lindsay Pollock as illustrator of this latter component. In chapter 1 of the thesis, Dix emphasizes both the collaborative nature of writing the novel and its grounding in anthropological research: 'We have produced a hybrid graphic novel – first in terms of the combination of text with illustration and photographs, and second with regards to a fusion between the "fictional" with "factual" – both deemed here as conventions of representing and engaging with real-life events' (pp. 12–13).

One of Dix's aims in developing the graphic novel was to reach a broader readership than that of the traditional PhD thesis and his hope is that it will play a role in promoting educational awareness and humanitarian advocacy about the Sri Lankan situation. The thesis has now been published as graphic novel, titled *Vanni: A Family's Struggle through the Sri Lankan Conflict* (2019).

Amanda Visconti's (2015) dissertation was also motivated by a desire to reach a wider public than the traditional PhD readership. Her dissertation in the digital humanities from the University of Maryland, "'How can you love a work, if you don't know it?': Critical code and design towards participatory digital editions', won that year's distinguished dissertation award. The University's online repository has a PDF of her Abstract that contains a link to her website, a title page and acknowledgements, while the *Infinite Ulysses* digital edition and a 123-page White Paper can be accessed at http://dr.amandavisconti.com/. The link to these latter components appears not to be working on the university website. *Infinite Ulysses* (www.InfiniteUlysses.com) is an open access, interactive, digital edition of the James Joyce novel, *Ulysses*, that lets anyone who wishes to annotate the text, in a sense broadening the notion of authorship. Apart from the white paper, the dissertation is entirely digital or, as is sometimes said, 'born digital'. In an interview, Visconti outlined what she saw as some of the unique features of her dissertation:

> There was no chapter-writing: there was no core of proto-monograph writing throughout the dissertation. I did produce analytics writing, but in non-traditional forms: blogging throughout the entire process, both about my research questions and around the meta-questions of doing a uniquely shaped DH [digital humanities] dissertation; and a final debriefing report (whitepaper) that was written entirely during the final month before my dissertation defense (usual for a math dissertation, unique for a literature dissertation). https://cags.ca/projects/rethinking-profiles/amanda-visconti/

'The water we call home: Five generations of indigenous women's persistence along the Salish Sea' is a Geography thesis submitted at the University of British Columbia by Jessica Wynne Hallenbeck in 2019 as part of the Public Scholar's Initiative (PSI) that we have referred to above in our discussion of authorship. While the first five chapters of the thesis take a topic-based format, Chapter 6 is a twelve-minute film called *In Defiance of All That*, filmed and edited by Hallenbeck and directed by Rosemary Georgeson, the Indigenous woman who collaborated with Hallenbeck throughout the thesis as she sought to find her family. The video of the film is embedded in the PDF at the beginning of the chapter and is followed by four pages of explanatory text. The dissertation adopts what Hallenbeck calls a 'non-linear' structure that seeks to 'connect seemingly disparate events through the lives of five generations of Coast Salish Indigenous women. The story of finding Rosemary's ancestors and relatives is told throughout the seven chapters, as is the story of our research relationship and decisions about what to include or exclude from the dissertation' (p. 9). Chapter 7 is the co-authored article discussed above.

Gregory Gan's (2019) anthropology thesis, '"Russia outside Russia": Transnational mobility, objects of migration, and discourses on the locus of culture amongst educated Russian migrants in Paris, Berlin, and New York' in which he investigates transnational Russian identity through ethnographic, autoethnographic and visual anthropology methods is also part of the PSI at the University of British Columbia. While the macrostructure of the written component contains six chapters and is topic-based, the thesis also comprises an interactive multi-media installation titled *Still Life with a Suitcase* that draws on interviews with the research participants that were recorded and edited into short vignettes. The videos can be accessed on the *vimeo* platform from the List of Supplementary Materials on page ix of the thesis. As Gan explains in chapter 3 of the thesis, part of his intention in developing the video and exhibiting it internationally was to make his research more accessible to a wider public. The written text is also multimodal in that Gan deploys different typefaces to capture the different 'academic voices' in his text: personal vignettes are italicized and bold; a lighter typeface is used for more autobiographical and reflexive text, and a bolder typeface is used for more conventional 'social science discourses' (p. 4). In what could be seen as a crossover with the practice-based theses in the visual arts, he also recreated in clay nine material objects that participants shared with him in the course of the interviews, and visitors to the exhibitions were asked to place these inside an empty suitcase and are filmed doing this.

Omer Aijazi's (2018) 'Fictions of social repair: Chronicity in six scenes' is a PSI dissertation in Educational Studies that is reminiscent of the new humanities theses we discussed in Chapter 5 in that it disrupts the typical topic-based macrostructure through adopting a more poetic, narrative approach presenting the research 'findings' in six 'scenes' with titles such as Betrayal, Muslim Poetics, Anger and Opacity rather than chapters. The study investigates how vulnerable disaster survivors engage in processes of social repair following large-scale natural disasters. The thesis contains eighty-seven photographs taken by Aijazi and his research assistants in the course of field work carried out in remote areas of Pakistan affected by such disasters and other forms of violence. The text does not follow a conventional layout and contains passages written as poetry and narrative or 'creative non-fiction'. It is decorated with Hindu numerals that sit in blank space and is deeply influenced by feminist theory and other theorists common to the new humanities, including decolonialiality.

In our brief survey of these re-imagined PhDs, we see the centrifugal forces for change and diversity in play with the centripetal forces for stability and uniformity that for Bakhtin ([1935] 1981) are always at work in any discourse. Our study raises several questions for future scholars of the doctoral genre.

Will the proto-monograph survive? Will it continue to produce new variants? Will the PhD by publication edge out the monograph? Will 'born digital' dissertations increase in number? Will creative practice doctorates and the new humanities combine in the digital space? Or could we see a 'radically reimagined doctoral dissertation' as envisioned by Sidone Smith in her 'Manifesto for the Humanities' that 'might involve a multiyear collaboration of doctoral students and faculty in a large project' (Smith, S. A. 2015: 42)? When we gave a talk on our research at a recent conference, mentioning the composition submissions at the University of Toronto where students submit the score for an original work rather than a traditional dissertation, a member of the audience asked, 'Is the PhD now dead?' Our answer was: 'No, it's not, but there are now many alternatives to the traditional dissertation that are being accepted as doctoral level work and accepted for the award of the degree.'

So, what might the doctorate of the future in the social sciences and humanities look like? It is hard to answer this question with any precision. In the areas of the visual arts and music we have already seen a shift from the submission of traditional type theses and we wouldn't be surprised to see more changes in these areas. In other areas however, such as Education, apart from one exception we didn't find any major changes in what students are submitting for their doctorate in most parts of the world. That said, however, the EdD by Patrick Stewart (2016) we have referred to in this book did break many rules and challenge academic writing expectations and could pave the way for further changes in EdD submissions, at least at the university where it was awarded. The PhD by publication (as opposed to the PhD by published work), by contrast, seems to have settled into a new set (or sets) of conventions and could stay that way for some time. And at some institutions, such as the University of Toronto, doctoral submissions in composition are not required to contain a thesis, whereas in its sister area, performance, they are. Beyond this, however, all the submissions we have discussed in this book are still located within the realities of the academy (Molinari 2022) where they are required to meet the criteria for the award of doctoral degrees. That is, they need to be based on previous work in the area and need to contribute to knowledge. That is, as one of the participants in Mary-Helen Ward's (2013) examination of PhD students' experiences said, 'A thesis has to tell you something you didn't know before you started reading it' (p. iii). There are however an increasing number of ways, in some areas at least, in which this can be done.

Certainly, the ways in which theses and dissertations are produced, disseminated, received and archived are subject to continual change. In this chapter and previously, we have identified how digital affordances are a force for change in doctoral theses and dissertations and that universities may experience challenges when engaging with 'non-print ecologies' (see Deegan 2017: 31, cited above). Gossett and Potts (2021: 50) note that there is currently 'no mechanism to adequately archive and publish' born-digital projects and that 'doctoral candidates often find themselves having to produce two versions of their dissertations: one representing their born-digital scholarship (e.g., interactive webtexts, software, apps, games, etc.) and another satisfying the need to deposit the dissertation into an archive (e.g., print-based PDF, etc.)'. The work to date that has enabled the rapid development of online repositories of theses and dissertations in universities around the globe has enabled the studies reported on in our book. It is vital that we now work to find ways to preserve nascent digital and multimodal doctoral work for future scholarship.

Appendix A

Interview questions: Students

- What are the expectations and conventions for a doctoral thesis at your institution and in your area of study?

- Tell us about the thesis you wrote for your degree. What was it about and why did you choose this topic?

- Was your thesis based on a single empirical study, several empirical studies or a thesis by publication (or other type of thesis)?

- Why did you choose this particular type of thesis?

- Were you given any advice on the writing of your thesis? If you were, who gave you the advice and what was it?

- What did you find most straightforward about writing your thesis?

- What did you find most challenging about writing your thesis?

Interview questions: Supervisors

- What are the expectations and conventions for a doctoral thesis at your institution and in your area of study?

- What kind of thesis do students typically write in your area of study? Are they based on a single empirical study, several empirical studies or a thesis by publication (or other type of thesis)?

- Why do students write this kind of thesis?

- What advice do you give students on the writing of their thesis?

- What, in your view, are features of high-quality doctoral theses in your area of study?

- What, in your view, are features of poor theses in your area of study?

- What do students find most straightforward about writing a doctoral thesis in your area of study?

- What do students find most challenging about writing a doctoral thesis in your area of study?

References

Accurso, K. (2019), 'Learning linguistics, teaching for change: Preparing secondary educators to more equitably teach disciplinary literacies', PhD diss., University of Massachusetts Amherst.

Aijazi, O. (2018), 'Fictions of social repair: Chronicity in six scenes', PhD diss., University of British Columbia.

Ali-Khan, C. (2011), 'In these bones the economy of the world: A multi-logical, multi-representational cultural study', PhD diss., City University of New York.

Allen, R. (2020), 'An adaptable approach to expertise: The application of Ivan Galamian's violin pedagogy to trumpet practice and teaching', DMA diss., University of California San Diego.

Allen, C. M., Smyth, E. M. and Wahlstrom, M. (2002), 'Responding to the field and to the academy: Ontario's evolving PhD', *Higher Education Research & Development*, 21: 203–14.

Allen, J. R. (2014), 'The structure, function and specificity of the rhodobacter sphaeroides membrane-associated chemotaxis array', DPhil thesis, University of Oxford.

Allori, P. E., Bateman, J. and Bhatia, V. K. (2014), 'Evolution in genre: Emergence, variation, multimodality', in P. E. Allori, J. Bateman and V. K. Bhatia (eds), *Evolution in Genre: Emergence, Variation, Multimodality*, 9–16. Bern: Peter Lang.

Amell, B. (2022), 'Not all who want to, can—not all who can, will: Extending notions of unconventional doctoral dissertations', PhD thesis, Carleton University.

Anderson, T. (2016), 'Negotiating academic discourse practices, ideologies and identities: The socialization of Chinese PhD students', PhD thesis, University of British Columbia.

Anderson, T. and Okuda, T. (2019), 'Writing a manuscript-style dissertation in TESOL/applied linguistics', *BC TEAL Journal*, 4, 1: 33–52.

Anderson, T. and Okuda, T. (2021), 'Temporal change in dissertation macrostructures', *English for Specific Purposes*, 64: 1–12.

Anderson, T., Alexander, I. and Saunders, G. (2020), 'An examination of education-based dissertation macrostructures', *Journal of English for Academic Purposes*, 45: 100845.

Anderson, T., Saunders, G. and Alexander, I. (2022), 'Alternative dissertation formats in education-based doctorates', *Higher Education Research & Development*, 41: 593–612.

Andrews, R. and England, J. (2012), 'New forms of dissertation', in R. Andrews, E. Borg, S. Boyd Davis, M. Domingo and J. England (eds), *The Sage Handbook of Digital Dissertations and Theses*, 31–46. London: Sage.

Archer, A. (2010), 'Multimodal texts in higher education and the implications for writing pedagogy', *English in Education*, 44: 201–13.

Archer, A. (2013), 'Voice as design: Exploring academic voice in multimodal texts in higher education', in M. Böck and N. Pachler (eds), *Multimodality and Social Semiosis: Communication, Meaning-Making, and Learning in the Work of Gunther Kress*, 150–61. New York: Routledge.

Ascenzo, A. E. (2020), 'Digital landscape: An annotated list of works for solo cello and electronics', DMA thesis, University of Toronto.

ASU Mary Lou Fulton Teachers College (2021), *Doctor of Education in Leadership and Innovation Program Guide, 2020–2021 Academic Year*. Tempe, AZ: Arizona State University.

Atkinson, D. (1999), *Scientific Discourse in Sociohistorical Context: The Philosophical Transactions of the Royal Society of London, 1675–1975*. Mahwah, NJ: Lawrence Erlbaum.

Ausländer, S. B. (2019), 'On tangibility, contemporary reliefs, and continuous dimensions', PhD thesis, Slade School of Fine Art, University College London.

Australian Qualifications Framework Council (2013), *Australian Qualifications Framework*. Second edition. Adelaide: Australian Qualifications Framework Council.

Auton, E. (2018), 'Performance or presence? Examining the private parts of Australian medical education', PhD thesis, University of New South Wales.

Ayers, G. (2008), 'The evolutionary nature of genre: An investigation of the short texts accompanying research articles in the scientific journal Nature', *English for Specific Purposes*, 27: 22–41.

Ayres, T. L. R. (1923), 'Ionisation by electrons travelling with small velocities in various gases', DPhil thesis, University of Oxford.

Badenhorst, C. and Xu, X. (2016), 'Academic publishing: Making the implicit explicit', *Publications*, 4, 3: 1–16.

Badley, G. (2009), 'Publish and be doctor-rated: The PhD by published work', *Quality Assurance in Education*, 17: 331–42.

Bailey, K. D. (2011), *Typologies and Taxonomies*. Thousand Oaks, CA: Sage.

Bakhtin, M. M. ([1935]1981), 'Discourse in the novel', in M. Holquist (ed.), *The Dialogic Imagination: Four Essays by M. M. Bakhtin* (trans. C. Emerson and M. Holquist), 259–422. Austin, TX: University of Texas Press.

Bakhtin, M. M. (1981), *The Dialogic Imagination: Four Essays*, M. Holquist (ed.), C. Emerson and M. Holquist (trans.). Austin, TX: University of Texas Press.

Banks, D. (2008), *The Development of Scientific Writing: Linguistic Features and Historical Context*. Sheffield: Equinox.

Bao, Y., Kehm, B. M. and Ma, Y. (2018), 'From product to process: The reform of doctoral education in Europe and China', *Studies in Higher Education*, 43: 524–41.

Barbero, E. J. (2008), 'Journal paper requirement for PhD graduation', *Latin American and Caribbean Journal of Engineering Education*, 2: 51–3.

Barros, A. S. (2012), 'Transcriptional regulation by non-coding RNAs in saccharomyces cerevisiae', DPhil thesis, University of Oxford.

Bateman, J. A. (2008), *Genre and Multimodality: A Foundation for the Systematic Analysis of Multimodal Documents*. Basingstoke, England: Palgrave Macmillan.

Bateman, J. A., Allori, P. E. and Bhatia, V. K. (2014), 'Evolution in genre: Emergence, variation, multimodality', in P. E. Allori, J. Bateman and V. K. Bhatia (eds), *Evolution in Genre: Emergence, Variation, Multimodality*, 9–16. Bern: Peter Lang.

Bazerman, C. (1988), *Shaping Written Knowledge: The Genre and Activity of the Experimental Article in Science*. Madison, WI: The University of Wisconsin Press.

Beauton, J. A. (2020), 'Systems of value: Societal influences on, and the mediation of, the classical interpreter percussionist', DMA diss., University of California San Diego.

Becher, T. and Trowler, P. R. (2001), *Academic Tribes and Territories: Intellectual Enquiry and the Culture of Disciplines*. Second edition. Buckingham, England: Open University Press.

Beetz, R. (2017), 'The winter stars', DMA diss., University of California San Diego.

Bentley, P. J. and Meek, V. L. (2018), 'Development and future directions of higher degree research training in Australia', in J. C. Shin, B. M. Kehm and G. A. Jones (eds), *Doctoral Education for the Knowledge Society*, 123–46. Cham, Switzerland: Springer.

Berkenkotter, C. (2007), 'Genre evolution? The case for a diachronic perspective', in V. K. Bhatia, J. Flowerdew and R. H. Jones (eds), *Advances in Discourse Studies*, 78–191. London: Routledge.

Berkenkotter, C. and Huckin, T. N. (1995), *Genre Knowledge in Disciplinary Communication*. Hillsdale, NJ: Lawrence Erlbaum Associates.

Biber, D. (1988), *Variation across Speech and Writing*. Cambridge: Cambridge University Press.

Birman, H. (2017), 'Reading between the lives: The sociality of volunteering in palliative care', PhD thesis, University of New South Wales.

Black, P. (2016), 'Explanatory essays and seven articles', PhD thesis, University of Glasgow.

Blair, K. A. (2018), 'Performer/Co-composer: A self-analysis of performer-contributed compositional choices in microcosm and macrocosm as relevant to the interpretation of four solo piano works of Stuart Saunders Smith', DMA diss., University of California San Diego.

Bogle, D. (2018), '100 years of the PhD in the UK'. Available online: https://discovery.ucl.ac.uk/id/eprint/10068565/1/Bogle_History%20of%20PhD.pdf (accessed 17 August 2023).

Bok, G. (2017), 'Understanding alienation, subjectivity and relations among the beauty employees in the retail beauty industry', PhD thesis, University of New South Wales.

Bolter, J. D. and Grusin, R. (1999), *Remediation: Understanding New Media*. Cambridge, MA: MIT Press.

Booij, G. (2017), 'Inheritance and motivation in construction morphology', in N. Gisborne and A. Hippisley (eds), *Defaults in Morphological Theory*, 18–39. Oxford: Oxford University Press.

Borg, E. (2007), 'Writing in fine arts and design education in context', *Journal of Writing in Creative Practice*, 1: 85–101.

Bowden, S. L. (2018), 'Max Roach and M'Boom: Diasporic soundings in American percussion music', DMA diss., University of California San Diego.

Brady, J. (2020), 'Preparing teachers for diverse classrooms: Developing intercultural competence', EdD diss., Arizona State University.

Britton, G. (2015), 'Bonfire of the humanities'. Council of Graduate Schools Future of the Dissertation Workshop, 15–18. Available online: https://www.humanitiescareers.pitt.edu/sites/default/files/CGS%20Future%20of%20the%20Dissertation%202015.pdf (accessed 4 May 2022).

Brown, H. C. (2001), 'The development of social work practice with lesbians and gay men', PhD thesis, Middlesex University.

Buchanan, A. L. and Hérubel, J. P. V. M. (1995), *The Doctor of Philosophy Degree*. Westport, CO: Greenwood Press.

Buckley, B. (2009), 'What is with the Ceiling! The artist, higher degrees and research in the University Art School', in B. Buckley and J. Conomos (eds), *Rethinking the Contemporary Art School*, 76–86. Halifax, Canada: The Press of the Nova Scotia College of Art and Design.

Bui, T. H. G. (2015), 'Using collaboration and technology to enhance Vietnamese students' English writing skills', EdD thesis, Queensland University of Technology.

Bukhatir, S. A. (2018), 'Learning from experiences and investing in opportunities: A narrative inquiry about the career progress of public kindergarten principals in the United Arab Emirates', EdD thesis, University College London.

Bunton, D. (2002), 'Generic moves in PhD thesis introductions', in J. Flowerdew (ed.), *Academic Discourse*, 57–75. London: Longman.

Burgess, H., Sieminski, S. and Arthur, L. (2006), *Achieving Your Doctorate in Education*. London: Sage.

Burland, K., Spencer, M. and Windsor, L. (2017), 'Exploring, enhancing and evaluating musical 'Doctorateness': Perspectives on performance and composition', in F. Nilsson, H. Dunin-Woyseth and N. Janssens (eds), *Perspectives on Research Assessment in Architecture, Music and the Arts*, 114–27. London: Routledge.

Burnard, P. (2016), 'The professional doctorate', in P. Burnard (ed.), *Transformative Doctoral Research Practices for Professionals*, 15–28. Rotterdam: Sense Publishers.

Burnard, P., Dragovic, T., Ottewell, K. and Lim, W. M. (2018), 'Voicing the professional doctorate and the researching professional's identity: Theorizing the EdD's uniqueness', *London Review of Education*, 16: 40–55.

Burns, E. and Rajcan, A. (2019), 'Publishing outputs of sociology PhD candidates at New Zealand universities, 2013–2017', *New Zealand Sociology*, 34: 51–7.

Butler, J. (2009), *Frames of War: When Is Life Grievable?* London: Verso.

Campbell, K. (2022), 'The retrospective PhD by publication: A lesser doctorate?' in S. W. Chong and N. Johnson (eds), *Landscapes and Narratives of PhD by Publication*, 95–117. Cham, Switzerland: Springer.

Canadian Association for Graduate Studies (2018), *Report of the Task Force on the Dissertation – Purpose, Content, Structure, Assessment*. Ottawa, Canadian Association for Graduate Studies.

Candlin, F. (2000), 'Practice-based doctorates and questions of academic legitimacy', *International Journal of Art and Design Education*, 19: 96–101.

Candy, L. (2006), *Practice-Based Research: A Guide*. Creativity and Cognition Studios. Sydney: University of Technology Sydney.

Cano, P. J. G. (2016), 'Modern guitar techniques: A view of history, convergence of musical traditions and contemporary works', DMA diss., University of California San Diego.

Capezzuto, M. (2021), 'The hands of Johannes Whisler: A historical study of handwriting and drawing', EdD diss., Columbia Teachers College.

Carlin, N. (2016), 'Written through blood: The moral complexities of Jewish ritual circumcision', PhD thesis, University of New South Wales.

Caroll-Dwyer, E. (2015), 'Forging cooperative gender relations among youths in the gilded age and progressive era: The case of the Christian Endeavor Movement', PhD thesis, University of New South Wales.

Carson, A. D. (2017), 'Owning my masters: The rhetorics of rhymes & revolutions', PhD diss., Clemson University.

Casanave, C. P. (2019), 'Performing expertise in doctoral dissertations: Thoughts of a fundamental dilemma facing doctoral students and their supervisors', *Journal of Second Language Writing*, 43: 57–62.

Casanave, C. P. (2020), *During the Dissertation: A Textual Mentor for Doctoral Students in the Process of Writing*. Ann Arbor, MI: University of Michigan Press.

Cayley, R. (2020), 'Using genre to teach the publication-based thesis', in L. E. Bartlett, S. L. Tarabochia, A. R. Olinger and M. J. Marshall (eds), *Diverse Approaches to Teaching, Learning, and Writing Across the Curriculum*, 153–63. The WAC Clearinghouse; University Press of Colorado.

Cerfeda, D. (2019), 'The performance of perversion in Kafka's literature and its adaptations', PhD thesis, University of Melbourne.

Chang, K. (2004), 'From oral disputation to written text: The transformation of the dissertation in early modern Europe', *History of the Universities*, XIX, 2: 129–87.

Chang, K. (2007), 'Kant's disputation of 1770: The dissertation and the communication of knowledge in early modern Europe', *Endeavour*, 31, 2: 45–9.

Chang, K. (2010). 'Collaborative production and experimental labor: Two models of dissertation authorship in the eighteenth century', *Studies in History and Philosophy of Biological and Biomedical Sciences*, 41: 347–55.

Chong, S. W. (2020), 'PhD by published work and "doctorateness": My experience at a UK university', *Innovation Practice in Higher Education*, 4: 1–12.

Chong, S. W. (2021), 'Demystifying commentary guidelines of PhD by published work in the UK: Insights from genre analysis', *Innovations in Education and Teaching International*. doi: 10.1080/14703297.2020.1871396

Chong, S. W. (2022), 'The retrospective PhD by publication in the UK: A rapid review on educational research commentaries', in S. W. Chong and N. Johnson (eds), *Landscapes and Narratives of PhD by Publication*, 47–71. Cham, Switzerland: Springer.

Christianson, B., Elliot, M. and Massey, B. (2015), *The Role of Publications and Other Artifacts in Submissions for the UK PhD*. Lichfield, England: UK Council for Graduate Education.

Clark, A. (2012), 'Ways of knowing: Developing the Mosaic approach with young children and adults', PhD thesis, The Open University.

Clarke, P. (2004), 'Life lines to life stories: Some publications about women in nineteenth century Australia', PhD thesis, Griffith University.

Clemson Rhetorics, Communication and Information Design (2019), 'About RCID', Clemson, SC: Clemson University. Available online: https://www.clemson.edu/cah/academics/interdisciplinary-studies/programs/rcid/about-us/index.html (accessed 17 August 2023).

Clerke, T. and Lee, A. (2018), 'Mainstreaming the doctoral portfolio?' in M. Kiley and G. Mullins (eds), *Quality in Postgraduate Research: Research Education in the New Global Environment*, 17–30. Adelaide: Proceedings of the Quality in Postgraduate Research Conference.

Clucas, T. (2014), 'Romantic reclusion in the works of Cowper and Wordsworth', DPhil thesis, University of Oxford.

Coleman, K. S. (2017), 'An a/r/tist in wonderland: Exploring identity, creativity and digital portfolios as a/r/tographer', PhD thesis, University of Melbourne, Australia.

Collante, R. Q. (2019), 'Yawar para (Blood rain)', PhD diss., San Marcos University, Lima, Peru.

Collyns, D. (2019), 'Student in Peru makes history by writing thesis in Incas' language', *The Guardian*, 27 October 2019.

Cotterall, S. (2011), 'Stories within stories: A narrative study of six international PhD researchers' experiences of doctoral learning in Australia', PhD thesis, Macquarie University, Australia.

Cowden, M. (2012), 'Do children have rights? Five theoretical reflections on children's rights', PhD thesis, Australian National University.

Cowden, M. (2013), 'A PhD by publication or how I got my doctorate and kept my sanity', *The Conversation*, 14 February. Available online: https://theconversation.com/a-phd-by-publication-or-how-i-got-my-doctorate-and-kept-my-sanity-11012 (accessed 28 November 2022).

Crombie, W. (1989), 'Post-structuralism and the denial of mental processes', *Parlance*, 2, 1: 36–54.

Culvenor, C. C. J. (1945), 'Report on research carried out during 1945 in the University of Melbourne', MSc thesis, University of Melbourne.

Culvenor, C. C. J. (1948), 'The chemistry of the ethylene sulphides and some related topics', PhD thesis, University of Melbourne.

Curry, M. J. (2016), 'More than language: Graduate student writing as "Disciplinary Becoming"', in S. Simpson, N. A. Caplan, M. Cox and T. Phillips (eds), *Supporting Graduate Student Writers: Research, Curriculum, & Program Design*, 78–96. Ann Arbor: University of Michigan Press.

Curry School of Education and Human Development (2019), 'PhD Dissertation Manual', Charlottesville, VA: University of Virginia School of Education and Human Development.

Dalziell, J. (2018), 'The blindness of the seeing eye: Testing anthropocentrism'. PhD thesis, University of New South Wales.

Day, S. (2020), 'Why you should do your doctorate in 'real time': By publication', FERSA University of Cambridge Blog. Available online: https://fersacambridge.wordpress.com/2020/01/20/why-you-should-do-your-doctorate-in-real-time-by-publication/ (accessed 17 August 2023).

de Beaugrande, R. and Dressler, W. (1981), *Introduction to Text Linguistics*. London: Longman.

Decker, S. I. (2017), 'Gender, religious difference, and the notarial economy in medieval Catalonia', PhD diss., Yale University.

De Cambiaire, E. (2016), 'Enlightened alliance: Nature, botany and France's expansion to the East Indies: The colonization of the Mascarenes (1665–1775)', PhD thesis, University of New South Wales.

de Lange, T. and Wittek, A. L. (2014), 'Research genres as knowledge practices: Experiences in writing doctoral dissertations in different formats', *Journal of School Public Relations*, 35: 383–401.

Deegan, M. (2017), *The Academic Book of the Future Project Report: A Report to the AHRC and the British Library*. Available online: https://bl.iro.bl.uk/concern/reports/97e5819f-5def-4b69-b31a-6d4f3fe5fb91 (accessed 22 November 2022).

Deem, R. and Dowle, S. (2020), 'The UK doctorate: History, features and challenges', in M. Yudkevich, P. Altbach and H. de Wit (eds), *Trends and Issues in Doctoral Education: A Global Perspective*, 152–78. London: Sage.

Devitt, A. (2004), *Writing Genres*. Carbondale, IL: Southern Illinois Press.

Dewey-Hagborg, H. (2016), 'Postgenomic identity: Arts and biopolitics', PhD diss., Rensselaer Polytechnic Institute.

Di Mauro, S. (2015), 'Stories in search of a perfect home: Sebastian Di Mauro's visual arts practice 1995–2015', PhD thesis, Queensland College of Art, Griffith University.

Dix, B. (2016), 'Graphic violence: Representing conflict and migration through visual narratives', PhD thesis, University of Sussex.

Dix, B. and Pollock, L. (2019), *Vanni: A Family's Struggle through the Sri Lankan Conflict*. University Park, VA: Penn State University Press.

Dobson, I. R. (2012), 'PhDs in Australia, from the beginning', *Australian Universities Review*, 54: 94–101.

Dong Y. R. (1998), 'Non-native graduate students' thesis/dissertation writing in science: Self-reports by students and their advisors from two U.S. institutions', *English for Specific Purposes*, 17: 369–90.

Dudley-Evans, T. (1999), 'The dissertation: A case of neglect?', in P. Thompson (ed.), *Issues in EAP Writing Research and Instruction*, 28–36. Reading, England: Centre for Applied Language Studies, University of Reading.

Dunn, M. (2015), *A Valley in a Valley: Colonial Struggles over Land and Resources in the Hunter Valley, NSW 1820–1850*. PhD thesis, University of New South Wales.

Edminster, J. and Moxley, J. (2002), 'Graduate education and the evolving genre of electronic theses and dissertations', *Computers and Composition*, 19: 89–104.

Egan, R. B. (2019), 'Power and dysfunction: The New South Wales Board for the Protection of Aborigines 1883–1940', PhD thesis, University of New South Wales.

Elkins, J. (2014), 'Remarks on the Studio-art PhD around the world', in L. Ravelli, B. Paltridge and S. Starfield (eds), *Doctoral Writing in the Creative and Performing Arts*, 9–31. Faringdon, England: Libri.

Ellis, A. and Anderson, A. (2019), 'A snapshot of Australian professional doctorates', in P. Miller and T. Marchant (eds), *Professional Doctorate Research in Australia: Commentary and Case Studies from Business, Education and Indigenous Studies*, 7–14. Lismore, NSW: Southern Cross University Press.

Estima, S. (2020), 'Multimodal meaning making and the doctoral dissertation – An exploration of academic forms', EdD diss., University of Illinois, Urbana-Champaign.

Evans, D., Gruba, P. and Zobel, J. (2014), *How to Write a Better Thesis*. Third edition. Cham, Switzerland: Springer.

Evans, M. (2022), 'Genre: Some sociological foundations and implications', in A. Ding and M. Evans (eds), *Social Theory for English for Academic Purposes*, 15–38. London: Bloomsbury.

Evans, T. (1997), 'Flexible doctoral research: Emerging issues in professional doctorate programs', *Studies in Continuing Education*, 19: 174–82.

Evans, T., Macauley, P., Pearson, M. and Tregenza, K. (2003), 'A decadic review of PhDs in Australia', in NZARE/AARE, *Educational Research, Risks and Dilemmas*, 1–15. Coldstream, VIC: Australian Association for Research in Education.

Fairskye, M. (1993), 'Frankly, I may be a genius, but don't call me Dale, I'll call you', in *Ornithology and Art? A Bird's Eye View of Conceptual Rigour in Contemporary Art Practice*. Brisbane: Queensland Art Gallery.

Fenton, D. (2007), 'Unstable acts: A practitioner's case study of the poetics of postdramatic theatre and intermediality', PhD thesis, Queensland University of Technology.

Fiedler, S. (2000), 'Beyond Pinochet: Class, power and desire in Pinochet's Chile'. PhD thesis, University of New South Wales.

Finkelstein, J. (2022), 'Unprofessional and fundamentally corrupt', *Inside Higher Ed*, 12 March 2022. Available online: https://www.insidehighered.com/advice/2022/03/11/problem-co-authored-chapters-dissertation-opinion (accessed 17 August 2023).

Flanders, E. (2014), 'What isn't there: Imaging Palestine', PhD diss., York University, Canada.

Forbes, A. M. (2014), 'Doctoral research through music performance: The role of the exegesis', in L. Ravelli, S. Starfield and B. Paltridge (eds), *Doctoral Writing in the Creative and Performing Arts*, 263–79. Faringdon, England: Libri.

Fortais, S. E. (2018), 'Defining cool through a bricoleur's studio practice', PhD thesis, Slade School of Fine Art, University College London.

Fox, C. (2019), 'Craft and the contemporary geographies of manufacturing: Local embeddedness, new workspaces, and the glamourization of work in the craft brewing sector', PhD diss., University of Toronto.

Foxton, K. (2016), 'Reasoning without words: Envisioning the multimodal thesis and its challenges'. Available online: https://academicbookfuture.org/2016/09/21/multimodal_thesis/ (accessed 20 May 2022).

Fraser, C. J. (2007), 'Secondary school girls in conversation about school success: Implications for practice and policy', EdD thesis, University of British Columbia.

Freedman, A. (1999), 'Beyond the text: Towards understanding the teaching and learning of genres', *TESOL Quarterly*, 33: 764–8.

Freedman, S., Jr. (2018), 'The manuscript dissertation: A means of increasing competitive edge for tenure-track faculty positions', *International Journal of Doctoral Studies*, 13: 273–92.

Gaietto, D. (2019), 'What is happening here? [exploits of the nonhuman]', PhD thesis, Slade School of Fine Art, University College London.

Gan, G. (2019), '"Russia outside Russia": Transnational mobility, objects of migration, and discourses on the locus of culture amongst educated Russian migrants in Paris, Berlin, and New York', PhD diss., University of British Columbia.

Gao, D. (2019), 'D-brane chan-paton factors and orientifolds', PhD diss., University of Toronto.

Geertz, C. (1980), 'Blurred genres: The refiguration of social thought', *The American Scholar*, 49: 165–79.

Genette, G. (1997), *Paratexts: Thresholds of Interpretation*. Cambridge: Cambridge University Press.

Gibson, J. J. (1977), 'The theory of affordances', in R. E. Shaw and J. Bransford (eds), *Perceiving, Acting, and Knowing*, 67–82. Hillsdale, NJ: Lawrence Erlbaum.

Gishen, F. (2020), 'Evaluating a curriculum map for undergraduate medical education: A critical analysis through different stakeholder lenses', EdD thesis, University College London.

Golde, C. M. and Walker, G. E. (eds) (2006), *Envisioning the Future of Doctoral Education. Preparing Stewards of the Discipline. Carnegie Essays on the Doctorate*. San Francisco: Jossey-Bass.

Goldstein, L. (1999), 'Wittgenstein's Ph.D. viva – a re-creation', *Philosophy*, 74: 499–513.

Gopalan, S. (2018), 'The PhD in studio arts: An examination of the parameters of practice-led research in the United Kingdom', PhD diss., Indiana State University.

Gosset, K. and Potts, L. (2021), '#digidiss: A project exploring digital dissertation policies, practices and archiving', in V. Kuhn and A. Finger (eds), *Shaping the Digital Dissertation: Knowledge Production in the Arts and Humanities*, 49–63. Cambridge: Open Book Publishers. https://doi.org/10.11647/OBP.0239.04

Green R. J. (1997), 'Community perceptions of town character: A case study', PhD thesis, Queensland University of Technology.

Green, J. and Bloome, D. (1997), 'Ethnography and ethnographers of and in education: A situated perspective', in J. Flood, S. B. Heath and D. Lapp (eds), *Handbook of Research on Teaching Literacy through the Communicative and Visual Arts*, 1–41. New York: Macmillan.

Gross, D., Alhusen, J. and Jennings, B. M. (2012), 'Authorship ethics with the dissertation manuscript option', *Research in Nursing & Health*, 35: 431–4.

Guerin, C. (2016), 'Connecting the dots: Writing a doctoral thesis by publication', in C. Badenhorst and C. Guerin (eds), *Research Literacies and Writing Pedagogies for Masters and Doctoral Writers*, 31–50. Leiden: Brill.

Guerin, C. (2018), 'Feedback from journal reviewers. Writing a thesis by publication', in S. Carter and D. Laurs (eds), *Developing Research Writing. A Handbook for Supervisors and Advisors*, 136–8. London: Routledge.

Guerin, C. (2020), 'What's the formula for writing a thesis?' in S. Carter, C. Guerin and C. Aitchison, *Doctoral Writing: Practices, Processes and Pleasures*. Cham, Switzerland: Springer.

Guillén-Galve, I. and Bocanegra-Valle, A. (eds) (2021), *Ethnographies of Academic Writing Research: Theory, Methods, and Interpretation*. Amsterdam: John Benjamins.

Gustavii, B. (2012), *How to Prepare a Scientific Doctoral Dissertation Based on Research Articles*. Cambridge: Cambridge University Press.

Haak, J. S. (2012), 'Early language/literacy and behavior problems: Identification of developmental pathways and contextual contributors', PhD diss., University of Virginia.

Hallenbeck, J. W. (2019), 'The water we call home: Five generations of indigenous women's persistence along the Salish Sea', PhD diss., University of British Columbia.

Hamilton, J. (2014), 'The voices of the exegesis: Composing the speech genres of the practitioner-researcher into a connective thesis', in L. J. Ravelli, B. Paltridge and S. Starfield (eds), *Doctoral Writing in the Creative and Performing Arts*, 369–88. Faringdon, Oxfordshire: Libri Publishing.

Hannan, M. (2008), 'Unruly rules: Guidelines for Australian practice-based doctorates in music', in W. L. Sims (ed.), *Proceedings: International Society for Music Education*, 125–9. *28th World Conference, Bologna, Italy*.

Harron, P. (2016), 'The equidistribution of lattice shapes of rings of integers of cubic, Quartic, and quintic number fields: An artist's rendering', PhD diss., Princeton University.

Harwood, N. (2006a), 'Political scientists on the functions of personal pronouns in their writing: An interview-based study of "I" and "we"', *Text and Talk*, 27: 27–54.

Harwood, N. (2006b), '(In)appropriate personal pronoun use in political science: A qualitative study and a proposed heuristic for future research', *Written Communication*, 23: 424–50.

Hatch, T. and Skipper, A. (2016), 'How much are PhD students publishing before graduation? An examination of four social science disciplines', *Journal of Scholarly Publishing*, 47: 171–9. doi: 10.3138/jsp.47.2.171

Haultain-Gall, M. (2017). 'A battlefield of "Imperishable Memory"? The 1917 Belgium campaigns in Australian collective memory', PhD thesis, University of New South Wales.

Hawkes, D. and Taylor, S. (2016), 'Redesigning the EdD at UCL Institute of Education: Thoughts of the incoming EdD program leaders', in V. A. Storey (ed.), *International Perspectives on Designing Professional Practice Doctorates*, 115–25. London: Palgrave Macmillan.

Hawkes, D. and Yerrabati, S. (2018), 'A systematic review of research on professional doctorates', *London Review of Education*, 16: 10–27.

Heaton, J. (2020), 'Beyond the baton: An investigation of the intangibles of conducting', DMA thesis, University of Sydney.

Hemmings, B. (2012), 'Sources of research confidence for early career academics: A qualitative study', *Higher Education Research & Development*, 31: 171–84.

Hepfer, J. D (2016), 'Conducting, teaching, curating: Re-channelings of a percussive education', DMA diss., University of California San Diego,

Herman, C. (2017), 'Looking back at doctoral education in South Africa', *Studies in Higher Education*, 42: 1437–54.

Higher Education Student Statistics (2022), 'Higher education student statistics: UK, 2020/21 – Student numbers and characteristics'. Available online: https://www.hesa.ac.uk/news/25-01-2022/sb262-higher-education-student-statistics/qualifications (accessed 7 August 2023).

Hirst, N. (2019), 'Early childhood studies as a site for education for sustainability, eco literacy and critical pedagogy', PhD thesis, Liverpool John Moores University.

Hodge, B. (1995), 'Monstrous knowledge: Doing PhDs in the new humanities', *Australian Universities' Review*, 2: 35–9.

Holbrook, A., Bourke, S., Lovat, T. and Dally, K. (2004), 'Investigating PhD thesis examination reports', *International Journal of Educational Research*, 41: 98–120.

Holland, A. (1998). '"Saving the Aborigines": The white woman's crusade. A study of gender race and the Australian frontier 1920s– 1960s'. PhD thesis, University of New South Wales.

Hood, S. (2010), *Appraising Research: Evaluation in Academic Writing*. Basingstoke, England: Palgrave Macmillan.

Huang, C. W. and Archer, A. (2017), 'Academic literacies' as moving beyond writing: Investigating multimodal approaches to academic argument', *London Review of Education*, 15: 63–72.

Huang, Y. (2020), 'Doctoral writing for publication', *Higher Education Research & Development*. doi: 10.1080/07294360.2020.1789073

Hudson, R. (2015), 'Word Grammar', in B. Hiene and H. Narrog (eds), *The Oxford Handbook of Linguistic Analysis*. Second edition, 1–27. Oxford: Oxford University Press.

Hussey, C. (1999), 'Of swans, the wind and H.D.: An epistolary portrait of the poetic process', PhD diss., McGill University.

Hutchinson, B. (2015), 'UBC student writes 52,438 word architecture dissertation with no punctuation - Not everyone loved it', *National Post*, 8 May 2015. Available online: https://nationalpost.com/news/canada/ubc-student-writes-52438-word-architecture-dissertation-with-no-punctuation-not-everyone-loved-it (accessed 24 June 2022).

Hutchinson, V. (2020), 'Adults' perceptions of their writing practices and development as writers', EdD thesis, University College London.

Hyland, K (2000), *Disciplinary Discourses: Social Interactions in Academic Writing*. London: Longman.

Hyland, K. (2004), 'Disciplinary interactions: Metadiscourse in L2 postgraduate writing', *Journal of Second Language Writing*, 13: 133–51.

Hyland, K. (2005), 'Stance and engagement: A model of interaction in academic discourse', *Discourse Studies*, 7: 173–92.

Hyland, K. (2013), *Disciplinary Discourses: Social Interactions in Academic Writing*. Second edition. Ann Arbor, MI: University of Michigan Press.

Hyland, K. and Jiang, F. K. (2019), *Academic Discourse and Global Publishing: Disciplinary Persuasion in Changing Times*. London: Routledge.

Inside Higher Ed, (2012). 'Ending the first Ed.D. program', *Inside Higher Ed*, March 28, 2012. Available online: https://www.insidehighered.com/news/2012/03/29/country's-oldest-edd-program-will-close-down (accessed 17 August 2023).

Ivanič, R. (1998), *Writing and Identity. The Discoursal Construction of Identity in Academic Writing*. Amsterdam: John Benjamins.

Jackson, D. (2013), 'Completing a PhD by publication: A review of Australian policy and implications for practice', *Higher Education Research & Development*, 32: 355–68.

Jackson, P. (1993), 'The interrelationship between religious education and religious studies', PhD thesis, University of Warwick.

Jackson, P. A. (2013), 'Better late than never? Identity work, trajectories, and persistence of latecomers to science', PhD diss., McGill University.

Jamil, F. M. (2013), 'Understanding teacher effectiveness: Theory and measurement of teacher skills, knowledge and beliefs', PhD diss., University of Virginia.

Jamieson, I. and Naidoo, R. (2007), 'University positioning and changing patterns of doctoral study: The case of the University of Bath', *European Journal of Education*, 42: 363–73.

Jansen, E. (2015), 'Creativity unbound: An analysis of open collaboration between experience design and poietic practice', PhD thesis, University of New South Wales.

Jenkins, K. (2003), 'The cold war: The politics of being inside and outside a visual art space', PhD thesis, University of Sydney.

Jewitt, C. (2017), 'An introduction to multimodality', in C. Jewitt (ed.), *The Routledge Handbook of Multimodal Analysis*. Second edition, 15–30. London: Routledge.

Jewitt, C., Bezemer, J. and O'Halloran, K. (2016), *Introducing Multimodality*. London: Routledge.

Johns, A. M. (1990), 'L1 composition theories: Implications for developing theories of L2 composition', in B. Kroll (ed.), *Second Language Writing: Research Insights for the Classroom*, 24–36. Cambridge: Cambridge University Press.

Johns, A. M. (1997), *Text, Role and Context: Developing Academic Literacies*. Cambridge: Cambridge University Press.

Johns, A. M. (2016), 'Reader-culture-text mergence (RCTM): Seven pedagogical principles', in L. C. de Oliveira (ed.), *The Common Core State Standards in Literacy in History/Social Studies, Science and Technical Subjects for English Language Learners: Grades 6-12*, 107–22. Alexandria, VA: Teachers of English to Speakers of Other Languages.

Johnson, W. C. (2009), 'Preparing to appear: A case study of student activism', EdD thesis, University of British Columbia.

Jones, P. M. (2009), 'The Doctor of Musical Arts in music education: A distinctive credential needed at this time', *Arts Education Policy Review*, 110, 3: 3–8.

Jones, T. E. (2009), 'The studio art doctorate in America', in J. Elkins (ed.), *Artists with PhDs: On the New Doctoral Degree in Studio Art*, 81–5. Washington, DC: New Academia Publishing.

Jowsey, T., Corter, A. and Thompson, A. (2020), 'Are doctoral theses with articles more popular than monographs? Supervisors and students in biological and health sciences weigh up risks and benefits', *Higher Education Research & Development*, 39: 719–32.

Jung, J. H. (2015), 'Self-care and care-for-others in education', PhD diss., University of British Columbia.

Kamler, B. (2008), 'Rethinking doctoral publication practices: Writing from and beyond the thesis', *Studies in Higher Education*, 33: 283–94.

Kamler, B. and Thomson, P. (2014), *Helping Doctoral Students Write. Pedagogies for Supervision*. Second edition. London: Routledge.

Kamler, B. and Threadgold, T. (1997), 'Which thesis did you read?' in Z. Golebiowski (ed.), *Policy and Practice of Tertiary Literacy*, Proceedings of the First National Conference on Tertiary Literacy: Research and Practice. Volume 1. Melbourne: Victoria University of Technology.

Karikis, M. (2006), 'The acoustics of the self', PhD thesis, Slade School of Fine Art, University College London.

Kay, M. J. (2019), 'Spectralism decomposed: An exploration of process and transformation through the improvisational network', DMA thesis, University of Sydney.

Keating, J. (2017), 'Antipodean crossings: Australasian suffragists and the limits of internationalism', *1885–1914*, PhD thesis, University of New South Wales.

Kern, I. B. (2017), 'The proliferation of medical specialisation: A participatory account', PhD thesis, University of New South Wales.

Kinuthia, H. J. (2021), 'Teacher professionalism, education reform and 21st Century Skills in the United Arab Emirates', EdD thesis, University College London.

Kirchherr, J. (2017), 'The anti-dam protest cycle: Evidence from Asia', DPhil thesis, University of Oxford.

Kirchherr, J. (2018), *The Lean PhD*. London: Palgrave Macmillan.

Koh, S. K. (2017), 'Spaces-in-between: A swing-informed approach to performing jazz- and blues-influenced Western art music for violin', DMA diss., University of Toronto.

Kot, F. C. and Hendel, D. D. (2011), 'Emergence and growth of professional doctorates in the United States, United Kingdom, Canada and Australia', *Studies in Higher Education*, 37: 345–64.

Kuhn, T. (1962), *The Structure of Scientific Revolutions*. Chicago: University of Chicago Press.

Kühnast, A. (2017), 'Theorising race and evolution – German anthropologie's utilisation of Australian Aboriginal skeletal remains during the long nineteenth century', PhD thesis., University of New South Wales.

Kuteeva, M. and McGrath, L. (2015), 'The theoretical research article as a reflection of disciplinary practices: The case of pure mathematics', *Applied Linguistics*, 36: 215–35.

Lakoff, G. (1987), *Women, Fire and Dangerous Things. What Categories Reveal about the Mind*. Chicago: Chicago University Press.

Lander, B. (2017), 'Coping mechanisms: An improvised opera for non-improvising opera singers', DMA diss., University of California San Diego.

Larivière, V., Gingras, Y., Sugimoto, C. R. and Tsou, A. (2015), 'Team size matters: Collaboration and scientific impact since 1900', *Journal of the Association for Information Science and Technology* (JASIST), 66: 1323–32.

Larson, J. (1910), 'A computation of the orbit of E3062', PhD diss., Yale University.

Latimer, M. E. (2010), 'The nation's first D.M.A. in choral music: History, structure, and pedagogical implications', *Journal of Historical Research in Music Education*, XXXII, 1: 19–36.

Lemke, J. L. (1992), 'Intertextuality and educational research', *Linguistics and Education*, 4: 257–67.

Lemke, J. L. (1995), *Textual Politics. Discourse and Social Dynamics*. London: Taylor and Francis.

Leonarder, R. A. (2016), 'Ethical decision making by school leaders in a period of neoliberal reform', EdD portfolio, Western Sydney University.

Levin, K. L. (2021), 'Holding on to millennial teachers: Learning from aspiring leaders' experiences about why they stay', EdD diss., Columbia Teachers College.

Levine, A. (2007), *Educating Researchers*. New York: The Educational Schools Project.

Li, Y. (2016), "Publish SCI papers or no degree": Practices of Chinese doctoral supervisors in response to the publication pressure on science students', *Asia Pacific Journal of Education*, 36: 545–58.

Li, Z. (2021), 'Authorial presence in research article abstracts: A diachronic investigation of the use of first person pronouns', *Journal of English for Academic Purposes*, 51: 1–13.

Liardét, C. and Thomson, L. (2020), 'Monograph v. manuscript: Exploring the factors that influence English L1 and EAL candidates' thesis writing approach', *Higher Education Research & Development*, 41: 436–49.

Lillis, T. M. (2008), 'Ethnography as method, methodology, and "deep theorizing"', *Written Communication*, 25: 353–88.

Lillis, T. M. and Curry, M. J. (2010), *Academic Writing in a Global Context: The Politics and Practices of Publishing in English*. London: Routledge.

Lillis, T. and Scott, M. (2007), 'Defining academic literacies research: Issues of epistemology, ideology and strategy', *Journal of Applied Linguistics*, 4: 5–32.

Lim, J. (2018), 'Unsuk Chin's Piano Music: 6 Piano Etudes (1995–2003) and Piano Concerto (1996–1997)', MDA thesis, University of Sydney.

Lin, L. and Evans, S. (2012), 'Structural patterns in empirical research articles: A cross-disciplinary study', *English for Specific Purposes*, 31: 150–60.

Lipkin, A. (1999), *Understanding Homosexuality, Changing Schools: A Text for Teachers, Counselors, and Administrators*. Boulder, CO: Westview Press.

Liu, Y. (2019), 'An exploration towards the enrichment of a personal musical language in musical composition', DMus Final Submission Commentary, Royal College of Music London.

Liu, Y. (2021), 'Going home: Professional integration of Chinese graduate degree holders from United States colleges and universities in art education', EdD diss., Columbia University.

Lovett, L. (2019), 'Making a scene in London and Rio de Janeiro: Invisible theatre and urban performance after Augusto Boal (1931–2009)', PhD thesis, Slade School of Fine Art, University College London.

Lowry, S. (2014), 'Strategies for artists becoming writers: Tackling the written component of practice-based research in the creative and performing arts (a report from the regions)', in L. Ravelli, B. Paltridge and S. Starfield (eds), *Doctoral Writing in the Creative and Performing Arts: The Researcher/Practitioner Nexus*, 337–52. Faringdon, England: Libri.

Lowy, M. (2017), 'Maternal experience: Encounters with love and ambivalence', PhD thesis, University of New South Wales.

Luckmann, T. (2009), 'Observations on the structure and function of communicative genres', *Semiotica*, 173, 1–4: 267–82.

Lunt, I. (2018), 'Introduction to 'The EdD at 20: Lessons learned from professional doctorates' – a special feature for the London Review of Education', *London Review of Education*, 16, 1: 4–9.

Luzón, M. J. and Pérez-Llantada, C. (eds) (2019), *Science Communication on the Internet. Old Genres Meet New Genres*. Amsterdam: John Benjamins.

Ma, V. W., Dana, N. F., Adams, A. and Kennedy, B. L. (2018), 'Understanding the problem of practice: An analysis of professional practice in EdD dissertations', *Impacting Education. Journal on Transforming Professional Practice*, 3: 13–22.

MacEntee, K. (2016), 'Can participatory visual methods make a difference? Responding to HIV and AIDS in rural South African schools', PhD thesis, University of Toronto.

MacLeod, K. and Holdridge, L. (2004), 'The doctorate in fine art: The importance of exemplars to the research culture', *International Journal of Art and Design Education*, 23: 155–68.

Madsen, L. M. (2008), 'Fighters and outsiders, linguistic practices, social identities, and social relationships among urban youth in a martial arts club', PhD thesis, University of Copenhagen.

Madsen, L. M. (2015), *Fighters, Girls and other Identities. Sociolinguistics in a Martial Arts Club*. Bristol, England: Multilingual Matters.

Malloch, M. (2016), 'Trends in doctoral education in Australia', in V. A. Storey (ed.), *International Perspectives on Designing Professional Practice Doctorates*, 63–77. London: Palgrave Macmillan.

Manton, C. (2016), 'Multimedia PhD research and non-text theses' Available online. http.//blogs.bl.uk/digital-scholarship/2016/09/multimedia-phd-research-and-non-text-theses.html (accessed 25 May 2020).

Marcus, G. and Fischer, M. (1986), *Anthropology as Cultural Critique: An Experimental Moment in the Human Sciences*. Chicago: University of Chicago Press.

Marsh, D. D. and Dembo, M. H. (2009), 'Rethinking school leadership programs: The USC EdD program in perspective', *Peabody Journal of Education*, 84: 69–85.

Mason, S. (2018), 'Publications in the doctoral thesis: Challenges for doctoral candidates, supervisors, examiners and administrators', *Higher Education Research & Development*, 37: 1231–44.

Mason, S. and Frick, L. (2022), 'Ethical and practical considerations for completing and supervising a prospective PhD by publication', in S. W. Chong and N. Johnson (eds), *Landscapes and Narratives of PhD by Publication*, 31–45. Cham, Switzerland: Springer.

Mason, S. and Merga, M. K. (2018a), 'A PhD by publication is a great way to build your academic profile, but be mindful of its challenges', *LSE Research Online*, 20 August 2018. Available online: https://blogs.lse.ac.uk/impactofsocialsciences/2018/08/20/a-phd-by-publication-is-a-great-way-to-build-your-academic-profile-but-be-mindful-of-its-challenges/ (accessed 10 August 2021).

Mason, S. and Merga, M. K. (2018b), 'Theses by publication in humanities and social sciences', *International Journal of Doctoral Studies*, 13: 139–53.

Mason, S. and Merga, M. K. (2018c), 'Integrating publications in the social science doctoral thesis by publication', *Higher Education Research & Development*, 37: 1454–71.

Matzler, P. P. (2022), *Mentoring and Co-Writing for Research Publication Purposes*. London: Routledge.

Maxwell, T. W. (2016), 'Australian EdDs: At a crossroad?', in V. A. Storey (ed.), *International Perspectives on Designing Professional Practice Doctorates*, 79–98. London: Palgrave Macmillan.

Mayr, E. (1982), *The Growth of Biological Thought. Diversity, Evolution, and Inheritance*. Cambridge, MA: Belknap Press.

McCarthy, P. X. and Wienk, M. (2019), *Advancing Australia's Knowledge Economy. Who are the Top PhD Employers?* Melbourne: Australian Mathematical Sciences Institute and CSIRO.

McCarty, R. and Swales, J. M. (2017), 'Technological change and generic effects in a university Herbarium: A textography revisited', *Discourse Studies*, 19: 561–80.

McCausland, O. W. (2017), 'PhD 'Turning landscape into colour', PhD thesis, Slade School of Fine Art, University College London.

McGrath, L. (2014), 'Parallel language use in academic and outreach publication: A case study of policy and practice', *Journal of English for Academic Purposes*, 13: 5–15.

McGrath, L. (2015), 'Writing for publication in four disciplines: Insights into text and context', PhD thesis, Stockholm University.

McGrath, L. (2016a), 'Open Access Writing: An investigation into the online drafting and revision of a research article in pure mathematics', *English for Specific Purposes*, 43: 25–36.

McGrath, L. (2016b), 'Self-mentions in anthropology and history research articles: Variation between and within disciplines', *Journal of English for Academic Purposes*, 21: 86–98.

McLennan, J. C. (1900), 'Electrical conductivity in gases transversed by cathode rays', PhD diss., University of Toronto.

Merandy, J. A. (2019), 'Vanishing leaves: A study of Walt Whitman through location-based mobile technologies', PhD diss., The City University of New York.

Merga, M. K., Mason, S. and Morris, J. E. (2019), ' "What do I even call this?" Challenges and possibilities of undertaking a thesis by publication', *Journal of Further and Higher Education*, 44: 1245–61.

Mestek, L. (2011), 'Phenotypic characterisation of the C. elegans latrophilin homolog, lat-1', DPhil thesis, University of Oxford.

Meurant, C. L. (2019), 'The bow and the lyre: Harmonious structures and opposite tensions – collaboration and extramusical inspiration in composition', DMA thesis, University of Sydney.

Miller, C. M. (2016), 'Genre innovation: Evolution, emergence, or something else?', *The Journal of Media Innovations*, 3, 2: 4–19.

Miller, C. M. (2017), "Where do genres come from?" in C. R. Miller and A. R. Kelly (eds), *Emerging Genres in New Media*, 1–33. London: Palgrave Macmillan.

Molinari, J. (2019), 'What makes writing academic: An educational and philosophical response', PhD thesis, University of Nottingham.

Molinari, J. (2021), 'Re-imagining doctoral writings as emergent open systems', in C. Badenhorst, B. Amell and J. Burford (eds), *Re-imagining Doctoral Writing*, 49–69. Louisville: WAC Clearinghouse and University Press of Colorado.

Molinari, J. (2022), *What Makes Writing Academic: Rethinking Theory for Practice*. London: Bloomsbury.

Murphy, M. (2016), 'Reconceptualising parent involvement in a culturally and linguistically diverse (CALD) school community', EdD portfolio, Western Sydney University.

Myers, R. H. (1948), 'The preparation and properties of tantalum and some of its alloys', PhD thesis, University of Melbourne.

National Association of Schools of Music (2021), *Handbook 2020–2021*. Reston, VA: National Association of Schools of Music.

National Science Foundation (2016), 'Number of doctorates awarded by US institutions in 2016 close to all-time high'. Available online: (accessed 14 May 2020).

National Science Foundation (2022), *Doctorate Recipients from U.S. Universities: 2021*. Alexandra, VA: National Science Foundation.

Necas, B. and Poli, S. (2021), 'A tale of two languages: First language attrition and second language immersion', in M. Savva and L. P. Nygaard (eds), *Becoming a Scholar: Cross-Cultural Reflections on Identity and Agency in an Education Doctorate*, 27–42. London: UCL Press.

Nestor, R. D. (2018), 'This is not a drill: The siren as a symbol and musical instrument', DMA diss., University of California San Diego.

Nethsinghe, R. and Southcott, J. (2015), 'A juggling act: Supervisor/candidate partnership in a doctoral thesis by publication', *International Journal of Doctoral Studies*, 10: 167–85.

Neumann, R. (2005), 'Doctoral differences: Professional doctorates and PhDs compared', *Journal of Higher Education Policy and Management*, 27: 173–88.

Newman, M. (n.d.), 'Housed memory'. Available online: https://urielorlow.net/work/housed-memory/ (accessed 14 May 2020).

Newton, S. J. (2009), 'Resisting education: A capital idea', EdD thesis, Queensland University of Technology.

Nguyen, B. D. (2016), 'Wavicles', DMA diss., University of California San Diego.

Niven, P. and Grant, C. (2012), 'PhDs by publication: An "easy way out?"', *Teaching in Higher Education*, 17: 105–11.

Nixon, S. A. O'S. (2007), 'A study of the reading experiences of "at risk" grade 10 students', EdD thesis, University of Alberta.

Noble, K. A. (1992), 'An international prognostic study, Based on an acquisition model of degree philosophiae, Doctor (PhD)', PhD diss., University of Ottawa.

Noble, K. A. (1994), *Changing Doctoral Degrees. An International Perspective*. Buckingham, England: Society for Research into Higher Education/Open University Press.

Noss, L. (1968), 'Yale university school of music doctor of musical arts', *College Music Symposium*, 8, Fall: 42–3.

Nygaard, L. A. P. (2019), 'Ready or not: Negotiating gender and institutional environment on the path to professorship', EdD thesis, University College London.

Nygaard, L. P. and Solli, K. (2021), *Strategies for Writing a Thesis by Publication in the Social Sciences and Humanities*. London: Routledge.

Nyquist, J. D. and Woodford, B. J. (2000), *Re-envisioning the PhD: What Concerns Do We Have?* Seattle: University of Washington Center for Instructional Development and Research.

O'Brien, L. J. (2016), 'All in the game of school. Structuring a socially cohesive school', EdD portfolio, Western Sydney University.

Okuda, T. (2017), 'The writing centre as a global pedagogy: A case study of writing centres in Japan', PhD diss., University of British Columbia.

O'Keeffe, M. B. (2016), 'Exploring higher education professionals' use of Twitter for learning', EdD thesis, University College London.

O'Keeffe, P. (2022), 'The PhD by Publication as Preparation for Work in the "Performative University"', in S. W. Chong and N. Johnson (eds), *Landscapes and Narratives of PhD by Publication*, 199–213. Cham, Switzerland: Springer.

Okuda, T. (2018), 'Policy borrowing in university language planning: A case of writing centers in Japan', in J. Crandall and K. Bailey (eds), *Global Perspectives on Educational Language Policies*, 73–83. New York: Routledge.

Okuda, T. (2019a), 'Policy borrowing for a world-class university: A case of a writing center in Japan', *Current Issues in Language Planning*, 20: 503–20.

Okuda, T. (2019b), 'Student perceptions of non-native English speaking tutors at a writing center in Japan', *Journal of Second Language Writing*, 44: 13–22.

Okuda, T. (2020), 'The writing center and international students in a Japanese university: A language management perspective', *Higher Education Research & Development*, 39: 778–91.

O'Mullane, M. (2005), 'Demonstrating significance of contribution to professional knowledge and practice in Australian professional doctorate programs: Impacts in the workplace and professions', in T. W. Maxwell, C. Hickey and T. Evans (eds), *Working Doctorates: The Impact of Professional Doctorates in the Workplace and Professions*, 8–23. Geelong, Victoria, Australia: Deakin University.

Orlow, U. (2002), 'Housed memory', PhD thesis, University of the Arts, London.

Orth, A. M. (2015), 'International students' perceptions of their experience of higher education in Australia: A focus on Saudi Arabian students in their first year of a business course in a major Australian university', EdD thesis, Queensland University of Technology.

Ottewell, K. and Lim, W. M. (2016), 'PhD: Been there, done that: So why do a (second), professional doctorate?' in P. Burnard, T. Dragovic, J. Flutter and J. Alderson (eds), *Transformative Doctoral Practices for Professionals*, 29–41. Rotterdam: Sense Publishers.

Oxley, R. (2014), 'Attending to fathers with postnatal depression: Lived embodiment and bio-graphical systematicity', PhD thesis, University of New South Wales.

Palma, R. (2019) 'De(ar)anged. Ornamenting the six cello suites BWV 1007–1012 by Johann Sebastian Bach: The evidence in arrangements by Bach and his contemporaries', DMA thesis, University of Sydney.

Palmer, M. (1894), 'Determination of the Orbit of the Comet 1847 VI', *Transactions of the Astronomical Observatory at Yale University*, 1, iv: 187–207.

Paltridge, B. (2002), 'Thesis and dissertation writing: An examination of published advice and actual practice', *English for Specific Purposes*, 21: 125–43.

Paltridge, B. (2004), 'The Exegesis as a Genre: An ethnographic examination', in L. J. Ravelli and R. A. Ellis (eds), *Analysing Academic Writing*, 84–103. London: Continuum.

Paltridge, B. (2008), 'Textographies and the researching and teaching of writing', *Iberica*, 15: 9–24.

Paltridge, B. and Starfield, S. (2020a), *Thesis and Dissertation Writing in a Second Language. A Handbook for Students and Their Supervisors.* Second edition. London: Routledge.

Paltridge, B. and Starfield, S. (2020b), 'Change and continuity in thesis and dissertation writing: The evolution of an academic genre', *Journal of English for Academic Purposes*, 48: 100910.

Paltridge, B., Starfield, S., Ravelli, L. and Nicholson, S. (2011), 'Doctoral writing in the visual and performing arts: Issues and debates', *The International Journal of Art and Design Education*, 30: 242–55.

Paltridge, B., Starfield, S., Ravelli, L., Nicholson, S. and Tuckwell, K. (2012a), 'Doctoral writing in the visual and performing arts: Two ends of a continuum', *Studies in Higher Education*, 37: 989–1003.

Paltridge, B., Starfield, S., Ravelli, L. J. and Tuckwell, K. (2012b), 'Change and stability: Examining the macrostructures of doctoral theses in the visual and performing arts', *Journal of English for Academic Purposes*, 11: 332–44.

Paltridge, B., Starfield, S., Ravelli, L., Tuckwell, K. and Nicholson, S. (2014), 'Genre in the creative-practice doctoral thesis: Diversity and unity', in G. Garzone and C. Ilie (eds), *Evolving Genres and Genre Theory: Specialized Communication across Contexts and Media*, 89–106. Boca Raton, FA: Brown Walker Press.

Paltridge, B., Starfield, S. and Tardy, C. M. (2016), *Ethnographic Perspectives on Academic Writing*. Oxford: Oxford University Press.

Pantelides, K. L. (2013), 'Mapping dissertation genre ecology', PhD diss., University of South Florida.

Paré, A. (2014), 'Rhetorical genre theory and academic literacy', *Journal of Academic Language & Learning*, 8: A83–A94.

Paré, A. (2019), 'Re-writing the doctorate: New contexts, identities, and genres', *Journal of Second Language Writing*, 43: 80–4.

Park, C. (2005), 'New variant PhD: The changing nature of the doctorate in the UK', *Journal of Higher Education Policy & Management*, 27: 189–207.

Park, C. (2007), *Redefining the Doctorate*. York, England: The Higher Education Academy.

Parks, W. A. (1900), 'The Huronian of the basin of the Moose River', PhD thesis, University of Toronto.

Peacock, S. (2017), 'The PhD by publication', *International Journal of Doctoral Studies*, 12: 123–35.

Pearson, I. E. (2014), 'Research degrees in the conservatoire context: Reconciling practice and theory', in S. D. Harrison (ed.), *Research and Research Education in Music Performance and Pedagogy*, 65–76. Cham, Switzerland: Springer.

Pérez-Llantada, C. (2013), 'The article of the future: Strategies for genre stability and change', *English for Specific Purposes*, 32: 221–35.

Pérez-Llantada, C. (2021), *Research Genres across Languages: Multilingual Communication Online*. Cambridge: Cambridge University Press.

Perkins, C. (2012), 'How school principals understand and respond to homophobia: A study of one B.C. school district using ethnodrama', EdD thesis, University of British Columbia.

Perry, J. A. (2014), 'What history reveals about the education doctorate', in M. M. Latta and S. Wunder (eds), *Placing Practitioner Knowledge and the Center of Teacher Education: Rethinking the Policies and Practices of the Education Doctorate*, 51–72. Charlotte, NC: Information Age Publishing.

Perry, J. A. (2017), 'The carnegie project on the education doctorate. Transforming education practice in multiple contexts', in J. Jiang, K. H. Mok and D. E. Neubauer (eds), *The Sustainability of Higher Education in an Era of Post-Massification*, 31–42. London: Routledge.

Phan, T. N. (2015), 'Approaches to curriculum development in Vietnams higher education: A case study', EdD thesis, Queensland University of Technology.

Phillips, M. (2016), 'Postmodernism and poststructuralism', in B. Warf (ed.), *Oxford Bibliographies*. Available online: https://www.oxfordbibliographies.com/display/document/obo-9780199874002/obo-9780199874002-0144.xml (accessed 10 August 2021).

Pilz, K. (1998), 'Literature and science in the works of Italo Calvino', PhD thesis, University of Melbourne.

Pilz, K. (2004), *Mapping Complexity. Literature and Science in the Works of Italo Calvino*. Leicester, England: Troubadour Publishing.

Pirler, S. (2019), 'Disruption, dis/orientation, and intra-action: Recipes for creating a queer utopia in audiovisual space', PhD diss., Rensselaer Polytechnic Institute.

Poli, S. (2017), 'Professional women in higher education management – Practices, career strategies and approaches to leadership', EdD thesis, University College London.

Poole, B. D. (2012), 'Perspectives on the EdD from academic at English universities', EdD thesis, University of Bath.

Poole, B. D. (2015), 'The rather elusive concept of "doctorateness": A reaction to Wellington', *Studies in Higher Education*, 40: 1507–22.

Porter, S., Young, L., Aarssen, L., Gibb, R., Klein, R., Paré, A., Ryoo, A. and Wood-Adams, P. (2018), *Report of the Task Force on the Dissertation - The Doctoral Dissertation – Purpose, Content, Structure, Assessment*. Ottawa: Canadian Association for Graduate Studies.

Powell, M. C. (2019), 'The environments of accreting supermassive black holes', PhD diss., Yale University.

Prentice, M. and Barker, M. (2017), 'Intertextuality and interdiscursivity'. *Oxford Bibliographies in Linguistics*. doi: 10.1093/obo/9780199766567-0171.

Pretorius, M. (2017), 'Paper-based theses as the silver bullet for increased research outputs: First hear my story', *Higher Education Research & Development*, 36: 823–37.

QAA (2012), *Royal College of Music, Institutional Review by the Quality Assurance Agency for Higher Education*. Gloucester, England: Quality Assurance Agency for Higher Education, UK.

QAA (2015), *Characteristics Statement: Doctoral Degree*. Gloucester, England: Quality Assurance Agency for Higher Education, UK.

QAA (2020), *Characteristics Statement: Doctoral Degree*. Gloucester, UK: Quality Assurance Agency for Higher Education, UK.

QUT (2021), 'Doctor of education'. Available online: https://www.qut.edu.au/courses/doctor-of-education (accessed 10 August 2021).

Rahman, A. and Jahan, Y. (2020), 'Confronting yourself: Reflections on academic publication in doctoral study', *The New Educational Review*. doi: 10.15804/tner.2020.59.1.12.

Ravelli, L. J. (2019), 'Multimodality and the register of disciplinary History: Challenges for new texts and old theories', *Language, Context and Text*, 1: 341–65.

Ravelli, L., Paltridge, B., Starfield, S. and Tuckwell, K. (2013), 'Extending the notion of text: The creative arts doctoral thesis', *Visual Communication*, 12: 395–422.

Ravelli, L., Starfield, S. and Paltridge, B. (2021), 'Re-imagining Doctoral Writing Through the Visual and Performing arts', in C. Badenhorst, B. Amell and J. Burford (eds), *Re-imagining Doctoral Writing*, 217–34. Louisville: WAC Clearinghouse and University Press of Colorado.

Rensselaer Polytechnic Institute (2021a), 'Electronic arts PhD'. Available online: https://hass.rpi.edu/arts/electronic-arts-0 (accessed 10 August 2021).

Rensselaer Polytechnic Institute (2021b), 'Electronic arts PhD'. Available online: https://hass.rpi.edu/arts/electronic-arts-0 (accessed 10 August 2021).

Richardson, L. (2000), 'Writing: A method of inquiry', in N. Denzin and Y. Lincoln (eds), *The Handbook of Qualitative Research*, 516–29. Thousand Oaks, CA: Sage.

Rigby, J. and Jones, B. (2020), 'Bringing the doctoral thesis by published papers to the social sciences and the humanities: A quantitative easing? A small study of the doctoral thesis submission rules and practice in two disciplines in the UK', *Scientometrics*, 124: 1387–409.

Robertson, E. (2018), 'Transitions: Biophilia, beauty, and endangered plants', PhD thesis, Sydney College of the Arts, University of Sydney.

Robins, L. and Kanowski, P. (2008), 'PhD by publication: A student's perspective', *Journal of Research Practice*, 4, 2: 1–20.

Robinson, C. (2002), 'Being *somewhere*: Young homeless people in inner-city Sydney', PhD thesis, University of New South Wales.

Robinson, S. C. (2018), 'The lesbian presence in feminist, gay and queer social movements in Australia, 1970s – 1990s', PhD thesis, University of New South Wales.

Rosch, E. (1977), 'Human Categorisation', in N. Warren (ed.), *Advances in Cross-Cultural Psychology, Vol 1*, 1–72. London: Academic Press.

Rosch, E. (1983), 'Prototype classification and logical classification: The two systems', in E. K. Scholnick (ed.), *New Trends in Conceptual Representation: Challenges to Piaget's Theory?* 73–86. Hillsdale, NJ: Lawrence Erlbaum.

Rosch, E. and Mervis, C. B. (1975), 'Family resemblances: Studies in the internal structure of categories', *Cognitive Psychology*, 7: 573–605.

Rosenberg, R. P. (1961), 'The first American doctor of philosophy degree. A centennial salute to Yale 1861–1961', *The Journal of Higher Education*, 32, 7: 387–94.

Roth, L. (1922), 'A critical discussion of the sources of Spinoza with special reference to Maimonides and Descartes', DPhil thesis, University of Oxford.

Royal College of Music London (nd), 'Doctor of music'. Available online: https://www.rcm.ac.uk/courses/researchdegrees/dmus/ (accessed 10 August 2021)

Russell-Pinson, L. and Harris, M. L. (2019), 'Anguish and anxiety, stress and strain: Attending to writers' stress and the dissertation process', *Journal of Second Language Writing*, 43: 63–71.

Savage, S. L. (2008), 'Behind the text, beyond the sound: Investigations into processes of creative musical interpretation', PhD thesis, Queensland Conservatorium, Griffith University.

Savva, M. and Nygaard, L. P. (2021a), *Becoming a Scholar: Cross-Cultural Reflections on Identity and Agency in an Education Doctorate*. London: UCL Press.

Savva, M. and Nygaard, L. P. (2021b), 'The "Peripheral" student in academia: An analysis', in M. Savva and L. P. Nygaard (eds), *Becoming a Scholar: Cross-Cultural Reflections on Identity and Agency in an Education Doctorate*, 154–70. London: UCL Press.

Savva, M. and Nygaard, L. P. (2021c), 'Introduction', in M. Savva and L. P. Nygaard (eds), *Becoming a Scholar: Cross-Cultural Reflections on Identity and Agency in an Education Doctorate*, 1–9. London: UCL Press.

Sawaki, T. (2014), 'Interactions between ideology, dialogic space construction, and the text-organizing function: A comparative study of traditional and postmodern academic writing corpora', *English Text Construction*, 7, 2: 178-214.
Scharen, P. (2000), '*Famine and Prophecy: General Sir Arthur Cotton and the Poverty of India, 1844-84*', PhD thesis, University of New South Wales.
Schell, J. (2013), 'We rock long distance: Manifest and the circulations of diasporic hip-hop', PhD diss., University of Minnesota.
Schryer, C. (1994), 'The lab vs. the clinic: Sites of competing genres', in A. Freedman and P. Medway (eds), *Genre and the New Rhetoric*, 87-103. London: Taylor and Francis.
Schwandt, T. A. (2015), *The SAGE Dictionary of Qualitative Inquiry*. Thousand Oaks, CA: Sage.
Scott, D., Brown, A., Lunt, I. and Thorne, L. (2008), 'Specialised knowledge in UK professions. Relations between the state, the university and the workplace', in D. Boud and A. Lee (eds), *Changing Practices of Doctoral Education*, 143-56. London: Routledge.
Scott, F. H. (1900), 'The structure, micro-chemistry and development of nerve cells, with special reference to their nuclein compounds', PhD thesis, University of Toronto.
Segal, N. (2020), 'The flat diamond: The role of intimacy in a collaborative practice', PhD thesis, Slade School of Fine Art, University College London.
Seloni, L. (2014), '"I'm an artist and a scholar who is trying to find a middle point": A textographic analysis of a Colombian art historian's thesis writing', *Journal of Second Language Writing*, 25: 79-99.
Seto, K. (2016), 'The challenges and unintended impacts if the new school leaving age policy in one low socio-economic status school in Australia'. EdD portfolio, Western Sydney University.
Sharmani, S., Sproken-Smith, R., Goldman, C. and Harland, T. (2015), 'Assessing the doctoral thesis when it includes published work', *Assessment and Evaluation in Higher Education*, 40: 89-102.
Shibili, S. (2016), 'Performance analysis in sport and leisure management', PhD thesis, Sheffield Hallam University.
Solli, K. and Nygaard, L. P. (2022), 'Same but different? identifying writing challenges specific to the PhD by publication', in S. W. Chong and N. Johnson (eds), *Landscapes and Narratives of PhD by Publication*, 13-30. Cham, Switzerland: Springer
Simpson, E. M. (1924), *A Study of the Prose Works of John Donne*. Oxford: Clarendon Press.
Simpson, R. (1983), *How the PhD Came to Britain*. Guildford, England: Society for Research into Higher Education.
Simpson, R. (2009), *The Development of the PhD Degree in Britain, 1917-1959 and Since*. Lewiston, NY: The Edwin Mellen Press.

Simon, Y. (2019). 'Roxana Quispe Collante makes history by defending her PhD dissertation in Quenchua', REMEZCLA. Available online: https://remezcla.com/culture/roxana-quispe-collante-quechua-phd/ (accessed 28 November 2022).

Sizer, J. (2012), 'Textography as a needs analysis and research tool for English for academic purposes and learning development practitioners', *Journal of Learning Development in Higher Education*, 15: 1–21.

Sizer, J. (2021), 'Textography: Narrowing the gap between text and context in ethnographic explorations of situated academic writing', in I. Guillén-Galve and A. Bocanegra-Valle (eds), *Ethnographies of Academic Writing Research: Theory, Methods, and Interpretation*, 39–60. Amsterdam: John Benjamins.

Skamp, K. (2019), 'Emerging trends and themes in professional doctorate research – Doctoral research in education', in P. Miller and T. Marchant (eds), *Professional Doctorate Research in Australia: Commentary and Case Studies from Business, Education and Indigenous Studies*, 77–89. Lismore, NSW: Southern Cross University Press.

Skov, S. (2021), 'PhD by publication or monograph thesis? supervisors and candidates negotiating the purpose of the thesis when choosing between formats', in C. Badenhorst, B. Amell and J. Burford (eds), *Re-imagining Doctoral Writing*, 71–86. Louisville, CO: WAC Clearinghouse and University Press of Colorado.

Slade School of Fine Art (nd), 'MPhil/PhD Fine Art'. Available online: https://www.ucl.ac.uk/slade/study/mphil-phd/ (accessed 10 August 2021).

Smith, N. J. (2008), *Achieving Your Professional Doctorate*. Maidenhead, England: McGraw Hill.

Smith, S. (2015), *PhD by Published Work*. London: Palgrave Macmillan.

Smith, S. A. (2015), *Manifesto for the Humanities: Transforming Doctoral Education in Good Enough Times*. Ann Arbor: University of Michigan Press.

Smrekar, C. and McGraner, K. (2009), 'From curricular alignment to the culminating project: The Peabody College EdD capstone', *Peabody Journal of Education*, 84: 48–60.

Sone, Y. (2005), 'Terrible twins: art & the academy', *Realtime* 68, Aug–Sept: 8. Available online: https://www.realtime.org.au/terrible-twins-art-the-academy/ (accessed 10 August 2021).

Sousanis, N. (2014), 'Unflattening', PhD diss., Columbia University.

Sousanis, N. (2015), *Unflattening*. Cambridge, MA: Harvard University Press.

Spinuzzi, C. (2004). 'Describing assemblages: Genre sets, systems, repertoires, and ecologies', University of Texas at Austin, Digital Writing & Research Lab. Available online: https://www.dwrl.utexas.edu/old/content/describing-assemblages.html (accessed 8 June 2022).

Starfield, S. and Ravelli, L. J. (2006), '"The writing of this thesis was a process that I could not explore with the positivistic detachment of the classical sociologist": Self and structure in New Humanities research theses', *Journal of English for Academic Purposes*, 5: 222–43.

Starfield, S., Paltridge, B. and Ravelli, L. J. (2012), '"Why do we have to write?" Practice-based theses in the visual and performing arts and the place of writing', in V. K. Bhatia, C. Berkenkotter and M. Gotti (eds), *Insights into Academic Genres*, 169–90. Bern: Peter Lang.

Starfield, S., Paltridge, B. and Ravelli, L. (2014), 'Researching academic writing: What textography affords', *International Perspectives on Higher Education Research*, 10: 103–20.

Steinman, O. (2019), 'An examination of the Doctor of Music as a comprehensive degree', PhD diss., Florida State University.

Stevenson, M. (2005), 'Reading and writing in a foreign language: A comparison of conceptual and linguistic processes in Dutch and English', PhD thesis., University of Amsterdam.

Stevenson, M., Schoonen, R. and de Glopper, K. (2003), 'Inhibition or compensation? A multi-dimensional comparison of reading processes in Dutch and English', *Language Learning*, 53: 765–815.

Stevenson, M., Schoonen, R. and de Glopper, K. (2006), 'Revising in two languages: A multi-dimensional comparison of on-line writing revisions in L1 and FL', *Journal of Second Language Writing*, 15: 159–87.

Stewart, P. (2016), 'Indigenous architecture through indigenous knowledge', PhD diss., University of British Columbia.

Stone, J. D. (1948), 'Virus haemagglutination: A review of the literature', PhD thesis, University of Melbourne.

Storey, V. A. (2013), 'Critical friendship: Facilitating innovative doctoral program adoption', in V. Storey (ed.), *Redesigning Professional Education Doctorates: Applications of Critical Friendship Theory to the EdD*, 1–6. London: Palgrave Macmillan.

Storey, V. A. and Hesbol, K. A. (2014), 'Can the dissertation in practice bridge the researcher-practitioner gap? The education professional doctorate and the impact of the Carnegie Project on the Education Doctorate Consortium', *Journal of School Public Relations*, 35: 324–47.

Storey, V. A., Caskey, M. M., Hesbol, K. A., Marshall, J. E., Maughan, B. and Dolan, A. W. (2015), 'Examining EdD dissertations in practice: The Carnegie Project on the education doctorate', *International HETL Review*, 5, Article 2. Available online: https://pdxscholar.library.pdx.edu/edu_fac/96/ (accessed 10 August 2021).

Sugimoto, C. R. (2015), 'Toward a twenty first century dissertation', Council of Graduate Schools Future of the Dissertation Workshop. Available online: (accessed 24 May 2022).

Susen, S. (2015), *The Postmodern Turn in the Social Sciences*. London: Palgrave Macmillan.

Svelte, D. (2019), 'Surprise and seduction: Theorising fashion via the sociology of wit', PhD thesis, University of New South Wales.

Swales, J. M. (1981), 'Aspects of article Introductions', *Aston ESP Research Reports*, No 1. Language Studies Unit. The University of Aston at Birmingham. Republished University of Michigan Press 2011.

Swales, J. M. (1985), 'ESP – the heart of the matter or the end of the affair?', in R. Quirk and H.G. Widdowson (eds), *English in the World. Teaching and Learning the Language and Literatures*, 221–3. Cambridge: Cambridge University Press.

Swales, J. M. (1990), *Genre Analysis: English in Academic and Research Settings*. Cambridge: Cambridge University Press.

Swales, J. M. (1993), 'Genre and engagement', *Revue Belge de Philologie et d'Histoire*, 71: 687–98.

Swales, J. M. (1998), 'Textography: Toward a contextualization of written academic discourse', *Research on Language and Social Interaction*, 31: 109–21.

Swales J. M. (2004), *Research Genres: Explorations and Applications*. Cambridge: Cambridge University Press.

Swales, J. M. (2018), *Other Floors, Other Voices: A Textography of a Small University Building*. Twentieth Anniversary edition. Ann Arbor: University of Michigan Press.

Swales J. M. (2019), 'The futures of EAP genre studies: A personal viewpoint', *Journal of English for Academic Purposes*, 38: 75–82.

Swales, J. M. and Luebs, M. (1995), 'Towards textography', in B.-L. Gunnarson and I. Backlund (eds), *Writing in Academic Contexts*, 12–29. Uppsala: Unit for Advanced Studies in Modern Swedish (FUMS), Uppsala University.

Swapan, A. Y. (2018), 'Sense of community: An investigation of the semi-public interface of a residential community', PhD thesis, Curtin University.

Talley, V. H. (1956), 'The Doctor of musical arts degree', *American Music Teacher*, 5, 5: 20–1.

Tan, R. (2015), 'The politeness ethic and the development of the public sphere in eighteenth-century England', PhD thesis, University of New South Wales.

Tardy, C. M. (2003), 'A genre system view of the funding of academic research', *Written Communication*, 20: 7–36.

Tardy, C. M. (2009), *Building Genre Knowledge*. West Lafayette, IN, Parlor Press.

Tardy, C. M. (2012), 'Current conceptions of voice', in K. Hyland and C. Sancho Guinda (eds), *Stance and Voice in Written Academic Genres*, 34–48. London: Palgrave Macmillan.

Taylor, J. (2008), 'Quality and standards: The challenge of the professional doctorate', *Higher Education in Europe*, 33: 65–87.

Texas A&M University (nd), 'Dissertation formatting guidelines', College Station, TX: Texas A&M University College of Education and Human Development.

Texas Tech University (2020), *Fine Arts Doctoral Program, Art Track Handbook*. Lubbock, TX: Texas Tech University.

Thacker, R. S. (2020), 'What is negentropy? A manuscript dissertation on "negentropic leadership" for innovation and change in higher education', PhD diss., University of Idaho.

The Modern Language Association of America (2014), *Report of the MLA Task Force on Doctoral Study in Modern Language and Literature*. Available https://www.mla.org/Resources/Guidelines-and-Data/Reports-and-Professional-Guidelines/Report-of-the-Task-Force-on-Doctoral-Study-in-Modern-Language-and-Literature-2014 (accessed 19 May 2022).

Thom, J. F. (2013), 'Embodied encounters: A performative, material reading of selected contemporary artworks by Santu Mofokeng, El Anatsui, Willem Boshoff and Johan Thom', PhD thesis, Slade School of Fine Art, University College London.

Thompson, P. (1999), 'Exploring the contexts of writing: Interviews with PhD supervisors', in P. Thompson (ed.), *Issues in EAP Writing Research and Instruction*, 37–54. Reading, England: Centre for Applied Language Studies, University of Reading.

Thompson, P. (2013), 'Thesis and dissertation writing', in B. Paltridge and S. Starfield (eds), *Handbook of English for Specific Purposes*, 347–66. Boston, MA: Wiley-Blackwell.

Thomson, P. (2021), 'Should you publish during your PhD?' *Patter*, 23 August 2021. Available online: https://patthomson.net/2021/08/23/should-you-publish-during-your-phd/ (accessed 24 August 2021).

Thompson, P. (2016), 'Genre approaches to theses and dissertations', in K. Hyland and P. Shaw (eds), *The Routledge Handbook of English for Academic Purposes*, 379–91. London: Routledge.

Thomson, P. and Walker, M. (2010), 'Doctoral education in context: The changing nature of the doctorate and doctoral students', in P. Thomson and M. Walker (eds), *The Routledge Doctoral Student's Companion Getting to Grips with Research in Education and the Social Sciences*, 9–26. London: Routledge.

Tidlen, W. A. (1918), 'The promotion of post-graduate work and research', *Nature*, 101, 2532: 184–6.

Torunczyk Schein, D. R. (2019), 'The PhD employment crisis is systemic', *Policy Options*, 30 July 2019.

Town, J. S. (2016), 'Integrative chapter in support of the award of a PhD by publication', PhD thesis, University of York.

UCL (2021), 'Education, practice and society EdD'. Available online: https://www.ucl.ac.uk/ioe/courses/graduate-research/education-practice-and-society-edd (accessed 10 August 2021).

UC San Diego (2021a), 'Visual arts'. Available online: https://visarts.ucsd.edu (accessed 10 August 2021).

UC San Diego (2021b), 'Music'. Available online: https://catalog.ucsd.edu/curric/MUS-gr.html (accessed 10 August 2021).

Uhrig, K. (2012), 'Business and legal case genre networks: Two case studies', *English for Specific Purposes*, 31: 127–36.

UK Council for Graduate Education (1997), *Practice-Based Doctorates in the Creative and Performing Arts and Design*. Coventry, England: United Kingdom Council for Graduate Education.

University of Alberta (2021), 'Doctor of education'. Available online: https://www.ualberta.ca/secondary-education/graduate-programs/doctor-of-education.html (accessed 10 August 2021).

University of Bath (2021), 'Doctor of Education (EdD)'. Available online: https://www.bath.ac.uk/courses/postgraduate-research/edd-doctor-of-education-part-time/ (accessed 10 August 2021).

University of Cambridge (2017), 'Guide to applicants: PhD degree under special regulations'. Available online: https://www.cambridgestudents.cam.ac.uk/files/phd_spreg_guide_for_applicants.pdf (accessed 13 April 2021).

University of Cambridge (2021), 'PhD under special regulations'. Available online: https://www.cambridgestudents.cam.ac.uk/your-course/examinations/graduate-exam-information/higher-degrees/phd-special-regulations (accessed 13 April 2021).

University of Sydney (nd), 'Doctor of musical arts'. Available online: https://www.sydney.edu.au/courses/courses/pr/doctor-of-musical-arts0.html (accessed 10 August 2021).

University of Technology Sydney (2019), *Graduate Research Candidature Management, Thesis Preparation and Submission Procedures, Sydney: Graduate Research School.* Sydney: University of Technology Sydney.

UNSW (2020), 'Thesis format guide', Graduate Research School, UNSW Sydney

van Leeuwen, T. (2005), 'Multimodality, genre and design', in S. Norris and R. H. Jones (eds), *Discourse in Action: Introducing Mediated Discourse Analysis*, 73–94. London: Routledge.

van Niele, I. (2005), 'Ambivalent belonging', PhD thesis, University of South Australia.

Vaughan, S. (2021), 'Practice submissions: Are doctoral regulations and policies responding to the needs of creative practice?' *Research in Post-Compulsory Education*, 26: 333–52.

Vella, R. (2005), 'Keeping the degree creative', *RealTime*, 68, 2 http://www.realtimearts.net/article/issue68/7916 (accessed 2 August 2022.

Vincs, R. (2014), 'Deleuze's hammer: Inter-textual tools for doctoral writing within practice-led research projects', in L. Ravelli, B. Paltridge and S. Starfield (eds), *Doctoral Writing in the Creative and Performing Arts: The Researcher/Practitioner Nexus*, 353–67. Faringdon, England: Libri.

Visconti, A. (2015), '"How can you love a work, if you don't know it?": Critical code and design towards participatory digital editions', PhD diss., University of Maryland.

Ward, M. H. (2013), 'Living in liminal space: The PhD as accidental pedagogy'. PhD thesis, University of Sydney.

Webb, C. (2019), 'Liberating the family: Education, aspiration and resistance among South African university students', PhD thesis, University of Toronto.

Webb, J., Brien, D. L. and Burr, S. (2012), 'Facing the final hurdle: Creative arts PhD programs and examination standards', *Encounters: Refereed Proceedings of 17th AAWP Conference*, 1–10.

Wessel, N. (2019), 'Accessibility beyond the schedule', PhD thesis, University of Toronto.

Wessell, A. (1999), 'History making history: Traversing the boundaries between contesting and commemorating Australia day and Columbus day', PhD thesis, University of New South Wales.

Western Sydney University (2017), 'Doctorate policy'. Available online: https://policies.westernsydney.edu.au/document/view.current.php?id=17&version=13 (accessed 28 November 2022).

Western Sydney University (2021), 'Doctor of Education (EdD). Available online: https://www.westernsydney.edu.au/future/study/courses/research/doctor-of-education#:~:text=The%20Doctor%20of%20Education%20offers,level%20of%20originality%20and%20quality. (accessed 10 August 2021).

Whitchurch, C. (2009), 'The rise of the blended professional in higher education: A comparison between the United Kingdom, Australia and the United States', *Higher Education*, 58: 407–18.

Whittington, K. and Barnes, S. (2021), 'The changing face of doctoral education', in A. Lee and R. Bongaardt (eds), *The Future of Doctoral Research*, 5–17. London: Routledge.

Williams, A. (2019), 'My Gothic dissertation: A podcast'. PhD diss., University of Iowa.

Williams, C. (2018), 'Embers in the ashes: Apocalyptic horror and the creative process', PhD thesis, University of Huddersfield.

Wilson, K. (2002), 'Quality assurance issues for a PhD by published work: A case study', *Quality Assurance in Education*, 10, 2: 71–8.

Wilson, S. (2000), 'The struggle over work: Conflict and debate over the distribution of employment, income and power', PhD thesis, University of New South Wales.

Wittgenstein, L. (1922), *Tractatus Logico-philosophicus*. London: Kegan Paul.

Wittgenstein, L. (1953), *Philosophical Investigations*. New York: Macmillan.

Wolff, E. C. (1948), 'A French-Australian writer: Paul Wenz', PhD thesis, University of Melbourne.

Wright, C. (2020), 'Dimensions of perceived reality for soprano and modular orchestra', DMA diss., University of Toronto.

Yahav, A. (2018), 'From text to sound: Revisiting some performance indications in Chopin's works', DMA Portfolio and Commentary, Royal College of Music London.

Yale University (1961), *Doctors of Philosophy 1861–1960*. New Haven, CN: Yale University.

Ye, R. (2009), 'Homing in and reconstructing native American identity. Identity collision and fusion in Leslie Marmon Silko's writing', PhD diss., Fudan University.

York U Graduate Admissions (nd), 'Visual arts'. Available online: https://futurestudents.yorku.ca/graduate/programs/visual-arts (accessed 10 August 2021).

York University Faculty of Graduate Studies (2020), *Graduate Program in Visual Arts. MFA/PhD Student Handbook 2020–2021*, Toronto: York University.

Yu, T. F. (2017), 'Class differences among gay men in Hong Kong: Local history, queer modernity', PhD diss., Chinese University of Hong Kong.

Yu, T. F. (2018), 'Class as a method to localise Queer Studies in Hong Kong', *Gender, Place & Culture, A Journal of Feminist Geography*, 25: 309–12.

Yu, T. F. (2020), 'Reconfiguring queer Asia as disjunctive modernities: Notes on the subjective production of working-class gay men in Hong Kong', *Journal of Homosexuality*, 67: 863–84.

Zamudio-Suárez, F. (2017), 'An activist defends his dissertation in rap', *The Chronicle of Higher Education*. Available online: https://www.chronicle.com/article/an-activist-defends-his-dissertation-in-rap/ (accessed 10 August 2021).

Zhang, Y. (2017), 'Masculinities in transcultural spaces – Negotiations of masculinities in Ang Lee's films', PhD diss., Humboldt University of Berlin.

Zhao, M. (2014), 'Distribution of appraisal resources in English newspaper texts', PhD diss., Shanghai Jiao Tong University.

Zubrzycki, J. (2018), 'Transnational exchanges in magical knowledge and methodologies between India and the West, 1813–1940', PhD thesis, University of New South Wales.

Index

The Academic Book of the Future Project 239
Accurso, K. 236
Aijazi, O. 245–6
Alexander, I. 35, 43–4, 46, 197, 200, 213, 235
Ali-Khan, C. 206–8
Allen, J. R. 54
Allen, R. 174
Ambivalent Belonging (van Niele) 23
Amell, B. 39–40
Anderson, T. 24, 35–7, 43–4, 46, 105, 117, 120, 197, 200, 213–14, 217, 235
Andrews, R. 27, 243
Archer, A. 27
Arizona State University 105–6, 108–9, 126–7
article-based thesis 193, 233
Arts and Humanities Research Council (AHRC) 239
Ascenzo, A. E. 179–80
Atkinson, D. 9, 31, 61
Ausländer, S. B. 149–50
Australia
  Doctor of Musical Arts (DMA) 183–91
  EdD 118–23
  The 'new humanities' PhD 66, 71, 75, 81, 94, 97, 100
  PhD 158–64
  PhD by publication 218–24
  practice-based doctorates in the visual arts 133–5, 158–64
Australian Qualifications Framework 118
authorial voice 75, 237, 242–3
authorship 35, 157, 196, 201, 204, 214, 233–7, 244
Auton, E. 85
Ayers, G. 33
Ayres, T. L. R. 53–4
Azoulay, A. 154

Bakhtin, M. 15, 246
Banks, D. 32
Bao, Y. 134
Barros, A. S. 54
Bateman, J. A. 27
Bazerman, C. 31–2
Beauton, J. A. 174
Becher, T. 25
Beetz, R. 170, 174
Bentley, P. J. 230
Birman, H. 80–1, 85
Black, P. 210
Blair, K. A. 174
Bocanegra-Valle, A. 30
Bok, G. 83, 85
Booij, G. 14
Bourdieu, P. 70
Bowden, S. L. 174
Brady, J. 126
British Library (BL) 239
British Library Electronic Digital Thesis Online Service (EThOS) 47
Britton, G. 233
Brown, H. C. 213
Buckley, B. 134
Burland, K. 192
Burns, E. 232
Butler, J. 154

Canada
  Doctor of Musical Arts (DMA) 168, 178–83
  EdD 114–18
  PhD 152–7
  PhD by publication 213–17
  practice-based doctorates in the visual arts 135, 152–7
Canadian Association for Graduate Studies (CAGS) 63, 231
Cano, P. J. G. 172
Capezzuto, M. 124
Carlin, N. 87

Carson, A. D. 10–11, 237, 241–2
Cerfeda, D. 59
Chang, K. 234
Chong, S. W. 212
City University of New York (CUNY) 242–3
Clarke, P. 218
Clemson 26
Clerk, T. 121–2
Coleman, K. 243
Collante. R. Q. 63, 228
Collins, S. 139–40, 144, 149–50, 165
Columbia Teachers College 103, 106–8, 124, 126
complex traditional thesis 2, 17, 19, 34, 61, 68, 78, 164, 197
composition theses 190–1
contributorship model 235
Cool Mind Map 143
coping mechanisms (Lander) 171–2
Cotton, A. 74
Council for Graduate Schools (CGS) 231
Cowden, M. 222–3
creative component 41, 133, 135, 144, 154, 156–7, 163–4, 173, 192, 236
Culvenor, C. C. J. 60
Curry, M. J. 30

Dalziell, J. 87
Day, S. 210
de Beaugrande, R. 14
Decker, S. I. 52
Deegan, M. 239
Deem, R. 230
default inheritance 14
Dembo, M. H. 130
Devitt, A. 62
diachronic change 10, 30, 33, 60
digital dissertations 237, 246
Di Mauro, S. 218–19, 221
dissertation component 169
Dix, B. 243–4
Dobson, I. R. 47
doctoral authorship 234–5
doctoral student writers 13–14
doctorates by publication 193–6, 202, 224–6
   Australia 218–24
   Canada 213–17

thesis types and 197–200
two-part model 199
UK 209–13
United States 203–8
writing challenges 201–2
Doctor of Education (EdD) 1, 3, 41, 103–5
   Bath 113–14, 128
   and new humanities theses 123–9
   Queensland University of Technology (QUT) 119–20, 128
   University College London (UCL) 111–13, 149
   Western Sydney University (WSU) 120–3
Doctor of Music (DMus) 167–70, 175–6, 191–2
Doctor of Musical Arts (DMA) 1, 7, 167–74, 177–80, 182–3, 185–9, 191–2, 238–9
Dong, Y. R. 36, 46, 179
Dowle, S. 230
DPhil at the University of Oxford 53–4, 233–4
Dressler, W. 14
Dudley-Evans, T. 17, 20
Dunn, M. 92–3, 95

Eastman School of Music 168
Edminster, J. 27, 237
Elkins, J. 135
England, J. 27, 243
Estima, S. 39, 241
EThOS 202
Evans, S. 33–4
Evans, T. 47
examination guidelines 225
exegetical perspective 192
exemplars 10, 13, 60, 134, 189, 227, 240

family resemblances 10, 13, 49, 61, 101, 227–8
Fenton, D. 23–4
Fiedler, S. 71, 75
Flanders, E. 152–7, 236
Forbes, A. M. 183
Fortais, S. E. 140–4, 148, 150
Fox, C. 17
Foxton, K. 239

Gaietto, D. 140, 144–5, 147
Gan, G. 245
Gao, D. 57
Gaultier, J. -P. 82
Gebhard, M. 236
Geertz, C. 67
Genette, G. 66
genre change 1, 5, 13, 15, 28, 30–1, 33, 36, 40, 42, 45, 60–1, 100, 129–30, 165, 227, 238
genre emergence 10, 28, 36
genre evolution 10, 39, 60, 131, 227
geography PhDs 57–8
Georgeson, R. 236
Gingras, Y. 235
Gishen, F. 127
Gosset, K. 247
Grant, C. 196
Guerin, C. 13
Guillén-Galve, I. 30
Gustavii, B. 198, 200

Hallenbeck, J. W. 236, 244–5
Hamilton, J. 134
Harron, P. 11–12
Hatch, T. 232
Haultain-Gall, M. 93–5
Heaton, J. 185–7
Hendel, D. D. 114
Hepfer, J. D. 173
Herman, C. 47
Hesbol, K. A. 130
Hirst, N. 211–12
historiography 50, 71–2, 77, 90, 93, 96, 98–9
history dissertations 50, 52–3
history PhDs 2, 5–9, 35, 46, 50, 52–3, 66, 75–6, 90, 95, 99, 229
Hodge, B. 65–8, 75, 77, 100–1
Holbrook, A. 16–17
Holdridge, L. 134, 240
Hood, S. 89
Hudson, R. 14
hybrid SM (simple/manuscript) 35
hybrid TM (topic/manuscript) 35
Hyland, K. 32

Infinite Ulysses 244
inheritance 10, 13–15, 129, 227

Institution Focused Study (IFS) 111
intertextuality 5, 13–15, 17
introduction-methods-results-discussion (IMRD) 2, 9, 17, 24, 33, 35, 38, 46, 54, 56, 60–2, 100, 197

Jackson, P. 210, 213, 215–16, 218
Jiang, F. K. 32
Johns, A. M. 29
Johnson, W. C. 129
joint authorship 235
Jones, B. 209

Kamler, B. 25, 86
Kanowski, P. 222
Karikis, M. 26
Kay, M. J. 186–7, 190–1
Kehm, B. M. 134
Kern, I. B. 96–7
Khalidi, W. 157
Kirchherr, J. 233
Koh, S. K. 168, 179–83, 186, 238–9
Kot, F. C. 114
Kristeva, J. 15
Kubrick, S. 144
Kuhnian revolution 65, 232
Kuteeva, M. 34

Lander, B. 171–4
Larivière, V. 235
Larson, J. 49–50
Latimer, M. E. 169–70
The Lean PhD 233
Lee, A. 121–2
Leonarder, R. A. 122
Levin, K. L. 124–5
Liardét, C. 222–3
Lillis, T. 29–30
Lim, J. 184–5
Liu, Y. 126, 176–8
Li, Z. 32–3
location-based mobile experience (LBME) 242
Lovett, L. 150

MacEntee, K. 217
MacLeod, K. 134, 240
macrostructure, topic-based 78–89
Malloch, M. 119

Manton, C. 239
manuscript-style dissertation 35–6, 193, 197–8, 203, 213–15, 218, 224, 235
Marsh, D. D. 130
Master of Fine Arts (MFA) 133, 135–6
Maxwell, T. W. 119
Ma, Y. 134
Mayr, E. 14
McGrath, L. 8, 34, 199
McLennan, J. C. 6, 56
Meek, V. L. 230
Merandy, J. A. 242
Meurant, C. L. 186–7
Middlesex University 211, 213
Miller, C. M. 10, 14, 26, 60, 227
MLA Taskforce 234–5, 237–8
Molinari, J. 10–12
monographs 89–95
Moore, G. E. 12
Moxley, J. 27, 237
multimodality 165, 192, 238–9

narrative voice 172
National Endowment for the Humanities 230–1
natural categorization (Rosch) 13
Nestor, R. D. 173
Nethsinghe, R. 222
new humanities PhDs 65–6, 89, 100–1, 164, 207, 225, 229
  features 67–75
  genre blurring 99–100
  macrostructure 78–89
  monographs 89–95
  participatory and oral histories 95–8
  sociology 77–8
  2020 corpus 75–7
new technologies 1, 5, 26–8, 79, 239
Newton, S. J. 128–9
Next Generation Humanities PhD Planning Grant 230–1
Next Gen PhDs 230–1, 242
Nguyen, B. D. 174
Niven, P. 196
Nixon, S. A. O'S. 115–16, 128
non-traditional doctorates 240
Nygaard, L. 110–12, 129, 193–4, 198, 225

Ohio University 135
O'Keeffe, M. B. 112–13
Okuda, T. 35–6, 105, 197, 214, 217

online thesis and dissertation repositories 3 n.1, 24–6, 34–6, 136, 169
oral history 89–90, 95–9, 101, 233
Orlow, U. 26
Orth, A. M. 128
Owning my masters (Carson) 10–11, 237, 241
Oxley, R. 79–80

Palmer, M. 49
Paltridge, B. 24, 36, 38, 44
Pantelides, K. L. 39, 131
paratext 66, 78, 83, 97, 99, 101, 138, 154, 159, 207
Paré, A. 62–3, 233
Park, C. 229–30
Parks, W. A. 56
Pérez-Llantada, C. 10, 33
performing arts doctorates 23–4, 38, 44, 148–9, 222, 229, 238
Perkins, C. 116–17, 128
Phan, T. N. 128
PhDs. *See also* new humanities PhDs
  Australia 158–64
  Canada 152–7
  Geography 57–8
  history 2, 5–9, 35, 46, 50, 52–3, 66, 75–6, 90, 95, 99, 229
  by publication 1, 8, 24, 44, 46, 157, 194, 197–200, 229, 232–4, 236, 246 (*see also* doctorates by publication)
  social sciences and humanities 238–47
  UK 139–52
  United States 136–9
  University of Melbourne 58–60
  University of Toronto 56–8
  visual arts 135, 144, 149, 154
  Yale University 49–53
Philosophical Transactions of the Royal Society of London (Atkinson) 9, 31–2, 56, 61
Pilz, K. 60
Pirler, S. 138–9
Poli, S. 112, 129
Poole, B. D. 110, 113–14, 127–8
post-modernism 65–7, 70–1, 74–5, 77–8, 95, 123, 129
Potts, L. 247
Powell, M. C. 50–1
practice-based doctorates 23, 40–1, 133, 158, 164–5, 167, 174, 181, 191–2

practice-based PhDs 135, 143, 159, 161, 229
practice-led PhDs 139–40, 144, 149–51, 165
Prince of Wales Hospital (POW) 95
productivity 15, 79, 130
professional doctorates 7, 28, 40–1, 103–4, 113–15, 118–20, 127, 191, 227, 229
professional portfolios 128–9
ProQuest Dissertations and Theses Portal 47, 202
prototype 5, 10, 13–15, 17, 33, 49, 61, 89, 99, 101, 227–8
Public Scholars Initiative (PSI) 150, 231, 234, 236–7, 244–5
Purington, S. 236

Quality Assurance Agency (QAA) 210
Queensland University of Technology (QUT) 119–21, 128

Rajcan, A. 232
Ravelli, L. 2, 34–5, 38, 46, 66–8, 71, 75–6, 89, 134, 164–5
reflective accounts 125–7, 137, 213
reflexivity 67, 70, 77, 87, 89, 99, 101, 123–4, 129, 131, 207
re-imagining the PhD 231, 238–47
Rensselaer PhD dissertations 136–7
research articles (RA) 9–10, 20–1, 25, 30–4, 46, 57, 61, 66, 193–5, 200–1, 203, 216, 223–4
research monographs 92, 99, 233
Richardson, L. 67
Rigby, J. 209
Robertson, E. 158–61
Robins, L. 222
Robinson, C. 68, 70, 75
Robinson, S. C. 95, 97–8
Rosch, E. 13, 15
Ross, D. 100
Roth, L. 53
Royal Australasian College of Surgeons (RACS) 96
Royal College of Music DMus 175, 177

sandwich style PhD by publication 200, 203–5, 215, 218, 220–2, 225
Saunders, G. 35, 43–4, 46, 197, 200, 213, 235
Savage, S. L. 218–19, 221
Savva, M. 110–11
Sawaki, T. 95

Scharen, P. 72, 74
Schell, J. 240
School of Art and Design (Ohio University) 135
School of Humanities and Languages (University of New South Wales) 76–7
School of Social Sciences (University of New South Wales) 76
Schwandt, T. A. 89
Segal, N. 151–2
Seloni, L. 39
Shibili, S. 211
simple traditional thesis 2, 17–18, 23, 36, 48, 58, 105–9, 112–16, 118, 120, 124–5, 129, 131, 164, 179–80, 182, 184, 187
Simpson, E. 53
Simpson, R. 47
Sizer, J. 41
Skipper, A. 232
Slade School of Art 26, 135–6, 139–41, 144–5, 149–51, 165, 237
Smith, S. 209, 212, 246
sociology theses 77–8
Solli, K. 193–4, 198, 225
Sousanis, N. 10, 26, 241–2
Southcott, J. 222
Spencer, M. 192
Starfield, S. 2, 34–6, 38, 46, 66–8, 71, 75–6, 89, 129
Stevenson, M. 200
Stewart, P. 12, 14, 63, 228, 246
Storey, V. A. 130
Sugimoto, C. R. 235
Svelte, D. 81–2
Swales, J. M. 29–31, 37–8
Swapan, A. Y. 218
Sydney College of the Arts (SCA) 158–9, 162–3
Sydney Conservatorium of Music 183
synchronic perspectives 40

Tan, R. 87–8
Tardy, C. M. 29–30
taxonomy 5, 13, 15–17, 225, 227
tenor 70, 78, 95, 165, 173, 237
Texas A&M University guidelines 196, 204
Texas Tech University 135
text-based approach 30–4
textography 1–2, 30, 36–41

textualist analytic lens (Lillis) 29
Thacker, R. S. 232
thesis and dissertation types 43–6
thesis by publication 2–3, 20–2, 28, 46, 48, 57–60, 193, 202, 222–3, 226, 234–6. *See also* doctorates by publication
Thom, J. F. 150–1
Thompson, P. 17, 100
Thomson, L. 222–3
Thomson, P. 86, 209
Threadgold, T. 25
topic-based thesis 20–1, 23–4, 35–6, 38, 43–5, 48, 52–60, 67–9, 73, 77–9, 87, 89, 96–100, 112, 116, 120, 136, 139, 159–60, 164, 171–2, 175, 177, 180, 182, 184, 227, 243–5
Tractatus Logico-Philosophicus (Wittgenstein) 11–12
Trowler, P. R. 25
Tsou, A. 235
Tuckwell, K. 38
two part PhD by publication 211, 219
typology 5, 13, 15–17, 212, 225, 227

UC San Diego DMAs 171, 174
the UK
   Doctor of Musical Arts (DMA) 174–8
   EdD 109–14
   PhD 139–52
   PhD by publication 209–13
   practice-based doctorates in the visual arts 139–52
UK Council of Graduate Education 134, 209
Unflattening (Sousanis) 10–11, 241
the United States
   Doctor of Musical Arts (DMA) 169–74
   EdD 106–9
   PhD 136–9
   PhD by publication 203–8
   practice-based doctorates in the visual arts 136–9
University College London (UCL) 110–14, 127, 129, 135, 139, 143, 148–9
University of Alberta 115–16, 128
University of British Columbia (UBC) 12, 105, 116–18, 128–31, 150, 157, 217, 231, 236, 244–5
University of California (UC) San Diego DMA 170, 172
University of California San Diego PhD 135, 167
University of Melbourne 7, 46, 48, 58–60, 168, 243
University of New South Wales (UNSW) 75, 93, 98
University of Oxford 6–7, 28, 28 n.1, 53–4
University of Southern California 130
University of Sydney 7, 119, 136, 158, 163, 168–9, 183, 185–6, 223–4
University of Technology Sydney (UTS) 8, 119
University of Toronto 6–7, 48, 56–60, 114, 168–9, 178–9, 246
UnstableActs (Fenton) 23
US National Association of Schools of Music 170

Vaughan, S. 133, 148
Vella, R. 192
Visconti, A. 244
visual arts doctorates 134–5
voice 26–7, 32, 41, 71, 75, 80–1, 83, 85–6, 112, 124–5, 159, 165, 171–2, 174, 177–8, 189, 237, 240, 242–3, 245

Ward, M. -H. 247
Webb, C. 57–8
Wessell, A. 71–2, 74–5, 99, 101
Wessel, N. 57
Western Sydney University (WSU) 120–3, 128, 131
What Makes Writing Academic (Molinari) 10–11
Williams, A. 237, 242
Wilson, K. 68
Windsor, L. 192
Wittgenstein, L. 10–12, 14
Wolff, E. C. 58
Wordsworth, W. 182
Wright, C. 182
written component 134, 138–40, 144, 146, 148, 151, 153–4, 156, 160, 162–3, 168, 171, 173, 175, 179, 185, 188–9, 192, 236–8, 245

Yahav, A. 175–7
Yale University 5–7, 48–53, 167, 169

Zubrzycki, J. 90

www.ingramcontent.com/pod-product-compliance
Lightning Source LLC
Chambersburg PA
CBHW071807300426
44116CB00009B/1230